ONE IN FOUR

By the same author

Tank, an autobiographical fiction
The Book of US

ONE IN FOUR

A year in the life of
a Channel Four Commissioning Editor

Michael Kustow

Chatto & Windus LONDON

Published in 1987 by
Chatto & Windus Ltd
30 Bedford Square
London WC1B 3RP

British Library Cataloguing in Publication Data

Kustow, Michael
 One in four: a year in the life of a
 Channel 4 commissioning editor.
 1. Channel Four
 I. Title
 384.55′4′0941   HE8700.9.G7

ISBN 0-7011-3255-8

The account of Peter Brook's
production of the *Mahabharata*
appeared in a different form in
the *London Review of Books*.

Photoset in Linotron Ehrhardt by
Rowland Phototypesetting Ltd
Bury St Edmunds, Suffolk
Printed in Great Britain by
Redwood Burn Ltd
Trowbridge, Wiltshire

CONTENTS

ACKNOWLEDGEMENTS

My thanks to Carmen Callil for seizing on it; Andrew Motion for godfathering it; Anthony Barnett for eliciting it in the first place, and for the title; Allegra Huston for weeding and trimming it; Michael Ignatieff, Colin Leventhal and Jenny Kay for reflecting on it; Jane Harter, Mary Harrison and Caroline Manuel for deciphering it; to Tom Phillips for being my mirror and my friend;
to Orna for helping me see straight about it, even when I didn't want to know: and for so much more.

The following copyright holders are gratefully acknowledged:

Walter Benjamin, 'The Work of Art in the Age of Mechanical Reproduction', in *Walter Benjamin* (*Illuminations* edition), translated by Harry Zohn, London: Fontana, 1969. Copyright © Walter Benjamin 1936; translation copyright © *Illuminations* 1969. Reprinted by permission of Collins/Fontana.
Tony Harrison, 'On Not Being Milton', from *Selected Poems*, London: Penguin Books, 1984. Copyright © Tony Harrison 1984. Reprinted by permission of Penguin Books Ltd.
Joseph Brodsky, 'The Keening Muse' and 'A Child of Civilisation', from *Less Than One*, London: Viking Press, 1986. Copyright © Joseph Brodsky 1982, 1986. Reprinted by permission of Viking/Penguin Ltd.
Andrei Tarkovsky, *Sculpting in Time*, London: The Bodley Head, 1986. Copyright © Andrei Tarkovsky 1986. Reprinted by permission of The Bodley Head.
Nam June Paik, 'La Vie, Satellites, One Meeting – One Life', from *Nam June Paik – Mostly Video*, translated by Yumiko Yamazaki, Tokyo: Metropolitan Museum of Art, 1984. Copyright © Nam June Paik 1984. Reprinted by permission of the author.
Peter Fiddick, 'May Market Force Be With You', in the *Guardian*, 29 December 1986. Reprinted by permission of *Guardian* Newspapers Ltd.
Iris Murdoch, *The Fire and the Sun*, Oxford: Oxford University Press, 1977. Copyright © Iris Murdoch 1977. Reprinted by permission of Oxford University Press.
Zbigniew Herbert, *Barbarian in the Garden*, translated by Michael March and Jaroslaw Anders, London: Carcanet Press, 1985. Copyright © Zbigniew Herbert 1985. Reprinted by permission of Carcanet Press.

For Tamara, for Yakov, who are no longer there.

'Daddy, I've been watching a terrible nightmare'

One of Mark Boyle's children, waking up in the middle of the night, 1968

'Miss, is it going to be in colour?'

*A pupil to a teacher, going into a schools matinee
performance at the National Theatre, 1975*

CAST OF CHARACTERS: CHANNEL FOUR, 1986

JEREMY ISAACS	Chief Executive
JUSTIN DUKES	Managing Director
PAUL BONNER	Programme Controller
EDMUND DELL	Chairman
MIKE BOLLAND	Senior Commissioning Editor, Entertainment
FARRUKH DHONDY	Commissioning Editor, Multicultural Programmes
LIZ FORGAN	Deputy Programme Controller
ALAN FOUNTAIN	Commissioning Editor, Independent Film and Video
RENEE GODDARD	European Editorial Consultant (Fiction and Arts)
ELLIS GRIFFITHS	Chief Engineer
CAROL HASLAM	Commissioning Editor, Documentary Series
MICHAEL KUSTOW	Commissioning Editor, Arts
COLIN LEVENTHAL	Head of Programme Acquisition
FIONA MADDOCKS	Assistant Editor, Music
FRANK MCGETTIGAN	Head of Administration and Industrial Relations
ADRIAN METCALFE	Commissioning Editor, Sport
GILL MONK	Deputy Head of Administration and Industrial Relations
JOHN RANELAGH	Commissioning Editor, Religion, Ireland
DAVID ROSE	Senior Commissioning Editor, Fiction
NAOMI SARGANT	Senior Commissioning Editor, Education
SUE STOESSL	Head of Marketing
GILLIAN WIDDICOMBE	Opera Consultant

More and more, the work of art reproduced becomes the work of art designed for reproducibility.

Walter Benjamin, 'The Work of Art in the Age of Mechanical Reproduction'

a forged music on the frames of Art.
The looms of owned language smashed apart.

Tony Harrison, 'On Not Being Milton'

I joined Channel Four as Commissioning Editor for the Arts in January 1982, ten months before it went on air. I had been chosen after an interview with the Channel's chairman, Edmund Dell, its chief executive Jeremy Isaacs, and board member Anthony Smith. I nearly blew the whole thing when the chairman asked me what I would do if I got the job, and I gave an answer that lasted twenty minutes. 'You almost talked yourself out of a job, Michael,' Jeremy said next day.

Jeremy Isaacs likes to say that he chose the first wave of commissioning editors not because of their television expertise or their fitness for a job specification, but because of what they were as individuals. One was recruited after Jeremy met him as a fellow member of the British Film Institute Production Board; another when she came to interview him for the *Guardian.* I saw Jeremy about the job because of a passing remark by a mutual friend. I certainly had little experience of television. When I was asked about this at my interview, I said, 'I may not know much about television, but I do know about production, about enabling talented people to make things well.'

In a variety of circumstances, that was what I'd been doing for the twenty years of my professional life. Unlike many of my creative contemporaries at Oxford at the start of the sixties (who included Melvyn Bragg, Dennis Potter, Ken Loach, John McGrath), I had not tried to get into the BBC, feeling it was too big and too British for me.

My model for the kind of institution I wanted to work in was a theatre, Brecht's Berliner Ensemble for preference. At Oxford, while acting and directing in as much university theatre as I could, I had gobbled up Brecht's poems, plays and anything I could learn about his life. The Berliner Ensemble seemed to me the image of a place where performance, poetry and politics met, where pleasure and enlightenment were combined. In the summer of my first term I went to the Avignon Festival, sat with two thousand people watching Germaine Montero tug Mother Courage's cart round the stage, and realised I could have all that without going to East Berlin. It was here that my romance with France began. French was the language of theatre and of the populist culture which stirred me. France was the doorway to Europe, where I sought an alternative self.

My other great hero at Oxford had been Kafka. I read and reread his diaries, painstakingly comparing what he was thinking and writing – especially about his father – with the thoughts I was having at the same age. I was looking for a deeper way of being Jewish than the traditions and outlook I had inherited from growing up in Golders Green. My father had a shop selling clothes in Tower Bridge Road; I was a scholarship boy. I was the first in my family to get to university; as a second-generation English Jew, I felt sharply the contradictions between my family and tribal customs and the immemorial Englishness I encountered at Oxford. Kafka and Brecht became my allies against the sense of not belonging.

So when I finished Oxford with a degree in English I was too confused about my place in England to start out along the regular paths, and I needed to find out more about my Jewish identity. My eyes opened by the New Left and CND, I went to a left-wing kibbutz in Israel, hoping to experience a socialist society in microcosm. It lasted three months. I learned some Hebrew, picked apples, emptied dustbins, became very fit and very bored.

I took a boat from Haifa to Marseilles, stopped at Lyon to see a Brecht-influenced French theatre and wound up spending the best part of the following year, my twenty-second, working with that theatre – Roger Planchon's Théâtre de la Cité. Planchon, a magnetic actor and director and the son of poor farmers from the Ardèche, was bringing the classics to new audiences in an industrial suburb, advertising Shakespeare's *Henry IV* Parts One and Two as 'un grand Western historique'. Planchon, the first of my series of professional father-figures, gave me an example of an outsider storming the citadels of culture. Although I had been to university and he was self-taught, I shared his sceptical attitude to the intimidating clubbiness of many cultivated people.

It was time to replant my discoveries into my own language and country. I spent the next year in Bristol as a postgraduate at the university drama department, acting, directing and trying to write a novel about my experiences in France. It was a good year to be living in Bristol; the university had just premiered a first play by Harold Pinter, Charles Wood and Peter Nichols were writing plays at either end of town, and the Bristol evening paper was employing a young show-business journalist called Tom Stoppard. Curious how British cities become the cradle of such sudden gatherings of talent: Bristol then, Glasgow now.

At the end of that year, I found a new friend and another provisional family in Arnold Wesker and his Centre 42 arts festivals, which attempted to build bridges between working people – reached through their trade unions – and the arts. We took plays, music theatre, exhibitions, folk-singers and a jazz band on the road. The festivals were neither triumphant nor traumatic, just a reminder that people who for centuries have been excluded from the arts by barriers of class and education can't be won round in a few weeks. Wesker was my image of a messianic Jew, trying to fuse politics, culture and family in a harmonious *seder*. We were both serious about life and we laughed a lot at the same things.

In the course of that year I married Liz Leigh, with whom I had been in love at Oxford. She went to work for BBC schools television; I, after a few months teaching Orwell and Wesker to Post Office engineers in a day-release college, wrote to Peter Hall and talked myself into a job with the Royal Shakespeare Company, which had just expanded into London. I was hired to write the programme booklets for the Shakespeare productions. John Goodwin, another mentor, gave me an invaluable training in editing and graphic design. He was gently merciless about my overheated, adjective-clogged prose: 'lapel-grabbing' he called it.

At the RSC, I began looking for ways to apply the lessons I had learned in France and with Centre 42. With Peter Hall's support I started Theatregoround, a travelling unit of RSC actors taking theatre to schools and workplaces. Peter Hall, another of my role models, stood for Leavisite standards – something he now calls 'militant classicism' – and a democratic sharing of quality. He helped me see that the entrepreneurial skills I had absorbed from my father and the shop in Bermondsey could be used in the arts as well as business.

The encounter at the RSC with Peter Brook mirrored other aspects of my personality. I travelled with him, as assistant, interlocutor and writer, along the path that led from Antonin Artaud's Theatre of Cruelty through Peter Weiss's play the *Marat/Sade* to *US*, a show about the British, the Americans and the Vietnam war. Brook was my cosmopolitan alter ego, an English Frenchman, a European hungering after modern extremes, a hard-headed mystic refuting English mildness.

After four years with the RSC, my marriage came to an end, and I moved from the theatre into the even more volatile world of the contemporary visual arts. I became director of the Institute of Contemporary Arts in autumn 1967, and led its move into the Mall in April 1968. I brought to the job a belief in the utopian modernism of the early part of the century, and strong showbiz instincts. The job gave me a crash course in the avant-garde, some bizarre late-sixties clothes, and a media notoriety which I found both enjoyable and alarming.

It was an intoxicating and controversial trip, but after four years I needed to get off the roller-coaster and the ICA needed a breathing space, something I was reluctant to contemplate. I had to be hauled away: I resigned in 1971, the beginning of my own third decade.

A line in Shakespeare which has always had special resonance for me is Polonius's 'By indirections find directions out.' It gives me an image for the zigzag course of my life, for my constant professional quest for new departures. Maybe I work best in new enterprises, which are still not fully formed. All the institutions I have worked in have been either just about to start, or in their early days: Centre 42, the RSC, the ICA in the Mall, the National Theatre, the American Repertory Theater, Channel Four. This has given me a useful awareness of the normal cycle of response in Britain to new institutions, especially in the arts.

The cycle begins with advance publicity, manifestos and high expectations. These last until the institution actually comes into being. Fierce attacks and vilification follow, often for a long time. And one day, while the shit still appears to be hitting the fan with unrelenting force, the third phase begins: 'How did we ever live without it?' This is often coupled with remarks about how much it has changed. In truth it has usually changed very little, although it may have improved. People have simply got used to what was unfamiliar. Sometimes it helps if there is a rival scapegoat for this apparently unassuageable need to attack the new. For the ICA, the Drury Lane Arts Lab drew the fire; for the National Theatre it was the Barbican; for Channel Four the musical chairs at TV-am.

But at the start of the seventies, after leaving the ICA, I didn't have this perspective. Nor did I feel like working for any institution, new or old. I freelanced on the margins of the arts, writing reviews and prefaces, helping to produce plays. The one thing I did do wholeheartedly was write a book, *Tank*, an autobiographical exorcism which swelled to three times its published length before I managed to tether it to the ground. At times I felt I was living merely in order to write about my living.

Things began to look up in January 1973, when I met Orna Spector, a redhaired Israeli television writer and producer. She had come to London to get out of a rut not unlike my own, and was staying with my friend Renee Goddard. Renee threw us together in a characteristically offhand fashion. Renee has a habit of intervening at crossroads of my life; this wasn't to be the last time she did so. A few weeks later Orna and I got married. We went into it the way people start a swim – we shut our eyes, gritted our teeth and dived in. We're still swimming.

In 1974 Peter Hall asked me to join the team of the new National Theatre on the South Bank, of which he was about to become director.

I was to be responsible for visiting foreign companies, and for animating the building with music and performances. I spent five years as an NT associate director, bringing leading European companies to London and starting Platform Performances – short early-evening plays, poetry or other texts performed by members of the company. They were good years under Peter Hall's flexible, pragmatic authority, working alongside yet feeling apart from my fellow associate directors: Pinter with his ferocious judgements, Christopher Morahan's soft-voiced rationality, Bill Bryden's stubborn populism, Harrison Birtwistle's laconic determination.

I was apart because I still felt like a special case, an intellectual or theorist in the theatre, part director, part literary manager, part producer. I thought I was improvising my own position, condemned to marginality not embracing it, as I had so often done. So when Robert Brustein, one of America's best drama critics, invited me to join his theatre it was hard to resist. He was the director of the American Repertory Theater, about to begin its second season in Boston attached to Harvard University. He wanted me to come for a year, as the theatre's literary manager and lecturer in drama at Harvard. Living and working in America was a mind-opening adventure, even though I tried to keep in mind my friend David Caute's warning: 'Remember, when they love you, they don't love you for yourself, but for being a member of the species Englishman.' My Jewishness was camouflaged by my English accent and my intellectuality was taken for granted; I had no need to shelter behind it as in England. My students were voracious, but Boston audiences for our theatre were sceptical at first; they needed the New York seal of approval. I was fascinated by the boundless power of a limited number of critics in monopoly positions, propelled and encouraged by an equally democratic spirit of possibility, a 'let's do it!' attitude.

Cambridge, Massachusetts, where we lived, felt so tidy after the diversity and eccentricity of London. Orna was enduring the blues of having a novel rejected, and a surfeit of wives and mothers striking ideologically correct feminist attitudes. In London, she said, no one cared what you did; here 'What do you do?' was the first question. If you weren't a writer, teacher, publicist or voluntary worker you were a freak. 'I'm Jewish and I shop,' was one of Orna's best replies. Had she not discovered personal computers and an obsession with computing science, she would have become quietly desperate.

We needed to come back to England. But in the intervening year, arts subsidies had been held back, and possibilities I had discussed with Peter Hall were out of the question. So with a heavy heart I signed up for a second year, and we came back to England for the summer holiday.

At this point my good fairy Renee Goddard waved her wand.

Renee, now living in Munich, had become the representative in Europe of Channel Four. Born in Germany, she had been brought up as a refugee child in England, and had careers as an actress, in theatre production and in commercial television, where she had got to know Jeremy Isaacs. At the end of our summer holiday in London in 1981, when Orna and I were cherishing every moment before returning to our American exile, she talked about me to Jeremy Isaacs. 'I asked him whether he'd chosen anyone to run the arts yet,' she told me, 'and when he said no, I said that you would be in town for a few days and he should talk to you.' That's Renee all over; an offhand matchmaker.

I spent an hour and a half with Jeremy, in Channel Four's temporary outpost in the Independent Broadcasting Authority in Brompton Road. He knew of my work at the ICA and the National and had read my autobiographical book *Tank*. I knew him chiefly from his magisterial television history of the Second World War, and from the occasional encounter at the theatre or on other social occasions. I knew he had worked for both ITV and BBC, and that he had lost out as programme controller in a power struggle at Thames Television. He was a man who had found direction by waywardness, who had not trod a regular path within a single institution. He asked me what I'd been doing and listened impassively, occasionally nodding. I had an initial impression of strong instincts, reserve, humour. When I said, 'I resigned from the ICA,' he said, 'Come on, Michael, you were fired!'

At the end of our talk he asked me to write him a paper about what I would do with the arts on television if I got the job. 'I'm going up to the Edinburgh Television Festival, where the world and his dog will be lobbying me for work in Channel Four,' he said. 'Let me have your paper when I get back.' I wrote something which must have been both utopian and sufficiently professional. At my interview a fortnight later, despite my attempts to glaze over the eyes of my listeners with polysyllabic explanations, I got the job. I would wind up my commitments in America over the autumn, and begin as Channel Four's Commissioning Editor for the Arts at Charlotte Street in January 1982.

Over my five years at Channel Four I have come to read the topography of Charlotte Street, where the Channel has its headquarters, as an allegory of many things Channel Four is and does. The Channel's building stands on the site of the Scala, originally a theatre, latterly one of London's enterprising independent cinemas. It is flanked by the electronics bazaars of Tottenham Court Road, embodiment of an era of new technology. Saatchi and Saatchi, emblem of the advertising agencies that have realised Channel Four can deliver an audience complementary to ITV's mass viewership, is up the road. Further up, in Fitzroy Square, plaques mark the house where George Bernard Shaw, challenger of intellectual and political orthodoxies, and Virginia Woolf, excavator of her individual sensibility, successively lived.

Going down towards Oxford Street you pass the Fitzroy Arms, where Dylan Thomas and other talented or merely bohemian inhabitants of Fitzrovia used to drink; some independent television programme-makers would say that the Channel continues to foster that tradition of impecunious creativity. Across huckstering Oxford Street, you come into the rabbit-warren of cutting rooms and video edit suites, stitching together film and tape where bespoke tailors once sewed worsted and gabardine.

Back up Charlotte Street, past the restaurants and bistros and kebab houses, past the old foreign shop signs APOTHEKE, PHARMACIE, JOURNAUX FRANCAIS, the Indian film posters and the Greek Cypriot demands to get the Turkish army out of Cyprus, past the Trot bookshop, the artists' materials stores, the neighbourhood help centre. A patchwork of special groups, particular communities, minority interests, like the Channel's various audiences.

Seen from the sky (or from the top of the Post Office Tower, our technological totem-pole), Channel Four is perched between BBC Broadcasting House and Bloomsbury; between the birthplace of the Reithian public-service credo, still the bedrock of British broadcasting, and the home of metropolitan liberalism. Each body of thought fed the debate that led to the creation of Channel Four; both are under pressure to evolve or be swept aside.

Little of this was clear to me when I arrived at Channel Four. Fifty people were working on one floor of the Charlotte Street building, housed in glass-walled boxes or open-plan booths. Crates of circuitry were being trolleyed into the basement where our Chief Engineer Ellis Griffiths and his staff were putting together the most modern computerised transmission system in Europe. I would wander down and look with bewilderment at forbidding racks of electronic tracery.

Once a week the commissioning editors would gather in the only meeting room we had, a triangular cell with burgundy-coloured walls, to listen to Jeremy and argue out the main lines of a policy and a schedule. The principles on which the Channel had been founded were clear to us all: to provide a distinctive service; to innovate in form and content; to deal with interests and groups not served by commercial television, or perhaps any television; to draw programmes from a wider range of production sources than those which constituted the existing industry. Weighing these principles against the undifferentiated mass of propositions and scripts, treatments, outlines, proposals, declarations, diagrams, schemes and fantasies which carpeted the desktops of each commissioning editor was not so simple. You sometimes had the impression that the entire British population thought it could make television on the strength of a letterhead and a blurb. But the sense of a new beginning, of boundless possibility, pumped adrenalin into all of us.

Then there was the question of how much a commissioning editor should allow his or her tastes and inclinations to colour decisions. Many editors in that triangular debating room felt that what was wrong with British television was the imprint of television apparatchiks, a professional class with a stake in the consensus constraining the dimensions of what television might attempt. 'Non-interventionist' was a good buzz-word in the early days; it meant interfering as little as possible in the making of a programme once we had commissioned it.

Others argued that Channel Four wasn't simply 'access' television, and that since we called ourselves a 'publishing-house' television station (rather than making programmes ourselves), we should have at least as much involvement as a good editor has with an author. Each editor was to find the position on the spectrum between detachment and control most appropriate for their subject area. In our zeal to foster independence, we probably began by underestimating programme-makers' need for a dialogue. It was an insecure as well as an exciting period for them – out in the world after years within the BBC or ITV, or starting to make television for the first time.

As we debated and argued with Jeremy each week, I began to get a sense of some of my fellow commissioning editors. David Rose (Drama – or Fiction, as we stubbornly called it): plucked from the BBC, bearded, tense, a man of few words and focused intensity. Naomi Sargant (Education): from the Open University, her heart as emotional as her head was analytical. Andy Park (Music): son of a Scottish miner, a composer and an elfin wit, came from commercial radio. Mike Bolland (Youth): another Scot, joky, ebullient, in love with the danger of live TV, came from BBC access programmes. Adrian Metcalfe (Sports): reminded me of John Cleese only much better dressed, a literate sports commentator who could talk about Flaubert as well as American football. Liz Forgan

(Actuality): used to edit the *Guardian* Women's Page, succinct, articulate, warily stepping out across the battlefield where accusations of lack of balance awaited her attempts to extend current-affairs TV beyond the familiar consensus. John Ranelagh (Ireland, Religion): a volatile and forceful arguer against the confusion of opinion with fact, formerly a speech-writer for Mrs Thatcher, collaborated with Jeremy on his tele-vision history of Ireland. Alan Fountain (Independent Film and Video): almost perpetually out on the road in those early days, setting up the network of film and video workshops which the Channel encouraged so that people and groups who had been previously excluded could make broadcast television. Alan had been a horse-racing correspondent and the film officer of a regional arts association; haggard, hurried and chain-smoking, he looked like the Channel's resident revolutionary, and often said, more than half-seriously, that Channel Four ought to be run as a collective.

Crammed together in our room, it wasn't possible to see each other clearly. And anyway there wasn't time; the months up to the start of transmission in November 1982 were an incessant, unsignposted journey for everybody; there was no let-up. We had to fill a hole measuring sixty hours of transmitted television per week, with material that would affirm our distinctive identity and not betray our principles. We had to estimate how much could be commissioned and made within the time, how much should be purchased, what the ITV companies should provide (and they professed themselves ready to fill our slots), what the new independent sector was capable of delivering.

Jeremy, who must have played a thousand different parts to a thousand people during those months, began to give us shape and parameters by laying out the main blocks of what, with only minor readjustments, has remained the Channel Four schedule: a twice-weekly soap opera set outside London, a long early-evening news, a viewers' right-to-reply programme, and so on. Each commissioning editor was given a budget and an estimated amount of airtime required. It began to be easier to find grounds for saying no to things.

Saying no was something we all had to learn to do swiftly and firmly. Each commissioning editor made his or her own priorities to deal with the flood of ideas, the stream of genuine makers, the cavalcade of glib hustlers. As I read outlines and scripts and watched tapes and films, I began to identify archetypal offers and identify the ideas of art on television that guided them. There were lots of proposals for series of classical music performed in stately homes, the gentility principle incarnate. There were almost as many offering the best of the fringe theatre, as if new subject matter alone would guarantee fresh television, without any attempt to find a televisual language for the formal experiments of many fringe productions. Waves of Americans rolled in, seeking our commitment to four plays a year from the National Theatre or the Royal Shakespeare Company, because they could find sponsorship for them in the USA and sell them to cultural cable and public television. When I said I wouldn't commit to any production on paper but only once I had seen and liked it, they couldn't understand: these were reputable cultural products, what was the problem?

There were umpteen profiles of performing artists, hardly any proposals about living composers. Multi-episode dramatised biographies of artists came and went, trailing promises of co-production funds in their wake. One steely American producer pursued me for months with a plan to do the Bauhaus as a drama in the original East German locations, with funding from the National Endowment for the Humanities. The only trouble was it didn't have a script yet, and I was concerned about the 'hello-Wassily-hello-Walter' problem which lies in wait for all bio-pics. A dramatised life of Brecht came and went in many guises. In its last incarnation it was to be written by a Spanish novelist and directed by Alain Resnais. Or so the febrile producer said. *Carry on Bertolt* was just around the corner.

Good directors offered films about theatre rehearsals, and I said no to most of them because I knew that what really happens in rehearsals is unreachable, and often takes place in the pub or the bathroom rather than in the rehearsal room. Perhaps such a film could be made one day, but it would require surveillance cameras and the equivalent of speeded-up nature filming. There were many proposals for a really original television book programme at last; the originality of most of them consisted in being about publishing and money rather than reading or writing. I was interested by a number of ideas for putting poetry on television, and tried some of them. I began to explore what happens to the dynamism of dance in front of the camera.

I steered away from most of the submissions about painting, either dressed-up lectures or cameras gliding across the surface of familiar masterpieces with appropriate musical background. I did not need to commission telerecordings of well-known ballets and operas: there were plenty that could be purchased at a fraction of the full production cost. I thought there would be a better chance of reinventing the relationship of art and television, and of giving people experiences that would surprise and lift them, if we concentrated on the contemporary and the unfamiliar rather than on hallowed heritage. Everywhere else in television, actuality and immediacy were the order of the day; in the arts (other than in topically based series) television tended towards timelessness and heritage. Sir Kenneth Clark in Tuscany was still archetypal arts TV.

I imagined new genres of programmes, mixed genres, that would not be easily pigeonholed as arts or drama or ideas; after all, we were running a channel which encouraged a more adventurous kind of viewing. 'Let's try to wrong-foot people into illumination,' I urged bewildered programme-makers. On the one hand there were mountains of proposals that saw art as a balm and solace, a comforting sanctuary in the avalanche of television, and in some sense a spiritual alibi for the crassness of much of it; on the other, there were some arts programme proposals which sought to make art, past or present, vivid in the context of the codes and conventions of television itself. I wondered whether they could be realised the way they had been imagined.

About twice a month I had a meeting with Jeremy. He began by seeing each of the commissioning editors personally and relating to their output himself. As the number of commissioning editors and the responsibilities of being chief executive grew, this became impossible. He decided to deal directly with news and actuality, our fiction output and the arts. I would bring to our meetings an agenda of programmes I wished to commission, possible ideas, scheduling suggestions, reports on work in production, themes and topics and problems. For an hour in his office, sitting on sofas under a turquoise abstract painting by William Scott, we would carve too many possibilities into a pattern of decisions, which entered the machinery and became commissions. Jeremy listened intently, considered swiftly but weightily, and was trenchant.

He talked to each commissioning editor with a mixture of respect for our specialist knowhow and the barnstorming instinct of the television professional questioning the practices and assumptions of his own craft. 'Michael, I want you to make a show of intellectual argument which has the standards of a serious weekly magazine,' he said; Udi Eichler and I invented *Voices*. 'Michael, are you being avant-garde enough?' he prodded, to my delighted amazement; I served him up three hours of the dance-theatre of Pina Bausch. 'Michael, we're going to give a commission for a series to Mike Dibb, and help him leave the BBC. He's an artist of the television documentary, you'll get on with him.' And the series *About Time*, to my mind the richest tapestry of ideas, experience and imagery I have commissioned, was made. 'Michael, if you can get Peter Brook's

Carmen for the Channel, you've earned your first year's salary.' And I did get it, against stiff competition from the BBC; it turned out to be three films each with a different Carmen, and they won the Prix Italia and an International Emmy for the Channel.

I was full of adrenalin, swept along by a blizzard of stimuli, by the torrent of television. I was also suspicious of television's speed and proliferation. Many articles of faith by which I had lived and worked in the live arts were being tested. The idea of a frame or focused space around a work of art – how could that survive the flood of an evening's television? The encounter of live audience and performers in a shared space, the presence of bodies in an event of unbroken time, qualities I had cherished in the theatre – what was to be done with them in television? Did the concepts of innovation or the avant-garde have the same meaning in a medium of information, entertainment and continual novelty as they do against a background of tradition? Could television be made the way poems and paintings are made, or was it condemned to reproduce pre-existing art? Was the very idea of high art or a 'classic' inappropriate for this essentially weightless medium that mingles high and low, serious and frivolous, in the window of one hugely democratic and indiscriminate machine?

The self-questioning, which began at the outset and continues in me still, reminded me of earlier debates about photography and the cinema. Like a rabbinical student or a Shakespeare scholar, I went back to the classic texts: Walter Benjamin's essay 'The Work of Art in the Age of Mechanical Reproduction', Susan Sontag's Benjamin-influenced book *On Photography*. 'Photography,' writes Sontag, 'is not, to begin with, an art form at all. Like language, it is a medium in which works of art (among other things) can be made.' Television, I said to myself, is an extension of the case of photography, a means of recording that can become art. So what kind of art can television become, and what new relationships (in tune with Channel Four's mission to innovate) can be built between the arts and television?

My pragmatic answers to these questions are in the arts output that I have commissioned for the Channel. But the questions are not stilled by a sum of programmes. In my third year at the Channel I found an image of the transactions between the arts and television. I thought of a pier and a boat, of that moment when you step across from one to the other and have a foot in each, and choppy waves force you to balance with extra care. Art and television are the boat and the pier, although which is the vessel and which the landing stage keeps changing. Accessibility or 'elitism', innovation or quality, industrial production or the individual vision, are some of the cross-currents which make the waves choppy. Keeping one's equilibrium, I thought, was harder than in any job I'd done. But also more interesting.

I started writing this book at the end of 1985, for a variety of reasons. It was Channel Four's fourth year on air, and although I now felt I had taken the measure of being in television, the television environment had not become something familiar and accepted. Many of its procedures and preconceptions still seemed strange, not to say unnatural. It could be so fast, and so ephemeral. There was such a lot of hype and bullshit, as there is in any industry or marketplace; there were also, especially in Britain, so many people who were trying to use television as a craft or an art, not an industry. Writing about the corner of Channel Four devoted to the arts might throw light both on television itself and on art in an age of technology and media.

Channel Four is an exceptional television institution: a lightweight organisation, still compact and changeable, not a monolithic fortress like so many other television stations in the world. There are some remarkable people in Charlotte Street, and an extraordinary man leading the team. I felt more a part of this restless, combative and volatile bunch than I had of any other group in my professional life. Yet I was also apprehensive about my future in Channel Four. All commissioning editors were on fixed-term contracts; 1986, my penultimate year, could well be the last regular working year I would have at the Channel. I wanted to record a unique period in the Channel's life and in my own before it was over. And I wanted to catch the imagination, talent and sometimes the genius of artists and programme-makers.

The only kind of writing I would have time for would be an immediate journal or diary, and I set out with dictation-machine, pen and finally word-processor to catch events and experience on the wing. I was painfully conscious of the slowness of writing compared with all the technological recording devices around me – whirr of tape-spool, spin of disc, slipstream of digital time-code. When I began I didn't want to leave out anything. My writing was like the rushes of a one-man documentary film, a surveillance camera of the self. As I got deeper in, I started to find a better selection of the feverish events of any week. Television was shaking me open and sharpening me up. Writing about my work was an attempt to put a frame and perspective around a life in an electronic medium that often seems to have no gravity at all.

One of the new breed of words which television has generated is 'timeshift'. It describes the act of taping a programme on a video recorder and playing it back after its transmission time. But timeshift is also a good way of describing the dislocation and lack of landmarks anyone coming to work in television feels at first and never quite loses. 'Your programmes will go out on Sundays from week 44,' says the scheduler, and you scurry to translate in your calendar. You travel with a production to its completion, but there's no immediate climax or pay-off for the temporary family of artists, directors and editors, as there is on a first night in the theatre. Months or years later, the result surfaces on the screen and by then – especially in the world of independent production – the original team is dispersed, everyone doing something else.

Television is gregarious and collective, yet immensely solitary: the solitude of the director and editor in an editing room, the solitude of the viewer who can shift time and escape the fate of watching the same thing at the same time as everyone else. I have tried to catch television's abrupt, simultaneous and kaleidoscopic remoulding of time in the form of this book. It's an immediate blow-by-blow diary, each entry written within days of the events described. Although there are close-ups of colleagues and programme-makers, it's not a now-it-can-be-told saga of life among the media people. Channel Four has not become like the Vatican or the Kremlin, a prerequisite for that kind of book. Not yet, anyway. *One in Four* is a personal account, about the effects on my life of working in television – one of which is to consume personal, domestic life. It is about some of the ironies and aspirations of television, seen from that edge of it that deals with the arts.

WEEK 47 *November 18, 1985*

Today is my forty-sixth birthday. Orna completely pulls the wool over my eyes, dragging me off to the Caprice, supposedly to have dinner with relatives. Instead seven of my favourite people greet me with a bellow of laughter: Jeremy and his wife Tamara; Tom Phillips, painter and fellow student with me at Oxford at the end of the fifties; Claire Bloom, whom I got to know when I directed her as the narrator in *The Soldier's Tale*; Sue Ockrent, actress and wife of Mike Ockrent who is out on the road licking his production of *Me and My Girl* into shape; Jeremy King, co-founder of the impeccable Caprice, and his wife Debra, a theatre organiser about to become an independent television producer.

Within an hour Jeremy and I are having a set-to at the top of our voices. Jeremy relishes and often provokes a good argument; now he accuses me of spending too much money and screen time translating work which had been made for the stage instead of creating something original for the medium itself. 'Like what? What's been so original on British television this season?' I ask. '*Edge of Darkness*,' he says, referring to Troy Kennedy-Martin's BBC thriller serial about the totalitarianism of a state that relies on nuclear power. 'It's well written, its themes are urgent, but formally it's a 1940s' film noir. Same abrupt cuts, same insistent music,' I reply. Jeremy splutters. Before he comes back with Monty Python or *Boys from the Blackstuff* whose televisual originality I would have to admit, I counter-attack. 'Why did David Mercer say that if he'd written his plays for the theatre and not for television he'd have the reputation of a Pinter? Why was the opera that Britten wrote specifically for television one of his weakest? And isn't it true that television has been hugely parasitic on writers and actors who learned their craft in the live theatre? All I'm trying to do by bringing Bill Bryden's version of *The Mysteries* or Peter Hall's Aeschylus' *Oresteia* from the National Theatre to television is to keep alive heightened expression, poetry in speech and classic form. Whatever else television has invented, it hasn't been a breeding ground for those things. And they matter.'

Jeremy thumps the table in a disagreement that is both angry and gleeful. Heads turn, along our table and beyond. Tamara is looking anxiously at Jeremy as his voice rises. 'Are you seriously trying to tell me, Michael, that the entire creative community of British television over the past twenty-five years hasn't managed to –' What is beginning to talk now is the wine. 'Jeremy, how about this? Has television given us any metaphors for life? Today I could write in my diary that I am forty-six, and ask why it still feels like the rehearsal when I'm already in the third act? People talk about the curtain falling at the end of a life, *finita la commedia*. Where are television's life metaphors?'

The most important thing about the argument is the fact that I can have it at all, and have it so openly and uninhibitedly. In most of the jobs in the arts I've had before – in the Royal Shakespeare Company, the Institute of Contemporary Arts, the National Theatre – I've felt over-heated, a one-man hothouse sprouting big, sprawling ideas and visions to father-figure bosses and colleagues who were more reserved than me, more sensible, tidy or 'grown-up'. Something about the sheer flood and indiscriminateness of television, and something expansive in Jeremy's temperament, have released these tensions. It is like being in a huge wardrobe where you can try on anything for size. Another theatrical metaphor.

And then there is also the suspicion, which probably everyone in television has somewhere in them, that none of it matters anyway, that it's 'only television'. So if I have managed to produce good television versions of Tippett's music or Tony Harrison's versions of Aeschylus or medieval popular theatre or the surreal psychic explorations of Pina Bausch's dance-theatre, what difference does it make? They all get swallowed up in the flood. There is no calm space around them, no silence in which they might stand forth. Art on television gets no pedestal, no frame.

But that, I thought over the following days, is also its opportunity. Reaching half a million people, a derisory number in television rating terms but three times the number that saw the *Oresteia* at the Olivier Theatre, means that some of those viewers are plunged into a classic for the first time. And if there's a marriage between the visual language and performance style of the theatre work and the codes of television, those viewers may stay tuned. And if you back the thing up with informative documentary and print, as we did with the *Oresteia* and *The Mysteries*, you may have opened new interests and appetites people didn't know they possessed. Because they are cumulative over years, these things are difficult to measure on television's 'appreciation index'.

As I argue with myself in this vein, I realise that something else has changed since I came to Channel Four, something about myself and my attitude to the arts. I arrived with a holy, almost messianic sense of art and its place in life. I still believe in the power of great stories and images to lift people and in the connections between a society's artistic expression and its moral and psychic health. But perhaps I now cling to these beliefs with a less religious fervour.

Is this because, for the first time in my professional life, I feel myself at home within a group? I've felt less attached to my stereotyped adversarial roles – as intellectual, Jew, modernist or cosmopolitan – than I did at the RSC, the ICA or the NT. It's been more like the opening out I experienced in America where there was no pantheon of establishment cultural values to respect or assault, a lot of talent around, a 'can-do' attitude and everything to go for.

Next day, Jeremy comes up to my office and points to his leg. 'Tamara kicked me black and blue under the table for attacking you on your birthday.' He tells me that he and Tamara had come to the dinner party straight from the hospital. Tests showed that secondary cancers, diagnosed in her fifteen months previously, were worsening.

WEEKS 48–51 *November–December 1985*

I am sitting in the production gallery at Limehouse Studios, watching the recording of Kent Opera's production of Michael Tippett's *King Priam*. We are coming up to the entry of Hermes in the thick of the Trojan War, and his aria celebrating the healing powers of music. Nicholas Hytner's staging of the piece, updating it to the First World War, looks even more forceful on the monitors than it did on stage. We know that war through the newsreels television reruns for us; seeing King Priam through the metaphor of trenches and barbed wire and mustard-gas might snatch thousands more television watchers into Tippett's heart-wrenching music.

Hermes' aria is beautiful but undramatic. The stage production had signalled a shift of convention by flying Hermes in from the skies, a *deus ex machina*. I'd urged the television director to find some equally strong shift of style, something abstract, separated from storytelling. He's placed Hermes at the very back of a white cyclorama surrounding an empty studio. Slowly the singer – wearing an army greatcoat but with his skin coated in gold – walks towards the camera singing his aria, a wraith-like apparition, abstracted by the off-focus lens into a Giacometti silhouette, moving slowly closer like a vision in a heat-hazed desert. But there is no pay-off to the shot. The singer arrives in sharp focus and a heightened image reverts to a factual record. So I ask the director to zoom in on the singer's mouth.

The camera moves in as the music weaves its patterns, it creeps up to the golden mask-like face, closer still, only the nostrils and lips visible now, the pores beneath the gleaming gold, now the lips alone, pulsing and pursing, framing and hiding the pink tongue and the white teeth.

Shooting, on film or video, is going on all the time. Geoff Dunlop and his crew are in Cologne, Frankfurt and Berlin for the German shoot of *State of the Art*, a six-part series about the painting, sculpture and other visual art of the eighties. Then they go to California to film artists, museums and the man who produces *Dynasty* and *The Colbys* for a living and also collects contemporary art.

Writers I have commissioned are producing scripts. David Rudkin delivers a screenplay for a fictionalised film of Shostakovich's life, full of pain, politics, musicality. Philip Roth makes me laugh out loud with the adaptation of his novella *The Prague Orgy*, its ironies even more fully worked through. And Julian Bond, flanked by a story editor and a group of young art historians, is turning the lives of the Impressionist painters into a drama series, trying to avoid the twin pitfalls of the cultural costume drama and the Hollywood bio-pic.

Getting the scripts of these three projects is only the start. Channel Four won't be able to finance them in full. The two films will cost not less than 1 million pounds each, the series around £400,000 an hour. Co-production partners will have to be found and, like any producer, I will have to start 'talking them up'.

In mid-November I am watching Derek Bailey's off-line edit of Bill Bryden's National Theatre production of *The Mysteries*. This three-night cycle of medieval mystery plays, restored and completed into alliterative Yorkshire verse by Tony Harrison, traced the Bible story from Creation to Doomsday. It was a promenade production, setting its players among the milling audience, carving paths through the crowd to make space for Noah's ark, the Nativity, the Massacre of the Innocents, ranting Herod, Hellmouth. Derek thrust a camera and sound crew into the throng during one feverish week in the summer, just before the Cottesloe Theatre went dark for lack of funds; they went for their hand-held shots like newsmen at a demonstration; cameras in the galleries followed the ebb and flow of players and public as if at a football match.

Now, as I watch the edited version of the second play in the trilogy, I am struck not just by the immediacy and intimacy of what the cameras have captured, the way actors buttonhole it, directly addressing the viewer; even more arresting are the faces of the audience in the Cottesloe Theatre, in the same space as the actors. As Christ drags his huge cross three times round the theatre past the kind of crowd you might see lining the Mall for a state parade, or as the soldiers hammer home nails and hoist Christ up on the cross, arguing about ropes and pulleys, the expression on the faces we watch watching is of real emotion, unfaked involvement. It makes you realise how synthetically most television audiences are made to behave, applauding on cue, tamed by the technology, rerunning reactions for the retakes.

Here there has been unbroken cumulative performance time. Here the space is hand-made for this one piece of work, not a technological tunnel for this week's production traffic. Here cameras and microphones and lights are absorbed into the strong ceremony of the performance itself, which is open enough to admit them without losing its own order. And the result: complex seeing and feeling. Adam and Eve pushing up through a tub of contractor sand, God clambering into a forklift truck for his entrance, a soundman squatting with a rifle mike, that pretty girl in the T-shirt, and the timelessness and timeliness of the tale being told – they are all gathered into a multiple perspective, available to millions.

Editing the introductory programme for *The Mysteries*, which is to be transmitted on three successive Sundays this Christmas, two remarks from the interviews I've done keep reverberating. Bill Bryden: '*The Mysteries* speaks to people's need to believe, to belong.' And Tony Harrison: '*The Mysteries* is written in short verse for street performance, verse to be immediately understood and imprinted on the ear and mind by alliteration. As an erstwhile impresario of the avant-garde, Michael, you should know that the most avant-garde thing anyone can do today is try to be direct. It's the same with my own poems; I write them to be understood now, because I can't be sure there'll be any posterity.'

WEEK 52 *December 22, 1985*

'WE SUCK HIM A LOT,' says Frances, the Scots girl from our press office, flirting with me over a pre-Christmas drink. 'That's what the letters of your name make. WE SUCK HIM A LOT.' And she giggles.

I'm too speedy to work out the anagram. I have just come back from a week in New York, buzzing and jet-lagged. At a meeting in their glossy Madison Avenue offices, the J. Paul Getty/Metropolitan Museum Program for Art on Film, of which I am an adviser, agreed to put up development money for teams of art historians and film-makers to propose specimen segments of 'innovatory films about art'. The Getty Trust must spend $90 million each year or lose their charitable status. As the price of oil fell, American public television executives were beginning to wonder whether oil companies like Exxon and Mobil who have sponsored their prestige and cultural programmes would continue to do so. New York's Museum of Broadcasting agreed to present a six-week season of Channel Four arts programmes in the spring. A rumour was going around that AIDS could be transmitted in tears. On Fifth Avenue black Santas shook handbells at hysterical shoppers.

Back in London there are no black Santas. No major disasters while I've been away. Yuri Lyubimov has left London for Italy, having fought me and the television director of his version of Dostoevsky's *The Possessed* to an exhausted standstill over making cuts in his work. A version of Michael Clark's dance film has been agreed so that bare bums and T-shirts with sexually provocative slogans won't prevent it getting transmitted at nine o'clock at night. 'You have to respond to a lot of voices,' Christopher Morahan says to me. 'I only to my own.'

Back home to catch up on domesticity and loved ones, and on sleep. Orna has put her own novel to one side and is subtitling and dubbing *Chateauvallon*, a French soap opera which Channel Four has purchased. It's already been nicknamed 'Dallas-sur-Loire'. As I pass her room I hear her trying out dubbing dialogue to see if it fits French lip movements. 'Hold the front page,' she exclaims. 'Take your hands off me you swine!' She asks me for synonyms for 'bastard', which can't be used on early-evening television. She is as obsessive as I am about working: work occupies some of the place of children for us both.

My stacks of weeklies and monthlies are full of memoirs and evaluations of artists who have died this autumn. Italo Calvino, who wrote books with the grace of music and the sad wisdom of an ancient Greek Stoic. Orson Welles, who once went to a party with a rabbit in his pocket, ready to do a conjuring trick, but nobody asked him to and the rabbit peed in his pocket. Was the magician of the American cinema trashed by Hollywood or wasted by self-sabotage? Philip Larkin, loping off, leaving one of the unforgettable images of time passing in old age: 'the sun's / Faint friendliness on the wall some lonely / Rain-ceased midsummer evening'. Beuys finally ambling over the skyline like one of the spindly Beckettian heroes he increasingly came to resemble. Beckett still there at eighty, slicing it finer and finer.

In last month's *TLS* George Steiner talks about the ego after Freud, Foucault or Lacan as 'a kind of Magellanic cloud of interactive and changing energies, partial introspections, moments of compacted consciousness, mobile, unstable, as it were, around an even more indeterminate central region or black hole of the subconscious'. At the end of another year in this job I know what he is on about. It doesn't even feel like an overheated way of putting things.

Over Christmas I find that I've lost my friend Arnold Wesker, who's been an inspirer, confidant and mentor since I was nineteen. For the past eighteen months we've hardly seen each other. I knew something was wrong, made conciliatory phone calls, sent chummy postcards – in vain. I see him across the room at Lisa Appignanesi's Christmas party, and am determined to take the bull by the horns and talk to him. It's late, I've had too much wine and I'm still in post-New York fatigue and extroversion, so I blurt out bewilderment, pinning him into a corner with words. 'This sounds like American talk, Mike,' he says. I persist; why is he avoiding me?

He thinks I've lied to him, or at least been cowardly and evasive, in the matter of getting one of his plays on television. It's been more complicated than that, and I start trying to explain, badly. 'I've been around long enough, Mike. I'd rather have had a straight no.'

A party is no place to patch this up; I ask him if he'd like to meet to talk things through. Doing so, I reach out to touch him and smudge his black shirt with icing sugar from a piece of cake I'm holding. It's one of those serio-comic meetings after a separation where nothing goes right.

He is noncommittal about meeting again. Two days later a card arrives from him saying that there would be no point in meeting; I had underrated his latest work, and (quoting Tynan on *Look Back in Anger*), he could not love anyone who did not love this play.

And that's that. The demise of this friendship reminds me, if I need reminding, how far I've moved from the self I was when I worked and lived under the sign of the theatre, how providential and provisional much of the attention I now get is. 'Dressed in a little brief authority . . .'

I try to look at a piece of music as if it were a three-dimensional object. The analogy is with sculpture: it's something you move round. And at no point do you see the total object. The total object is exactly like the conglomeration of memory.

Harrison Birtwistle.

I always thought that winter was the end of the year; but in the television calendar, it's the beginning.

Into the office to get some forward planning done while the telephones are quiet. My office, on the fourth floor of our Charlotte Street building, has glass walls looking out into the open-plan central area where secretaries and assistants work. Through the window there's a view of the Post Office Tower and the rooftops of Fitzrovia. Not much wall space that isn't filled with rows of black-cased videotapes (copies of our own shows, tapes of arts programmes from all over the world waiting to be viewed for possible purchase), shelves with scripts and proposals, and books that I hope to have time to read one day. A reconstruction of the Acropolis, a memory of last year's film about Lord Elgin; a punk-graphic poster for our dance season; prints of episodes in the King David story, by Ivan Schwebel, an Israeli painter, with David bewailing Absalom under an El Al sign in Jerusalem; a pair of Chinese kites dangling, to take the high-tech edge off my monastic cell.

Jenny comes in and we sit down to make lists and plans. Jenny Kay is much more than my secretary: she's transformed my working life in the year she's been here. A trained art historian and former secretary to the Art History department of Birkbeck College, she propelled herself into the job with a combination of elfin eagerness and systematic research.

On special sheets in my planner, a kind of mega-Filofax that causes much mirth, we list programmes in production or development this coming year. They include:

1. *State of the Art.* A six-part series by Geoff Dunlop, Sandy Nairne and John Wyver about ideas and images in the visual arts of the 1980s. Shooting now. To be delivered this autumn.
2. *The Mahabharata.* Peter Brook's nine-hour stage version of the Sanskrit epic poem, to be made into a film or a series, shooting in 1988. In search of additional finance.
3. *A TV Dante.* Dante's *Inferno* realised by Peter Greenaway and Tom Phillips, using film and videographics. One episode (Canto Five of the poem) of the projected thirty-four completed.

4. *The Painter's World.* A six-part series on 'the changing constants' of Western painting, devised and directed by Judith Wechsler.

5. *Diary.* Israeli film-maker David Perlov's 'camera diary' covering personal and political life from the Yom Kippur war to the Israeli invasion of Lebanon. Editing.

6. *Voices.* The fifth season of our intellectual discussion show, this time about 'Modernity and its Discontents', produced by Udi Eichler and chaired by Michael Ignatieff. Goes on air this spring. The new series, on Freud and his legacy, is recording this spring and summer.

7. *The Prague Orgy.* Philip Roth's screenplay of his novella about politics, sex, literature and freedom in East and West. Christopher Morahan will direct. Seeking co-funding.

8. *The Death of Webern and Others.* Peter Greenaway and Michael Nyman's 'film-opera' about the murders of Anton Webern, John Lennon and eight invented composers. A wonderfully inscrutable scenario, in search of a producer, an opera house, co-finance.

9. *There is a Happy Land.* John McGrath's people's history of the Highlands in song and story. To be filmed in performance by his theatre company on tour in the Highlands this spring.

10. *Naturally Creative.* Michael Dibb's and Peter Fuller's essay-film about creativity and imagination in nature, animals and humans. To shoot this summer.

11. *The Real Me.* Chris Rawlence will direct a programme built around a selection from a year's work at the Institute of Contemporary Arts. It looks as if Michael Nyman's chamber opera of Oliver Sacks's *The Man Who Mistook His Wife for a Hat* will be its centrepiece. Shooting this summer.

12. *Eduardo Paolozzi.* A film with and about the Scottish sculptor and contriver, by Barbara and Murray Grigor. Shooting in stages in London and Munich, where Paolozzi teaches half of each month.

13. *Callow's Laughton.* Simon Callow's investigation of the roots and disguises of Charles Laughton – one actor mirroring another. Half-shot, while Simon gets on with his book on Laughton.

14. *Peggy Ashcroft.* She speaks about her life for the first time in a profile by Derek Bailey and Michael Billington. Shooting this spring, to be transmitted this Christmas.

15. *Book Choice.* A straightforward attempt to bring books to television, through a weekly four-minute review immediately after the Friday evening news. Edited by Miriam Gross.

16. *Hail the New Puritan.* 'Punk Nijinsky': Michael Clark in Charles

Atlas's dance film tracing a day in his life in and around underground London. The film opens this year's *Dance on Four* season.

17. *Dancelines.* An experiment to create dance for television from scratch with two choreographers, Siobhan Davies and Ian Spink, eight dancers, a designer, a director and a crew, over a six-week period.

18. *Sinfonietta.* Transmission this spring of a six-part series made over two years, in which Paul Crossley and the London Sinfonietta explore key works by Schoenberg, Webern, Messiaen and other modern composers.

19. *Chasing Rainbows.* Transmission of Jeremy Marre's six-part series about music in England and its social and communal meanings.

20. *Harrison Birtwistle.* As part of a four-week season of Birtwistle's music, Andrew Snell will make a documentary built around the premiere of Birtwistle's opera *The Mask of Orpheus*, and Derek Bailey and David Freeman will tape his TV opera *Yan Tan Tethera* this summer.

21. *Ghosts in the Machine.* A six-part anthology, of video art from America and Europe made in the last decade, edited by John Wyver. Transmission this month.

The Ghosts in the Machine title-sequence uses a visual concept Magritte might have enjoyed. You see the vertical colour-bars and hear the high-pitched whine that normally signal the test card before transmissions begin. Has something gone wrong with your set? Then the colour-bars and the sound begin to bend, tugged apart like a curtain. Fingers, and then the bleached-out face of a prisoner appear: the phantom of innovation breaking open the bars of the box?

Nightmare. I'm arranging for friends to meet me in the Groucho Club, the watering-hole of the culture brigade, which opened in Dean Street last year. Only in my dream it's in South London and instead of looking like a chic Italian hotel it's an old club in the style of the Athenaeum, comfy and a little dusty. I phone the friends and then, as I'm waiting, start worrying how we could gracefully split the bill for such a large party. When the others turn up, it's Harold Pinter, Sam Shepard and their wives.

Another nightmare, four days later. I know the CIA has a contract out to kill me. Some civil war has been taking place, and there's a settling of accounts. A number of people are killed before our eyes in a big skyscraper, headquarters of some monolithic organisation. The killers move in on me. 'But this wasn't the agreement,' I say, backing out of the room. 'Oh yes it was,' they say, 'you signed an undertaking to be killed because you'd killed. It's a binding undertaking.' 'But that all happened in a different phase of the war,' I argue; they're playing by the rules of an earlier game. 'Tough,' they say. 'I'd better leave the country, hadn't I?' I say, and start running up to the top floor to get protection, assurances. But now I know their agents can bump me off anytime, anywhere. I'm a target.

I know this is a recurrence of my long-running dream saga, a twenty-year favourite in which I am relentlessly pursued for punishment or death in time of war. Now there's also a new night-time soap opera of the mind: how I got where I got by false pretences. The dream says that my reality isn't the world of Pinter, Shepard and the Groucho Club (transposed into an Athenaeum as a symbol of the British establishment) but South London, Bermondsey, where my father started out. I guess that both dreams are triggered by my inner clock noting that this is the start of the final two years of my contract. If nothing changes, the whole house of cards will come down at the end of next year. The 'undertaking' in the second nightmare is a grotesque version of the Channel Four contract of employment. The CIA comes from a conversation with John Ranelagh, who's just finished his book about American intelligence. (He gave me a lovely new coinage. To be 'duchessed' by the Agency means to have the wool pulled over your eyes.)

When the pressure of work lifts for a few days, this is what the uncorked bottle lets out.

Programme-makers begin to phone in, making contact again after the Christmas break. Colleagues reappear in Charlotte Street, their faces sharper, their eyes brighter. The word of mouth for *The Mysteries*, which we put out over Christmas, is very good. People seem to have felt a direct emotion they are unused to getting on television. Of course we were wiped out in the ratings by blockbuster movies and entertainment specials, and the press reviews are slow to come, though glowing. Still, more people saw *The Mysteries* over those three Sundays than would have seen it in the Cottesloe theatre over a year. And it felt like an authentic alternative to BBC and ITV. You can hardly get more alternative to Julie Andrews than medieval alliterative couplets in Yorkshire accents.

On the Friday of a comparatively calm first week of the year, I meet Anita Brookner for a drink at opening time in the deserted bar of Brown's hotel. A venue that could feature in one of her books – although she must be tired of people saying things like that. I wrote to her last spring to try to interest her in doing something on television about art history, which she teaches at the Courtauld Institute.

I won't easily forget our first meeting last year. She came into my office before we went out to lunch, and proceeded to examine it minutely – the tapes and books and pictures, the two grapefruits I had on a shelf: 'Are they for decoration or sustenance?' As we walked to the restaurant she told me how important offices were and how much time she spent in hers because she couldn't stand her apartment. Then she quizzed me about my travels, said how much she'd like to travel if only there was someone to travel with, and through the streets of Soho and the first two courses of our meal, talked about how difficult her life was. Was this a smokescreen, a test? Or the counterweight to the energy and drive of her writing? Then, as if a storm had passed or I had shown I could take it all on the chin like a man, she smiled, relaxed, said, 'Only in England would what I've said be regarded as frank or candid,' and we proceeded to talk about painting.

She reeled off a dozen topics and painters to go with them in five minutes. Like some frantic Boswell, I scribbled them down: they would be the basis of the programmes. Then, having opened up, she just as swiftly shut down. No question of doing anything before autumn 1986 at the earliest. 'I have my teaching in the winter and the spring,' she said, 'through the summer I condemn myself to write another book, and when I've finished I fall ill, regular as clockwork.'

In Brown's bar, she perches on the leather-padded fireguard. She has spent the afternoon with a friend, looking at paintings in the National Gallery. She has duly completed her summer assignments; the new book, she is convinced, is a dud (its heroine haunts the National Gallery, her loneliness rebuked by rosy eighteenth-century nymphs and cherubs). Because of financial cutbacks she is going to reduce the teaching she does. She agrees to make a pilot programme for me, leading an art-historical seminar with chosen participants. How would she start it off? 'By putting a painting – let's say an Ingres – in the middle of the table, and saying to everyone, "What do you see?"' But the pilot programme must wait on the completion of the next novel. And the next novel promises to be a long one. She has spent Christmas rereading Philip Roth, and thinks he writes like an angel. Would she like to meet him? She would. Will she come for dinner? No, we are to come for a drink to her, and dinner in the French restaurant round the corner. At the start of the evening in Brown's bar, now fully populated, we bid each other a happy new year.

I walk across to L'Escargot, where I have invited Jeremy Isaacs and Peter Hall to have dinner. It begins rather tentatively, perhaps because

Jeremy has hardly been out over Christmas; Tamara is not well. He asks Peter how he manages to find time to run the National Theatre and direct plays. Peter says he doesn't have the kind of time that his play directors do, but he sticks at directing plays 'because I don't want my gravestone to read, "He ran the National Theatre without a deficit"'. They talk about money for the arts. Jeremy says the arts budget should be doubled 'because it matters, because it makes us feel better, because it's one success story of this country'. Peter talks about the need to keep the classics alive: 'They teach Shakespeare in schools, but local reps can no longer afford to put on his plays.'

I feel like a Wimbledon-watcher between them, although it's mostly in my head that points are being scored, not off each other. Jeremy: 'Don't you think *Dallas* has all the basic elements of drama?' Peter: 'No, it's just crude moralising. It says, Look, the rich have sex, power and money, but they pay for it: it's better to remain safe at the bottom of the pile.' First Peter wins on flair, then Jeremy on reflectiveness. Jeremy comes out with less ego, Peter with more temperament; that may be because Jeremy is subdued tonight. Before he catches his train for Wallingford Peter makes a pitch to direct his whole Glyndebourne Verdi cycle for Channel Four. Is this chutzpah or a need to reaffirm his achievement as a director?

The second working week starts, as they say in video, to get up speed. Importunate phone calls from people who simply must have a decision by tomorrow or we'll miss a concert / gala / rare festival revival / fringe theatre first / positively last appearance and regret it for the rest of our lives. Piles of proposals, stacks of scripts, albums of artwork, volumes of videotape. Tony Palmer phoning up regularly about Shostakovich, irascible, glum and triumphant by turns, surprisingly vulnerable for someone with such a body of work behind him. Mike and Kate Westbrook wanting to mark Mike's many-sided jazz career for his fiftieth birthday: what would be the best form for his gutsy art jazz? The calmness and order of Paul Crossley's practice room, with its big black concert grand and black-rimmed, glass-fronted music shelves, as I discuss with him and Michael Vyner what the London Sinfonietta should do for us next: young British composers, great contemporary composers while they're still alive, or newly commissioned music-theatre works with Opera Factory.

I have a run-in with Sue Stoessl about the arts programme season at the New York Museum of Broadcasting. As head of marketing, she's responsible for selling the Channel and its deeds to 1) the audience, 2) the press, 3) the advertising industry, 4) our sometimes not-so-fraternal colleagues from ITV, 5) 'spheres of influence' – political parties, industry and business, international organisations and forums. A seasoned pragmatist after years marketing London Weekend Television, she contributed to the Channel's approaching a 10 per cent share of viewers by her advice to Jeremy about the strategic placing of popular items in our schedule. A real grafter, with a brain that seems to move like speeded-up film, she sometimes strikes me like a gentle-faced lion tensed to pounce.

Making a splash at an American Museum of Broadcasting doesn't rate high on her list of priorities, compared with pushing the ratings up. But if a festival of our work is going to happen – and Jeremy wants it to – then she wants to be in charge. Like many commissioning editors, I have found festivals and exhibitions abroad a useful source of contacts and connections and an opportunity for our programmes and the way we work to influence television in other countries. Anyway, I have devised this Museum of Broadcasting season, which will be called 'The Arts on Britain's Channel Four: Extending the Medium', and I intend to run it. There's a lot to be done in a short time if it's to happen in May.

This particular event is worth doing because it may shake up arts programming in American television, and make it less insular and gilt-edged. I have pre-purchased or co-produced a number of programmes from the *Great Performances* series, American public television's main arts slot, or from American independent producers. Dance by Balanchine, Baryshnikov, Twyla Tharp; plays by Sam Shepard and Jules Feiffer; documentaries on black dance, subway graffiti, Philip Glass. I have been unable to secure reciprocal interest in my projects. My counterparts in American television said they were either too way-out for them or too parochially British, or they simply threw up their hands and disarmingly said they had no funds and would have to go out and raise money from friendly foundations or patrons, a process usually too prolonged and laborious to be of practical help.

American public television, the Public Broadcasting System, is chronically underfunded. Such is their reliance on two big oil companies, Mobil and Exxon, to sponsor their prestige drama and arts programmes that some wit suggested that PBS ought now to stand for the Petroleum Broadcasting System. Small wonder that many of their arts programmes tend to be middle-of-the-road and predictably prestigious: they are in thrall to corporate America. And yet there is such adventure, zest, penetration and true modernity in new American art. If our season at the Museum of Broadcasting could show how we yoked contemporary art and television, it might encourage American television and its funders to take America's artists seriously before they become brand names or old masters. And to realise there is more to British culture than classic novel adaptations, nostalgia and gentility. Then reciprocity might begin at last.

WEEK 3 *January 13–17*

Andrew Snell comes in to talk about his film profile of Harrison Birtwistle. Andrew is one of the independents who left the existing system to become an independent when Channel Four started. He used to be a producer and director for *The South Bank Show*; I remember his deft documentary about the making of the Royal Shakespeare Company's *Nicholas Nickleby* and his fine film about Andrew Wyeth. He's done three programmes for me – a Sylvia Plath play, a documentary on the National Theatre's *Oresteia at Epidaurus* and a film on Dufy – as well as bringing the National Theatre of Brent's gently deflationary wit to the screen in their *Mighty Moments of World History*. For other editors he's done series on English vernacular architecture and on the psychology of perception. He's a typical middle-scale independent perpetually concerned lest the commissions from Channel Four, at present the sole outlet for most British independents, dry up.

He will hook the Birtwistle film on to the production of *The Mask of Orpheus* at the English National Opera this spring. I ask him to look for elements in that work from which he can branch out into a wider description of Harry's way of making music. I intend to devote four programmes to Birtwistle's music. But will the uncompromising sounds and slowly unfolding shapes of Harry's music survive reproduction through a tiny loudspeaker in a domestic television set?

Michael Ignatieff comes in for a freewheeling conversation. Michael has chaired the most recent series of *Voices* on 'Modernity and Its Discontents', which is going out in May. His acute book of social theory and political redefinition, *The Needs of Strangers*, brought him to my attention. *1919*, the film which he scripted with Hugh Brody, has just opened. It deals with two former patients of Freud who meet years later; it's about memory, the private life and the public winds of history. 'Everyone in analysis in London is flocking to it,' he says drily.

We start by talking about the last series of *Voices*. He says how difficult he finds it to look at himself on the screen, how awful his hands, tie and suit look. He criticises his own reluctance – in the name of a chairman's fairness – to call something bullshit when he thought it was. 'In general, I think the academics had much less to say on this series than the artists or poets or journalists.' He and I have been talking about the possibility of a live talk show in which different worlds – artistic and political – could argue. Michael says he's not sure he could do it himself; as a Canadian and cosmopolitan, teaching at the Sorbonne part of the year, he doesn't feel at home enough to be talking about what's happening in Britain. I say that this detachment could be an advantage.

The most interesting part of our talk is about decorum. I say that television has no decorum, it mixes everything up, it has, in the best and worst sense, no detachment. Presenters who have to go – at least on Channel Four – from *Hill Street Blues* to a programme about Schoenberg and Wittgenstein are asked to make impossible transitions. Michael is much involved with the idea of decorum and we jump into a discussion about the eighteenth century. He's writing a film script about Boswell at David Hume's deathbed, which he hopes Jonathan Miller will direct.

With Michael I always have a sense of someone who's trying to see what has happened to the old coherences and traditions of philosophy and art, while being as aware as any social anthropologist of the alienations and dispersals of modern life. He is an expatriate mind looking hard at the new times, knowing we can never return to the old homeland but unwilling to forget it.

Claude Guisard from the Institut National de Communication Audio-visuel, French television's research and archive organisation, tells me about forthcoming shifts in French television. There is to be a new company to produce cultural programmes. Pierre Desgraupes, the ebullient former head of Antenne Deux, looks the most likely to run it, although Claude would prefer Bernard Faivre d'Arcier, who used to run the Avignon Festival and is counsellor to Fabius, Mitterrand's Prime Minister. The right backs Desgraupes, the left would favour Faivre d'Arcier – and may yet impose him before the March elections. The public sector is divided as the transnational satellite tycoons – the Murdochs, the Berlusconis and their front men – gang up over Europe.

Claude speaks of a 'climate of torpor and guilt' among French public-service broadcasters, who have no ideas to combat neo-liberalism. He shows me a video version of *Répons* by Pierre Boulez, and some beautiful thirty-second 'video postcards' of European cities. We also look at a video version of Ravel's opera *L'Heure Espagnole*, full of ingenious effects, the kind of thing which in Britain you'd only find in pop videos. He wants co-production money and purchases, of course. Not being a broadcaster, INA can't help out much with my programme needs.

Simon Callow comes in with Nick Gray from YTV to talk about their television biography of Charles Laughton. Or rather Simon's personal interrogation of the meaning of Laughton's life and work – his quicksilver, changing identity until he came to terms with his homosexuality, his astounding transformations as a character actor who was also a star. I try to make sure that the programme will allow this to happen and not merely cram Simon into the codes of a conventional TV profile.

The *Guardian* this week is full of reports of the PEN writers' congress in New York. How depressing that so many of them wind up blaming television for society's cultural decline and the damage to the environment in which writers operate. There is no such thing as the blanket effect of television; there are only different ways of making and disseminating television, and better or worse ways of incorporating it into home life and educational values. But it's no wonder that American writers feel sore about American television. They neither get to write for it nor get their work seriously discussed on it, apart from plugging their books on talk shows. A series of documentary profiles called *American Masters* has been four years in the pipeline, and is still seeking funds.

WEEK 4 *January 20–24*

To the Independent Broadcasting Authority for a chairman's lunch with Richard Luce, the new Minister for the Arts. He immediately asks the ITV and IBA top people whether they could give better credit to sponsors, as this is going to be one of the growth areas of arts funding. David Plowright, programme controller of Granada, speaking for all the ITV companies, plunges in with a sharp warning that if the Peacock Committee recommends that the BBC take advertising then the stable base of revenue which enables ITV and Channel Four to support the arts will disappear. The minister, a low-key figure, nods sagely. We are all jockeying and lobbying as the ritual requires, but how much of this rhetoric and pressure will make any difference? This government has shown scant interest in the arts. Last year, when I said to Lord Gowrie, Richard Luce's predecessor, that the more people became interested in the arts the more the demand would grow, he sighed and said, 'Yes, that's the trouble.'

Later, Gina Newson, an ex-BBC independent film-maker, comes into my office. With the writer and historian Marina Warner she has made two acute and entertaining films for me. The first is about female stereotypes embodied in the legends and screen realisations of St Joan; the more recent considers the traditional use of women's bodies to allegorise Liberty and other abstract virtues, and how this is subverted by new generations of women artists. Gina explains to me their new idea, a film which is part drama, part documentary, about an actress hired to play the part of one of the 'surrealist muses', the women who inspired and were immortalised by male surrealist painters and photographers.

I like Gina. She's down-to-earth, quick and lets her feelings – whether of anxiety, enthusiasm or warmth – come to the surface. Marina and Gina are a terrific team. One furiously verbal and conceptual, the other visual and physical. I sometimes think of them as Hamlet and the Player King, or Groucho and Harpo. I notice myself becoming mildly avuncular with the two of them. Marina told me the other day that writing this film about the surreal muse will make her confront the stuff of being a woman itself, rather than the myths and legends about it, as she's done in her scholarly books.

Alan Yentob, head of Music and Arts at the BBC, comes in for a drink and a chat. Informally, we swap plans and ensure that we are not splitting the audience by scheduling similar programmes at the same time. This giving and taking has only started happening since Alan arrived. I tell him that for the time being I envy both the number of slots he's got and their regularity. I have not gone for a regular arts slot with an umbrella title, but rather grouped single programmes in seasons, or promoted them on special occasions. In the competition for airtime, this lack of regularity can be a liability; but when the programmes are really good, they attract special attention. He says that of course he's happy the way things are going at the moment, but worried about the future. The Controller of BBC2 is putting out as many of Alan's arts programmes as possible, he says, in order to show the Peacock Committee what would be lost if advertising forced the BBC to go downmarket. Alan is afraid that he's using up his programmes too fast.

Next day I go to the Coliseum to catch the end of the first stage run-through of Jonathan Miller's production of *The Magic Flute*, and to have lunch with Jonathan. Once more that wonderful secure feeling of sitting inside the darkened auditorium of an empty theatre, stealing a march on the world outside. Did I spend all those years in the theatre just to satisfy a need to sneak away from the workaday world and astonish it with some wonder I had hoarded up? Directing in the theatre begins as exhibitionism by proxy.

I'm struck again by the bony power of the Lutheran choral music for the two armed men at the beginning of the final scene when all the trials are resolved. Over lunch I ask Jonathan what he's learned about opera and Mozart doing his *Don Giovanni* and *Magic Flute* this year at ENO, and *Così Fan Tutte* for the BBC. 'Simply that these are works which I would like to do again and again,' he says. 'I'd like to be the director who has tried every possible way of doing the main Mozart operas. There's something in them quite unlike any other opera. Absolutely quintessential.'

We got on to talking about our business: he wants to make a movie of Kafka's *America*, based on the notion that Kafka had never seen America but imagined it in the 1920s after watching early Chaplin or Keystone Cops two-reelers with their images of America like shadows on the wall of Plato's cave. So he wants to shoot it in black and white in the style of those Chaplin films, and cast European actors for all the American parts: an immigrant dream-film. But will Jonathan find time even to write the script?

Our other topic is the theatre of philosophy. Remembering Jonathan's version of Plato's *Symposium* on BBC television and knowing his interest in the drama of thinking, I would like him to get a group of actors together and stage key philosophical arguments and debates: Plato, Diderot, Iris Murdoch's Plato-based philosophical discussions, a new play to be commissioned about Wittgenstein. I think that the works ought to be performed in a small theatre such as the Almeida first, so the actors can lose their fear of not having characters or a story to play.

'I'm beginning to think I've got a second chance in the theatre,' says Jonathan. 'It looks as if I will be asked to run the Old Vic at the end of next year. I'm going to New York to do *A Long Day's Journey into Night* with Jack Lemmon. Perhaps I've found a second wind, which is surprising for a fifty-year-old director. There are so many of us around stuck into old habits and attitudes. What keeps me modern, I think, is working with new designers. My encounter with Philip Prowse has really changed my whole outlook on things.' Since he knows that I worked for Peter Hall at the National Theatre, and since we both know the bitterness of his attacks on Peter Hall over the past decade, I'm surprised when he says that he thinks he ought to try to make things up at last.

The rest of the meal is taken up with Jonathan's magisterial account of Freud's 'Scientific Project', the first paper Freud ever wrote. Jonathan adopts a non-Freudian idea of the unconscious based on cognitive psychology, where the unconscious is more like a computer, constantly redefining bits of information into different categories. He tells a story about walking past the front of the National Gallery and trying to remember who designed it. He comes up with the name Winkie. He knows this isn't right, so when he gets home he looks it up and finds that it was in fact Wilkins. He then says 'Who else was working at this time

that I might have associated with the architect of the National Gallery?'
It turns out that the architect of the British Museum was called Smirke,
Sir Robert Smirke. Obviously, says Jonathan, two systems of classification
in the mind have got crossed, the phonetic and the semantic. Smirk
became Wink. I say that doubtless a Freudian would say that there was
some repressed psychic material there; isn't winkie baby-talk for prick?

Jonathan has given thinkers and audiences of this country a good deal
to relish. And he's used the theatre with sovereign irreverence and
impatience: his shoestring production of *Measure for Measure* set in a
1920s' Kafkaesque Vienna with Angelo as a bureaucrat out of *The Trial*
was my first revelation when I joined the National Theatre. He has
used his neurological knowledge to draw forth fresh and unexpected
performances: 'I give Erving Goffman's *The Presentation of Self in Everyday
Life* to all my actors,' he once said to me. And he has lifted the patina of
familiarity from classic plays and operas with the penetration of an art
historian and the curiosity of a philosopher. Doctors, professors and
theatre people alike look on Jonathan as a prodigious visitor to their
domain, soon to be off into another territory entirely. This sense of being
a visitor, of holding a provisional visa only, is something I identify
with, though I've never been able to play out all my contradictions as
full-bloodedly as he has. About once a year we sit down for 'a serious
talk'. Its subtext – for me at least – is often stammering and Jewishness,
which we have in common.

We wind up this lunch talking about Jewishness. He launches into a
vitriolic account of being sent to *shul* by his father. 'I had nothing in
common with all those accountants in bowler hats,' he says. 'The whole
thing made me want to throw up.' His father, the child psychiatrist
Emanuel Miller, was always telling him that he shouldn't assimilate, and
Jonathan would reply that he wasn't assimilating, he was already an
Englishman. For him the sound of hymns and a chapel choir moves him
to tears: I tell him that some of the East European and Oriental melodies
of a synagogue service have the same effect on me. But Jonathan is
unrelenting; he recalls Jerusalem with horror. 'All those people knocking
their heads against the Wailing Wall like lobotomised mental patients:
Jerusalem is the seat of the three great faiths – Judaism, Christianity and
Islam – which have killed millions and will probably go on doing so.'

Back at the office I tell an independent producer that I'm very disappointed in his proposal for a long documentary. 'If you really want me to
get it better, then I will take out another loan on my house to do so.'
How to make a commissioning editor feel guilty with one sentence.

Peter Greenaway comes in for an end-of-day drink. He is wearing a windcheater as if he's on a shoot, and carrying a briefcase stuffed with scripts, books and photographs. He starts talking, rapidly and telegraphically, not about *A TV Dante* but the film opera *The Death of Webern and Others* which he and Michael Nyman are devising. We skate through a lot of topics – heightened acting (which he acknowledges he didn't achieve fully in *A Zed and Two Noughts*), Rome (the setting of his next feature), Vermeer, whether there are any good new writers about and why he feels stuck in his favourites Pynchon and Beckett, and his enthusiasm for a new cameraman who has worked out a way of varying the speed of the camera motor while keeping the exposure constant so you can film something that imperceptibly speeds up and slows down.

Febrile is the best word for him. Whenever I see him advancing towards me with his loping walk I think of Monsieur Hulot, propelled towards some self-defined goal which the world would call quixotic. He listens impassively, with the faintest hint of impatience, and his interventions are always very economical. The emotionally carnivorous characters in his films and his obsession with catalogues, grids and symmetries – at times almost a delirium of taxonomy – point to fierce feelings inside, requiring strict formal controls.

I introduced him to Tom Phillips, the only artist I know who could outgun Peter intellectually. Their competitiveness produced the icono-graphic brilliance of Canto Five of *A TV Dante*. Now Tom feels pushed to one side by the demands of Peter's feature films. I say to Peter that I understand he must make the features he has written his first priority, but that the working relationship with Tom needs to be brought to a conclusion. And what am I supposed to do with a fifteen-minute episode from a television version of Dante's *Inferno* which, because of Peter's other commitments, looks as if it may never be finished? Poker-faced, Peter nods; he will talk to Tom. Then he digs into his case and slips me the libretto of an opera, parts of which will be seen in his next film, the whole of which he thinks worth staging somewhere. The man must feed his word-processor in his sleep . . .

WEEK 5 *January 28–February 1*

People all over the world are staring at enlarged video close-ups of the appalling last seconds of the American space shuttle *Challenger*, which blew up a minute after take off. The degraded colours of the video have some awful beauty – pink and orange against Prussian blue, a blazing blitz of light, a swirl of smoke. It all seems to be happening in total silence as the commentary from NASA has been cut off. A 35-year-old teacher is on board the shuttle, the first ordinary civilian on a manned space trip; her parents and her pupils, brought to Cape Kennedy to watch and celebrate, are seeing her burned up in front of their eyes. The television cameras watch them.

I first hear about this from Jenny, whose nine-year-old friend, a little girl, has just seen it on television and rings her up in panic. No one talks about the effect of such ferocities on children.

The accident happens two days after the jubilant razzmatazz of the Superbowl American football match in New Orleans which we put out on Sunday, 26 January. Two great American rituals: the biggest football match in the world, and space exploration, both of them examples of that American affirmative 'can do' spirit. President Reagan says that 'the quest into space' will continue. If you keep pushing outwards you don't have to look inside so much.

As facts fill out the news bulletins, further questions come: how much of the rush to get the shuttle into the air was due to the need to 'have something up there' just before the President's State of the Union speech? How much of it is to do with government through television, the politics of public relations? Or with the arms industries? Later that night a man appears on *Newsnight* saying that Star Wars systems were being tested in the space shuttle programme.

Next day, an all-morning meeting with a group from IPPA, Independent Programme Producers Association, the trade body of independent programme-makers. We spend £40 million a year with the independent sector, and for the time being we are their only British broadcasting outlet. Alasdair Milne, the BBC's Director-General, came to the Channel Four board dinner this week, and when pressed about the BBC employing an agreed proportion of independent programme-makers was very negative. The meeting, which IPPA's chairman John Gau calls 'a family discussion', is low-key and serious. We find some ways of improving the system, but there's no doubt that the anxiety of the independent programme-makers will not be assuaged by this. There will continue to be a greater desire to make programmes than Channel Four's ability to fund or transmit them. We have triggered the creation of an independent programme-making sector, which has produced some of the freshest programmes in British television. We cannot sustain it alone.

In the evening I go to a Steve Reich concert at the Dominion, which is packed to the rafters with a young and eager audience. Reich and his musicians are going on a tour of ten British cities. If you added together the audience that will come to these concerts and buy his records you've probably got something approaching half a million people. That is one of the special-interest minorities which Channel Four needs to feed.

The accuracy and precision of these musicians is astonishing, and soon familiar vertiginous feelings take hold of me. I have images of being on a rollercoaster or bobsleigh, swooping round curves; of birdsong; of big band riffs, African drumming. It's music for the age of information technology: its tapestry of simple figures and pulses is like the web of a video screen or a computer scanning process.

Next day I view the work print of Anthony Penrose's film about his mother, Lee Miller. Lee, whom I knew at the end of her life, her once beautiful face criss-crossed with wrinkles, her voice down to a croak and a glass rarely out of her hands, was the wife of Roland Penrose, my chairman at the Institute of Contemporary Arts. She had been the lover of Man Ray, the surrealist photographer, and the friend and probably the lover of many others of the surrealist group in Paris during the twenties and thirties. From her early fame as a fashion model she became a photographer, a surrealist muse who became a maker in her own right. The film is full of her striking images of London during the blitz, of the American army slogging across Europe, and of Europe's devastation in 1945: the shattered Vienna State Opera with a silhouetted soprano trying to sing in the wreckage, a Hungarian Nazi collaborator being shot by a partisan firing squad, a Nazi suicide. Something of Lee's whirlwind passions sweeps through the film, especially in the recollections of the men whom she must have hit like a tornado. I try to fulfil my task on these occasions: to act as a 'fraternal critic', helping to sharpen the focus and progression of the film, encouraging its makers to jettison what they cherish too much. Often it's a question of helping the maker decide what kind of film he or she is making. Here, the film starts too journalistically, with a report on an exhibition opening. Commissioning editor's detachment at this stage of a film can be as valuable as their initial encouragement and sympathy.

An end-of-day meeting with Christopher Morahan and his producer Mark Shivas about the Philip Roth film, *The Prague Orgy*. We're waiting to hear what the American production company and video distributors will offer towards the film. Christopher and Mark talk about getting Donald Sutherland and making the film an Anglo-Canadian production so that it has tax shelter advantages. A critical factor will be what the video distributors – who made a great deal of money by distributing Michael Jackson's *Thriller* video – will ask in terms of casting and script approval. I hadn't realised how important this was in setting up a film. Christopher says, 'Oh yes, the video rights have more and more become the hard part of the deal.' At the National Theatre when we met, Christopher and I used to talk about Shaw and Chekhov.

Next morning I see Jeremy for my routine meeting. He's just come back from the IBA, his spirits a bit dashed. 'It gets to you sometimes when all you hear from them about Channel Four is complaints.' The chairman and Director-General of the IBA have been critical about three matters. Two are political: the tendentiousness of a series on the Greek Civil War, and a film in Alan Fountain's *Eleventh Hour* slot about the welfare state which is judged to be crudely anti-Thatcherite. Since our aim is to go beyond consensual programmes and received ideas of balance, we keep pushing at the limits of the 'due impartiality' which the Broadcasting Act calls for. Similarly, we test notions of taste and acceptability, especially in sexual matters. Now Jeremy is getting a lot of stick for showing two Derek Jarman films, *Sebastiane* and *Jubilee*, late at night. Our temerity in screening these films, with their naked boys and defiant camp sleaze, is perceived by the IBA as having given ammunition to a private member's bill from Winston Churchill MP. He wants to bring the obscenity laws to bear on broadcasting, instead of self-regulation by the IBA and the BBC governors. This could mean that the author, director or publisher could be sent to jail. Jeremy is not his usual ebullient self so we zip through the agenda, scheduling arts programmes in the next six months and checking the progress of various productions. On my current contract, many things I'm engaged on now would not be even completed, let alone transmitted, until after I'd left Channel Four. That doesn't make me feel exactly my own exuberant self either, although I subscribe to the principle that there should not be a permanent establishment of apparatchiks.

To the BBC after lunch, to appear on *Did You See?*, to discuss the *Saturday Review, Spitting Image* and a programme about alcoholism that we showed. I enjoy the experience, not least because of Ludovic Kennedy, who is bright, warm and makes you want to say good things. When I watch it that night I can't help thinking how fast I'm talking, how much I'm waving my hands and what a lot of smiling I'm doing.

Next morning I drive down to Tom Phillips's studio in Camberwell for my portrait sitting. He said last year that he'd like to paint me, one of a batch of portraits he's doing. It's a good way of seeing each other regularly, two hours of peace and quiet every other Saturday morning. I've known Tom since we were both at Oxford in 1959. It's one of those friendships that has revived after years of hardly seeing each other. His keen mind and eye, his restrained warmth mean a lot to me. He's become one of the best painters of his generation. Last year he was elected to the Royal Academy, where he's joined Howard Hodgkin, Peter Blake, R. B. Kitaj and other recent arrivals in keeping the place central and not just conservative. As well as being a painter Tom is a composer and musician, and father of a cellist daughter and violinist son, both extremely talented. He's also a good writer and linguist; he translated Dante's *Inferno* himself, into good blank verse, and made images and typography and handmade paper and a binding for it. His marriage has recently broken up, and working on the video Dante last summer with Greenaway not only gave him an additional instrument of expression, the electronic paintbox; it also filled what could otherwise have been painful weekends.

When the painting is not going well Tom purses his lips, whistles, grunts. Or are they signs that it is going well? He's painting me with a background of his reproduction of Titian's *The Flaying of Marsyas*. I'm sitting underneath the figure of King Midas, with whom Tom connects me: 'He was a judge of artists,' he says. 'He made mistakes, and he's got funny ears.'

In Tom's studio, there are several things on the go at once: portraits of Iris Murdoch and Brian Eno, a theatre poster, autobiographical texts embedded in paintings. This is my sixth sitting. He began with a watercolour study, which made me look wounded. Then came a small-scale oil of my head, something vulnerable around the eyes that I recognise. Now he's begun the picture proper.

WEEK 6 *February 5–7 Paris*

The Carrefour International de la Communication is one of President Mitterrand's attempts to match the Centre Pompidou in Les Halles. It is in a much less prepossessing place: La Défense, a skyscraper city out west beyond the Étoile, an amalgam of downtown Houston and Alphaville. I'm here to make a presentation of Channel Four's programmes because we have been awarded a prize for 'the best television cultural policy'. It's given by the Conseil Audiovisuel Mondial Pour l'Edition et la Recherche sur L'Art. CAMERA is an organisation under the aegis of UNESCO, from which the British government has just withdrawn because it's become too politicised. Among the patrons of CAMERA are writers, artists, museum directors, scholars, members of the international brigade of the Great and the Good.

The room in which I will make the presentation has a wall-sized mosaic of monitors showing what is being transmitted on world TV. It is a patchwork of station identifications, jiggling puppets, smiling presenters, the same news clips coming up in different countries across the world, like lights chasing along the snakes and ladders of a pinball machine.

I talk about the antecedents of Channel Four to an audience of journalists, artists, scholars, video-makers, television executives. I start to play tapes, beginning with *Once in a Lifetime*, Geoff Dunlop's film about David Byrne and Talking Heads, which is at once a rollercoaster ride through world television imagery and an anthropological essay on the rituals of rock concerts. I have chosen the extracts to show that if culture or the arts are to make sense on television, they must take account of television. After two hours, the response is almost alarmingly enthusiastic. Because of fears about the future of French television since Mitterrand allowed the first two commercial channels in France last month, Channel Four is an encouraging model, showing that commercial needn't mean crass.

Jeremy arrives next evening for the award ceremony at the Carrefour de la Communication. In my room we go over his speech, which he wants to deliver in French. In the middle he has a key phrase about why Channel Four matters: 'We were given defined tasks, a free hand to execute them, and assured funding.' We add a sentence about giving broadcasters the stability to get on with their real work, which should certainly strike home to the current French situation. Then we talk about how he feels about Channel Four. Has he still got the zest for the job, I ask. He says he has, although the struggles with the IBA and with his own chairman have taken their toll.

Out at La Défense before an ambassadorial audience, Jeremy makes his speech, prefaced by an ad-lib: 'Prenez garde, comme disait Churchill dans un autre temps, je vais parler français.' He gets laughs, he gets applause, he gets belligerent towards the French language and batters its syllables into submission. Afterwards he says, 'I could see you wincing in the front row.' We flee the drinks party and go to La Coupole, where we have dinner with Annie Cohen-Solal, whose new biography of Sartre is the talk of France. Jeremy, his adrenalin up, launches into a scathing criticism of France's hasty and politicised decisions about their television. 'We have had more than twenty years' debate about ours, and even after a year we were scarcely ready to go on air; here your new commercial channels are going on air after three months.' He questions Annie about Sartre's relation to Simone de Beauvoir, and the recognition of intellectuals by French politicians. He's elated by the late-night Parisian exotics who parade up and down the aisles of La Coupole. 'Who's that? A fashion designer? A sculptor? I think I could very easily come and live in France. In fact I may be a bit of a Mediterranean really.' I ask him whether he considers himself a member of the English establishment. 'Well, I suppose someone like me probably is. But no one running a television company like Channel Four ought to get too close to the British establishment, which is why I go out of my way to insist on being a Scot and a Jew.'

WEEK 7 *February 10–16*

The pile of mail after three days out of the office is not quite as horrendous as I feared. But Jenny is off sick and I don't feel on top of things. The temporary secretary reels under the morning's fifty telephone calls. Even with the best acknowledgement system for proposals that I can devise, even with reiterated explanations that there is no money left in this year's budget and next year's proposals won't be examined until June at the earliest, every producer, artist, agent, salesman or foreign broadcaster demands attention immediately.

To lunch with Michael Billington and Derek Bailey to talk about the Peggy Ashcroft profile. Wearing his *Guardian* drama critic's hat, Michael is a member of the Arts Council Theatre Enquiry, which is going to report on the state of the British theatre by July, to give the Arts Council ammunition for its financial arguments in the autumn. Six months is a ridiculously short time to survey the entire British theatrical scene. I hope the enquiry will talk about the reasons for supporting theatre, not just how to spread the money around more efficiently and equably. Mrs Thatcher's attack on public spending and her pursuit of popular capitalism have had one side effect which the Arts Council is now trying to challenge, feebly and late in the day: they have undermined the idea of the arts as everybody's entitlement.

In this context, the Peggy Ashcroft programme will be a reminder of the kind of theatre she has always gone for: company or ensemble theatre, classical style rooted in language and Stanislavskian emotional truth; the sort of theatre threatened by costly buildings and the cult of the splashy musical. I hope the programme will explore what it meant to be an actress and a woman in the British theatre of Olivier, Gielgud and Richardson, though knowing Peggy's reticence I wonder how much she'll say that's not strictly professional.

In the evening, to the ICA to take part in a discussion about video art on television with John Wyver, who produced *Ghosts in the Machine*, the video anthology we started transmitting this month, and Jane Thorburn, ex-Royal College of Art video-maker whose company made *Alter Image*, an inventive video arts magazine in our first season.

John gives an account of the sources and funding for the works in his series. He says that the mainly American video-makers in *Ghosts* are the product of a childhood and youth drenched in television; its codes and conventions – and its sheer glut – are what they start out from. This glut, and the overwhelming awfulness of much American TV, are not such strong factors for British video artists. Given the comparative inventiveness of much British broadcast TV, what would prod the British, I ask, to make works as assured and bold as the best in *Ghosts*?

This question is largely sidestepped by the rest of the discussion which resurrects the good old conspiracy theory. A young man at the back, speaking with steely steadiness, accuses me and Channel Four of being part of the Oxbridge old-boy conspiracy, with literary rather than visual sensibilities and a journalistic rather than imaginative view of television. Many of his fellow video-makers nod agreement. Replying is like talking to armour plate.

The paranoia is depressing. Channel Four has already been cast in the minds of many in this room as part of the establishment, closed to new ideas. At the same time we are seen as a key source of financial support. I say that others have responsibilities to encourage innovation in video – the Arts Council Film Department, the ITV companies who could commission new works from video artists as well as giving philanthropic grants to orchestras and archives. But the grudge remains.

Next morning in early to meet the Controller of ZDF, West Germany's second channel, and his team. I stretch my legs on a bitterly cold morning by walking down Handel Street into a Bloomsbury churchyard. Gravestones, tombs, an obelisk, eighteenth-century italic and serif inscriptions. A bunch of stiff brooms in the gatehouse. One day when all this is over I'll retire and become a park-keeper, brewing tea in my hut, spearing leaves, writing a long novel through autumn afternoons.

The Germans arrive promptly at 9.30, and we settle in to discuss the things I'd like them to co-produce with us: a film by Pina Bausch, profiles of Polish composers Lutoslawski and Penderecki, *The Impressionists* series, Peter Brook's *Mahabharata*. The controller's eyebrows frown in bewilderment at the *Mahabharata*. 'An Indian Nibelungen,' explains one of his colleagues.

I read the first drafts of Julian Bond's *Impressionists* scripts. I want the series to have popular dramatic virtues as well as art-historical illuminations. The characters are starting to emerge: Manet, pioneer, precursor and a rat with women; Cézanne, stifled by his own intense search; Monet, singlemindedly after his artistic quarry; Renoir, expedient from the start; Pissarro, anarchist in politics, meek as a son and husband; Degas, sharp-tongued, sexually impotent; Zola, born polemicist, ambitious provincial. There's still too much undigested art-manifesto talk, and maybe it's too linear. But it's a fair start. Doubtless the art-historical community will raise its hands in horror at this attempt to combine drama with art history. Art historians or video-makers, every sect guards its preserve.

WEEK 8 *February 17–21*

After a weekend away near Bath, Orna is driving us back through a cold grey Wiltshire morning. We have become a very attuned couple. Orna, swamped in her father's over-demonstrative approval, distrusts praise; I, starved of recognition, need it more than is good for me. We have learned to be close but self-sufficient. She's swifter and more direct than me; stops me getting heavy or too earnest. I'm looking through a folder of submissions and proposals: a profile of Pasolini, a film about Piero della Francesca, a programme about the Cobra group of painters in Holland. Something really interesting from Don Taylor and Anthony Rooley of the Consort of Musicke: a long programme about the impact of the English Revolution on music, painting, poetry and polemic. In the seventeenth century, battles in the English Civil War were fought in the steely snowbound Wiltshire hills through which we are driving.

Peter Fuller and Mike Dibb are waiting in the office to talk about their film *Naturally Creative*, which will investigate the links between human creativity and creativity in biology and nature. It will be their fourth collaboration, and they now have a great shorthand with each other. With every film Mike enriches his search for a documentary form that is lyrical, informative, welcoming and human. I see his work as a continuation of the British tradition of poetic and inquiring documentary – Grierson, Humphrey Jennings, Living Cinema. Peter Fuller is now deep into an intellectual quest which started as art criticism but goes wider, testing the ground beneath the dislodged certainties of Marxism and modernism.

I get Mike to talk as much as he feels able to at this stage about the form of the film. I hope they push their concerns about visual art into considerations of music and poetry and other time-based art. They're going to talk to Alfred Brendel about expectation and silence in music, and to Tony Harrison about metre and breath. It sounds like a film that won't simply be an accumulation of discourse, but a balance between analysis and embodiment. Mike comes out with a lovely phrase: 'I keep seeing a film in which shapes turn into sounds and sounds into shapes.'

That night we cram into the black box of the Lyric studio for the first night of *Satie Day Night* written by Adrian Mitchell and designed and painted by Tom Phillips. I've known Adrian for twenty years; his courage and vulnerability have been an example to me. Like Lorca or Mayakovsky he's a poet in the theatre. His plays return to three themes: childlike innocence, cynicism, loss and death. His William Blake play in the sixties contrasted Blake with a Sir Joshua Reynolds seen as the David Bailey society portraitist of his time. In this play, Erik Satie is the childlike innocent and Claude Debussy the sophisticated success. Adrian is even-handed and doesn't say that one is better or more truthful than the other. 'Ravel has refused a prize,' says his Debussy. 'Yes, but all his music accepts it,' replies Satie.

In the interval Peter James, who runs the Lyric, tells me that he's heard that the Labour Party in Hammersmith Council, who are currently in opposition but will probably be elected next time round, have urged the Arts Council not to give a grant to the theatre because it will embarrass them when they come into power and withdraw support from the Lyric because it's too 'elitist'.

John Wyver, Geoff Dunlop, and Sandy Nairne have finished principal photography on *State of the Art*. If anyone can sort out the prophetic visions from the fashion and bullshit in today's art, they might. We talk about music, about the balance of argument and image within the films. They are going to try to make the films without an authoritative narrator and explainer, for they are dealing with a situation in art and ideas where authority has been unseated. Geoff shows me a box of black and white stills: the lean face and grey eyes of Joseph Beuys; Antony Gormley, naked and covered in plaster, using his own body to form a statue; a man doing an oil painting amid high-tech architecture.

After a punchy conversation with the Museum of Broadcasting in New York about the design and cost of the print for our season there, I apologise to my next appointment for keeping him waiting for half an hour. Then I look at him again. He is an eerily accurate copy of me as I looked in my early twenties. His name is Stephen Games, he edits and presents a sparky Radio Three arts review called *New Premises*, and he's come to talk to me about doing something like it for television. Everything he does reminds me of the way I was – the self-deprecating laugh that covers unease, the avidity about the latest books and art events, a nervous gesture of the hand to the top of the head and hair when bewildered. My clone. Uncanny.

I still haven't finished at the end of the day when Iris Murdoch comes up and sits while I sort myself out before driving her home for dinner. I first got to know her when I suggested that she write a Platonic dialogue for my early evening 'Platform Performances' at the National Theatre. The result was *Art and Eros*, in which she incorporates Plato's arguments about why the artist should be banished from the Republic, and adds her own characters expressing other arguments for and against this. It worked beautifully, with a humour and vigour of argument that was itself dramatic. Since then she's written another dialogue, *Above the Gods*, about how true religion is a mysticism which dispenses with God and gods. The dialogues are coming out in book form next month and she has dedicated them to me, something which gives me immense pleasure.

She sits there with her bright blue eyes and soft straw-coloured hair, something still girlish about her. This morning in the *New York Times Book Review* I read Harold Bloom's account of her latest book, *The Good Apprentice*. Her novels express a religious consciousness in a post-religious era. In her person, Iris demonstrates both fierce seriousness and a waggish gaze on the world. We drive north through Hampstead. 'I used to come here a lot years ago, when I was visiting Canetti,' she says. 'Hampstead always frightens me. It's as if something violent is about to happen to me.'

I tell her about this book and what I'm trying to do with it. She says that as well as narrative she's sure that it will have speculation about culture and television. 'You need to pick up where the Frankfurt school left off. Somebody needs to fill the void that Marxism has left, to make serious connections between culture, morality and politics.' This is one of the themes of her current philosophical inquiry, which she has been revising and enlarging for several years. Every time I ask her about this work she sighs deeply: 'Doing philosophy is contrary to nature, unlike writing novels.' I remind her that somewhere in the Platonic dialogues she makes Socrates encourage Acastos by telling him to jump in at the deep end with crude thinking as the way to start a philosophical argument. Is she saying that the reason for revising her philosophy book is that the thinking of the earlier versions was too crude? 'Not crude enough,' she says.

Back home, Iris kisses Orna. There's an enormous mutual warmth between them, and Iris is full of curiosity, about Israel, about Orna's planned novel. Tom Phillips, who is painting Iris as well, for the National

Portrait Gallery, joins us for dinner. We talk about politics. She speaks of the dangers of putting large moral expectations into political theory, as in the utopianism of the Marxist argument that it only needs a few more adjustments, changes and struggles, and we will all come out into a society of justice and plenitude. 'But politics isn't like that,' she says. 'It's largely a question of arrangements and reconciliations. The idea of the good life is at home in philosophy and religion and art. In politics we need good men, not dreams of an ideal society. Again and again her sense of the rigours and perils of thinking clearly and truly as a philosopher comes through. 'Mediocre art is art, but mediocre philosophy is not philosophy. Can one do philosophy at all if one is not a genius, why try?' When I attempt to describe my own political position since the certainties and faiths of the sixties, she calls it 'falling out of politics'.

At the end of the evening I look at her sitting in our front room with a whisky and water in her hand. She's listening with focused attention as Tom describes the ideal, haunting face he seeks behind and beyond all the actual faces he's painting. Plato, who wanted to get to the Form beyond forms, presides over the work of them both.

At Programme Review next morning, we discuss *Couples Arguing*, an American documentary in which couples about to have a row agreed to call up the film-makers and have the row on camera. I feel intruded upon by programmes like this. In the name of throwing light on feelings and guilts which people harbour as shameful secrets, they offer voyeurism or Californian psychobabble. Have we questioned ourselves sufficiently about exploiting people's exhibitionism, I ask, about television's intrusiveness, about the differences between British reticence (crippling as well as civilised) and democratic, fix-it American psychological engineering?

The meeting becomes almost an encounter group session in itself; someone jokes that cameras following our discussion through a one-way mirror would make a good programme. Carol Haslam, who commissions our health and documentary series, maintains the feminist position that there's no boundary between the private and the public life. I refute that. If there's no difference, aren't we losing a crucial distinction, one that non-totalitarian cultures are fortunate to enjoy? 'All personal life is political,' she says. Not totally; there is a politics of the personal life, and feminism has uncovered it; but that life is still personal, it doesn't elide into the political and public life.

'What's the difference,' asks Carol, 'between showing couples arguing in drama and doing the same thing in documentary? Doesn't the author load the dice to fit his or her point of view?' But a real writer is arguing with himself, not just propounding an authorial view. 'Was Tolstoy on Anna Karenina's side, or against her?' I ask.

'A question we will all ponder, Michael,' says our chairman Paul Bonner, moving us on to a discussion about gays and lesbians in television.

WEEK 9 *February 24–March 2*

To the Lyric Hammersmith after work for a crucial board meeting. The Lyric has become a political football in one of the post-GLC muddles facing arts institutions all over the country. The Arts Council for the first time has made an offer to Hammersmith of a grant for £400,000. £100,000 of this would come to top up the local council grant to the Lyric. But the real catch is that the money is conditional on the borough helping to support Riverside Studios. This is not acceptable to many Tories, nor to the Liberals who hold the balance of power. And the final twist is that Labour will probably win at the next elections and have said that they want to turn the Lyric into a gymnasium or a creche. A very depressing hour and a half of going round in circles. The whole thing has become an argument about deals and has nothing to do with artistic policy.

The Lyric could either close or be forced to run on a starvation diet by the summer. Peter James, who has led this theatre to metropolitan, national, and international status, looks tight-lipped as the discussion grinds on. But, as the local politicians on our board remind us, if we don't accept even an unsatisfactory form of recognition from the Arts Council we will simply be at the mercy of local political extremists.

The secretaries in the EEC glasshouse have pulled up the blinds and are sunning themselves in their offices as I drive into Brussels next day, and then out again the other side to an equally monolithic block which houses both Belgian televisions, the French and the Flemish. The meeting has been called by the Flemish to see whether cooperation could be increased between European Broadcasting Union members on arts and cultural programmes. 'This is an EBU tink-tank, with a loaded agenda,' announces our chairman in Eurospeak. He means think-tank, he means heavy.

But the two days of talk with the Belgians, Swiss, Germans, Dutch, Irish, the BBC and us are in fact fruitful. And almost overdue: it rapidly becomes apparent that in Europe cultural programmes are under pressure.

Everyone has similar problems: the reluctance of news editors to include arts stories in their bulletins ('although I bet viewers understand as much or as little about inflation as about ballet', says an arts presenter); accusations of 'elitism' in a mass medium; the dangers of sponsorship, the distorting influence of 'the culture industry', with its much-hyped stars doing the same familiar repertoire; smaller cultures complaining that they're swamped by the dominant ones.

WEEK 10 *March 3–7*

Catching up on the week's papers in London, there's one painful contrast. In France, as they wind up to their elections, the socialist Minister of Culture, Jack Lang, is a positive vote-getter for his government. Beckett, Graham Greene, García Márquez, Francis Ford Coppola, Ingmar Bergman, Maurice Béjart, Simone de Beauvoir and other artists have signed a statement applauding his and Mitterrand's cultural policy, and urging voters to make sure it continues.

Meanwhile among British art institutions there's a growing list of casualties: Jules Wright has thrown in the towel at Liverpool Playhouse, Pierre Audi's Almeida theatre is caught in the political crossfire as the Greater London Council is abolished. There's no arts policy left, just pragmatic patchwork and pious hopes of private-sector support.

Jeremy Isaacs appears with Brian Wenham and Michael Tracey of the Broadcasting Research Unit on *Thinking Aloud*, Bryan Magee's discussion show, which emulates our *Voices*. They're talking about the future of television. Tracey snaps away at the BBC's ankles, attacking it for moving substantial money from programmes like *Arena* or *Horizon* to daytime television, which is more than likely to turn out bland. Wenham counters that there are daytime viewers, and that the BBC has a right and a duty to reach them. With his hooded, intelligent face, he looks like a shrewd Renaissance cardinal.

Jeremy says that the new forms of television delivery and the proliferation of choice they will offer should not be seen as a threat to public-service broadcasting institutions, but rather as a reminder of their vocation, and a warning that they neither can nor should undertake everything. He obviously thinks that the BBC is doing too much, should clarify what is the heart of its activity, and articulate and sell that firmly to the public. Indeed Jeremy's insistence on support from the people for public broadcasting is one of the strongest threads of his argument: 'Public broadcasting needs to have the public behind it. Then it can persuade the politicians to enable it to do its job. It should not ever become an argument for the sake of the organisations themselves.'

Lunch next day with Reiner Moritz, one of the major distributors/ producers of arts programmes in Europe. When I first met Reiner, I thought he looked like a dashing, saturnine hero of a romance: penetrating black eyes, sleek hair, traditional tailoring. He's an enthusiast, a connoisseur and an energetic businessman, whose only fault – a fault which endears as much as it exasperates – is that sometimes he takes on too much. He deals with us, with LWT's *South Bank Show*, and the BBC, as well as with most European channels and the limited cable and broadcast outlets for the arts in America.

We talk about the changes in French television and the upsurge of Europe's TV tycoons; he has positive things to say about Berlusconi's arrival. 'The Italians work hard and they are utter professionals. No more of this "I don't know if I can receive anyone today."' Reiner thinks the ecology of British broadcasting – two popular channels, one financed by licence and one by advertising, and two minority specialised channels funded similarly – is still the healthiest system and should be protected.

I spend most of the rest of the day writing the blurbs for the brochure for our arts season at the Museum of Broadcasting in New York in May. Blurb-writing is a danger to the soul, and I suspect my facility at doing it. Granville Barker, when he was dreaming of the National Theatre, said that it would not need advertising, but it would be its own advertisement. He wasn't living in the age of umpteen television channels and page after page of arts listings.

To The Place off Euston Road, to see Ian Spink's new work for Second Stride, *The Bösendorfer Waltzes*. It's a sometimes infuriating but rarely boring piece of performance art. The dancers speak almost as much as they dance. There are references to Stravinsky's *Firebird*, to the argument between André Breton and Trotsky about art and revolution, to the performers' own dreams. Systems music by Orlando Gough that recalls Stravinsky's *Les Noces*, is played by amplified pianists with ultra-violet lights on their pianos. The set consists otherwise of lighting rigs, mike-stands, cables and projection screens, a technological apparatus that gives an unlocated sense of here and now. Many of the dancers look like children, and the movement is often reminiscent of children's games with their repetitions and utter seriousness, tennis balls and cornucopia of green apples rolling across the stage. The piece has a kind of calm graceful desperation, as if everything is happening after the Fall: no personalities, no aspirations, no hopes, just fragments and attempts to collage a world together.

A big round-table meeting next day at the Independent Broadcasting

Authority, with all their officers, our commissioning editors, Paul Bonner and Jeremy. Ostensibly it's for new IBA people and Channel Four people to meet; but in the current context of the Winston Churchill bill about obscenity and violence, it's obviously going to be about the regulatory role of the IBA. Jeremy, who introduces himself as 'commissioning editor without portfolio', gives an opening speech thanking and praising the IBA for helping Channel Four into being, and then trying to put into perspective the current crisis, which was intensified by our showing Derek Jarman's films. 'There's such an unnecessary tizz. The popular press loves saying the switchboards at Channel Four were jammed. In fact there were twenty calls after *Jubilee*. The switchboards were not jammed. What all of us know in this room is that there will never be an "anything goes" on British public broadcasting. We all have a tendency to forget the sophisticated great British public. But I find myself in a paradox: although I'm against broadcasting being nannied, I am also against deregulation. If we didn't have some regulation, other people with motives much less admirable than the IBA would control broadcasting. What is unsatisfactory at the moment is that because you the IBA own all the transmitters, you can interpose yourselves between us and the public in the final resort. I'm arguing that all television companies should be liable in the courts for what they do. I am responsible for my actions and I'm prepared to go to jail if necessary.'

I've had few formal dealings with the IBA, certainly less than Liz Forgan or Alan Fountain, whose factual programmes are continually under scrutiny for lack of political balance. In the non-factual area, Mike Bolland with his iconoclastic new comics performing live and David Rose, whose 'Films on Four' are deemed sometimes to have indulged in 'language', have had their run-ins. Does my lack of conflict with the IBA mean I'm doing something wrong?

Lunch with Udi Eichler, the producer of *Voices* and someone who's seen me in all my states since the beginning of Channel Four. Udi, as befits *Voices*, is a thoroughgoing European intellectual. He could come out of Chekhov; I've often thought that his combination of intellectual fervour and personal vulnerability would make him very good casting for Trofimov. The new series of *Voices* goes out from next week, and Udi is preparing a further series about the Freudian inheritance. He is in training as a psychotherapist, and when I tell him I'm writing this book he rises to the occasion. 'With so many people pushing their preoccupations and concerns towards you from all sides, what is the centre towards which you are trying to draw them?'

I say that one leitmotif I've become aware of is my interest in things Russian and East European – the David Rudkin Shostakovich script, the Lyubimov Dostoevsky production, Philip Roth's *The Prague Orgy*. I also keep upholding the truth of the encounter between performers and audience in unbroken time, setting it against the composed time and constructed truth of montage. Saying this reminds me how I defended what I called 'a proper inertia' when Jeremy attacked me last November for being too interested in translating theatre reality to the screen. I am less starry-eyed now about transmitting the power of theatre when you're not actually there in the same space. But there is some kinetic way in which the bodies of viewers can be reached by the sound of a singer's or an actor's voice, or by the physical immediacy of an unbroken set of dance movements. Ideas of human time, and our ability to distinguish them, are in play: shared time, live time, edited time, time stored and shifted and transmitted.

At the end of the day I go in to see our chief engineer Ellis Griffiths and ask him to explain high-definition television to me. I've been reading accounts in the trade papers of competition between an American-Japanese system that promises wall-size pictures with 35mm film definition and stereo sound, and a less radical European 'enhancement' of our existing television image. He launches enthusiastically into a fact-packed account of which I can understand about half, because there are so many technical terms I can't make sense of. I tell him that it would be nice if I could have a working idea of television technology, high-definition or not. He says he would like to understand what motivates me in my editorial decisions on what he calls 'the poofy side of the outfit'. But he thinks it's impossible for us both. 'My mind is trained for logic and has been from the start; yours has been trained very differently.'

Next day I go to the cutting room, where Geoff Dunlop and his team are watching the results of their first fortnight's editing of *State of the Art*. Luscious Howard Hodgkin oil paintings on the screen and a dissident voice from fellow artist Anthony Gormley in the darkened viewing room: 'I don't buy all that Proustian recollection Howard goes on about.' Impassive tracking shots through the Cologne Art Fair, where a stilettoed Mary Boone, queen of the New York new art scene, instructs dungareed Germans where to place Schnabels and Salles – the latest international art-chic, everyone must have one. The pictures, even in a roughly edited state, are poised and telling, the beginning of a clear description of a world of shifting and manipulated values.

Lunch with Melvyn Bragg in the Groucho Club, one of our most relaxed meetings yet. Melvyn and I were Oxford contemporaries, and he welcomed me publicly when I came to Channel Four. He has made *The South Bank Show* a landmark on ITV, popular and substantial. I admire his drive and directness. But I must find other ways for the arts on Channel Four. Melvyn is calmer today than at some of our previous meetings. He talks about the novel he's just finished: 'I hope I've incorporated much of what's been happening over the past ten years in fiction – the presence of the author, use of documents – into a mainstream novel.' I ask him to put in a word with Andrew Lloyd-Webber, who brought Melvyn's musical *The Hired Man* to the West End, to support Peter Greenaway's *Death of Webern* at the English National Opera. He's talked a lot about Neil Kinnock lately and I ask him whether he's thinking of going into politics. He says he isn't but if Labour got in, I think Melvyn could lead a revived Arts Council very well, if it was offered.

We talk about the motives of artists who win great success, forget where they started and go for the money. I begin an elaborate explanation, involving English puritanism and regional origins. 'Greed,' says Melvyn. 'Probably right,' I say, 'but you know me: I'll always look for the more complicated explanation if I can find it.' That's a key difference between Melvyn and me: I always go for the indirect, underground route, and he's a communicator, a responsible populariser. I'll never feel as much of a native Englishman as I imagine he does.

To Paris next day, to appear on *Droit de Réponse*, the two-hour live talk show on the first channel, the latest result of my new French celebrity. The first two-thirds of the show is about the French elections, with the Paris correspondents of eight European newspapers giving foreigners' views. We're sitting in a stepped-up version of a café, facing our host, an avuncular pipe-smoking journalist called Michel Polac. He's made his show a platform for heated and unrestrained encounters about French social and political ills and civil liberties.

I wait for the second part of the discussion, about the new French TV channels and the future of European television. It's 11.30 pm by the time this starts and the show has to end by midnight, so I'm pushed, and as always when I'm pushed and speaking French, I stammer. I am aware of myself weaving and feinting to avoid danger consonants and thrusting on fast because it's the sort of show where if you pause someone else cuts in. The result, I'm thinking as I talk, must look like some kind of voluble, flailing windmill; but I do nevertheless manage to get across some points about the hasty and politicised changes in French TV.

When it's over I'm shaking with the effort of it. The programme's producer drives me back into town from the farflung studios and tells a sad tale of reduced resources, damaging competition for ratings between public-service channels, and his own sense of betrayal. You can feel the direct political grip on French TV. At the end of tonight's show, one of the journalists said to Michel Polac, a well-known socialist, 'Will we still be seeing you on the screen after the elections?'

'*Tu avais le trac*,' you had stage-fright, says Micheline, Peter Brook's producer, as I sit with her and Peter in the café of their theatre, the Bouffes du Nord. It's 11.30 am the next morning, the audience is gathering for an all-day marathon performance of the *Mahabharata*. As we sift through various financing sources for the film version we're planning (which Peter, inspired by Kurosawa's *Ran*, now wants to make into a three-hour film) various spectators approach to press the maestro's hand. Brook has immense, gathered stillness. His eyes are a mineral blue. When he smiles, it's a big event. When he laughs, it's a boyish chuckle. He's like a man balancing on a wire. Brook nurses each perform-ance, by leading a pre-performance session or just by being there as often as possible, as if he cherishes the uniqueness of each occasion. He's just been in London and seen the latest RSC shows at the Barbican: 'Far too much industrialised acting,' he mutters.

WEEK 11 *March 10–14*

Leo Steinberg, one of America's great art historians, whom I met at the advisory meeting of the Getty Trust, lectures at the Architectural Association on 'Picasso's Intelligence'. The term 'art historian' seems inadequate to describe his own speculative mind, or his rich language-play, balancing Latinisms like 'recession' and 'planar' against Saxon monosyllables like 'brunt' with all the relish of the contrasts he loves in painting. He speaks for seventy-five minutes on two Picasso paintings, a 1904 self-portrait and a 1914 cubist table-top with pipe, jug, fruit bowl. He articulates something about painting itself: the way it superimposes what should be contradictory, makes you respond to several visions of reality at the same time without dismissing one as less real. Steinberg reasserts the astringency and adventure of so much modern art of this pre-First World War decade, the knots and clusters and sudden spaces and clarities of Picasso, Schoenberg, Stravinsky, Wittgenstein.

Tom, who comes with me to the lecture, is slowly won round. He disagrees when Steinberg dismisses students who say, 'But Picasso never thought all that, he just went ahead and did it.' They deny the artist the capacity of thought, Steinberg maintains. 'Not so,' says Tom, 'the artist does just do it; but the instant of just doing it is fed by years of thinking and storing up.'

Colin Leventhal has just rung through to tell me that Tamara, Jeremy's wife, has died.

Her funeral, at Golders Green Crematorium two days later. A bear-hug to Jeremy afterwards. Orna is weeping uncontrollably about Tamara, for whom she had an immediate fellow-feeling. It's also the first funeral she's been to. 'She treated me like one of her own,' Orna says. Once Tamara lent me a novel, and I lost it. On what turned out to be her last birthday, I gave her Dan Jacobson's memoir of growing up in South Africa. She wrote saying it had struck a lot of chords, because she was born there too. It's difficult getting to know your boss's wife. Orna and I only once spent an evening with Tamara, when Jeremy was abroad; at dinner afterwards she spoke calmly and clearly about living with cancer. She adored Jeremy, but that didn't stop her hacking his shins under the table when he went too far.

Colin Leventhal comes home for a bite before we go to say evening prayers with Jeremy and his family. He too is restive about the future: 'Things were bound to come to a head this year. We established new ground rules, now we must go deeper, keep it fresh. I want more challenge, I want us to do what we do better.'

Jeremy reads Kaddish with an ancestral Ashkenazi accent, in a crowded flat. As I will, I fear, for a parent, in the not too distant future, stumbling over the Hebrew syllables.

Matinee next day at the Pit of *Les Liaisons Dangereuses*, a tenacious piece of theatre wrought by Christopher Hampton from Laclos. The ruthlessly steady gaze Laclos brings to bear on his rapacious creatures is quintessential classicism, the spare production gives just the requisite dose of physicality to the book's epistolary exchanges. The allusion at the end to the oncoming French Revolution is almost an aside, and twice as devastating for that.

Is there an equivalent classicism for television? Or does classicism require the clear space of a stage or a page, the hierarchy of literary memory and tradition? Perhaps it is impossible in the cluttered profane space of the television screen, in which case no classicism, no sobriety would be possible, at best documentary immediacy or baroque excess, or some kind of event. But playwrights like David Mercer achieved a rigorous intensity in a body of work, and Dennis Potter is creating a highly-wrought form out of popular conventions.

Tonight the first of the new *Voices*, 'Modernity and its Discontents', goes out. Michael Ignatieff chairs Saul Bellow and Martin Amis debating the terrors and fascinations of what Bellow has labelled 'the moronic inferno'. They talk a lot about the pernicious effects of television culture: a paradox, since it's television, or at least one way of using it, that has brought this conversation about. In his courtly, quietly fervent manner, Bellow says two things that strike me. He pinpoints the promiscuity of television, the plethora of channels and the tyranny of the remote control, exactly when he describes a report on children's viewing habits. 'Kids no longer watch a programme through,' he says. 'They have the clicker in their hands and they are channel-hopping, and so they are interested only in fragments of programmes. And their chief interest is in the special effects ... And this means that all coherence has gone. This is a systematic destruction of coherence. Nothing is consecutive, everything is inconsequent, everything jumps out from strange corners. And really what this may create in the child, the adult too, is a sense of overwhelming sovereignty.' The other memorable remark is Bellow's reply to Ignatieff saying that if we could have a different kind of self, we might be able to withstand the contemporary onslaught better. 'It doesn't need to be a different kind of self,' says Bellow. 'It needs to be a self, however.'

Don Taylor comes in to talk about his project with Anthony Rooley and the Consort of Musicke on the impact of the Civil War and Revolution on English music, painting, poetry and polemic. Don, whom I've known since we were students at Oxford when he directed me as an evil Renaissance cardinal in *The White Devil*, is someone who could have stepped straight out of Cromwell's army of the righteous. Flaxen-haired, blue-eyed, rapid to the point of apparent impatience, he's driven his way through the theatre and television of the past twenty years as playwright, director and classicist. He's been obsessed by the seventeenth century for a long time, and has written plays about Marvell and Milton.

I suggest to Don that the form to be found should use television conventions that aren't normally connected with cultural or historical programmes – the way that Peter Watkins did for *Culloden*. He tells me that the Roundheads sold off Charles I's paintings to pay wages in their army 'just like selling off shares in North Sea oil today'.

What Don is after are the paradoxical links between the radical Republican John Milton and his political opponent but close friend, the Royalist composer Henry Lawes. And in the cross-currents of seventeenth-century society he seeks an image of today's arguments about culture and politics; between those who see culture as something safe for business sponsorship and grass-roots democrats who want a culture that speaks to the excluded and unprivileged.

I sometimes feel in this job as if I'm taking part in a university tutorial or seminar, sometimes as if I'm a publicist, a stage-manager, a sub-editor, or a salesman. Andrew Snell comes in to talk about his Harrison Birtwistle documentary which has now got a good shape on paper. But the budget is almost £40,000 more than I have set aside for it. Like every editor, I negotiate an annual budget with named projects and figures operating up to a budget ceiling – this year about 6 per cent. This negotiation is based on a notional number of hours in the schedule, but also on appealing to Jeremy's intuition. Because Jeremy is interested in the arts, there are periodic additions to my budget, sometimes for things he wants, sometimes for things I persuade him he wants and the channel could do with: it's a system of benevolent autocracy. I ring Birtwistle's publishers to ask whether they can either find a patron who would like to help, or whether they would consider reducing the fees they're asking for the use of Harry's music.

Over lunch I walk down through the spring sunshine to the National Gallery, to look at the Titians and Tintorettos before going to Venice next week, and to check out a Velázquez painting that Leo Steinberg described the other day. He'd said that this *Kitchen Scene with Jesus in the House of Martha and Mary* was the painting that had shown him the way he must take as an art historian. 'I had a real shock when I realised that if the top right-hand portion of the picture was a mirror, then Christ would be right behind me. Then I read all the literature, and realised no one was as concerned about pictorial ambiguities as I was.' There it is, placing tiny figures of Jesus, Mary and Martha on the wall at the top right-hand corner in what could be a picture, a window into a distant room, or indeed a mirror. A young woman in the foreground is grinding something in a pestle on a table, on which stand a bowl of fishes, a bunch of opened garlic, a jug, a plate with two eggs. It's one of the sharpest juxtapositions I've seen of the earthly and the holy.

WEEK 12 *March 17–22*

Karl Katz and Wendy Stein, from the Program for Art on Film, have flown in from New York for a meeting of British art historians. The Program has two parts: a critical inventory of art films and a 'production lab' to explore through film and video new ways of spreading knowledge and appreciation of the visual arts.

This meeting of British art historians is to begin to elicit ideas for these experimental programmes. Round a table in the Channel Four boardroom, six art historians have joined us. I present this opportunity as essentially a different form of publishing, requiring a definition of an art-historical topic different from a learned paper or a scholarly book or catalogue. 'It's an opportunity to go further than your specialist subjects,' I say, 'to come out of your professional stockade.'

There's an initial very British reserve, and some sharp criticism of the Getty as a purchaser not only of pictures, but of knowledge. Gradually, the defences of the scholars begin to melt. 'It's good to find art historians being asked to do more than justify the provenance of a painting,' says Marcia Pointon. 'Real scholarship always has a story behind it, a voyage of discovery,' says the medievalist John Mitchell. 'We're talking about the environment, the fabric of the world we live in. We tear it apart so easily if we don't know its memory and history. Scholars have a role to play, beyond the university, in keeping this sense of our world alive.' And Marcia Poynton adds: 'We need to find a wider justification for what we do, show that we can speak to a bigger audience. Otherwise governments and university managers will have every justification to cut our departments back, and we'll wind up teaching art history only to the children of the rich.'

When I arrive in Venice two days later for the Prix Italia meeting to discuss Channel Four's membership, I can't help remembering Italo Calvino's *Invisible Cities*, whose hidden subject is Venice. The most catlike novelist of Europe found a form to embody Europe's most elusive and intangible city.

On the hour, there's a reverberation of bells around the lagoon, a relay of sound surfing among the walls and quays. The buttresses of Santa Maria della Salute are giant cartwheels like whipped cream spirals, snail-shell whorls. The sparse brick walls of the Frari church enclose a space that soars and makes you want to rise like Titian's airborne Virgin in its altar painting. And then you look again and see that the brickwork is trompe l'oeil, and you know you're in the city where everything sideslips and shifts like the tide against mooring posts.

At tomorrow's meeting the BBC will oppose our separate membership, because it would mean that ITV and Channel Four will have twice as many entries as them. We know we're in for a struggle. Apart from the

BBC's opposition, many of the smaller broadcasters are afraid that our entry will open the floodgates for an avalanche of cable stations and satellite services that will swamp them and destroy the Prix Italia's character. I suppose there may also be some resistance to too many British programmes in competition: the Brits have managed to win a high proportion of the prizes in recent years. We give a drinks party to the delegates before dinner; our controller Paul Bonner, our European consultant Renee Goddard and I glad-hand our guests.

Up the Grand Canal next morning in a water-taxi to the Palazzo Labia, the imposing Venice offices of Italy's state broadcasters RAI, who organise the Prix Italia. We meet in a conference room next to the ballroom, which is decorated with Tiepolo frescos of scenes from *Antony and Cleopatra*, the play which contains a phrase which expresses for me the appetite that can be awakened in people for the arts: 'she makes hungry where she most satisfies'.

The morning is spent in listless debate about sharpening the categories for entry to the music and drama prizes. It looks as if Eckart Stein, from West Germany's ZDF, who proposed our admission last year, is right: after thirty-five years the Prix Italia has declined into 'a senile club'. Our chairman is indecisive, the discussion limp, my two colleagues restless.

Over lunch Souné Wade from TF1, the French first channel, says that after last week's narrow election majority for the right, they're slightly less scared of pre-election threats to privatise two of the three public channels. Elsewhere in Europe, deregulated commercial television marches on: Berlusconi, the condottiere of game-show and cheap series TV, has just signed a deal with Leo Kirch, the most powerful private producer in Germany, and Robert Maxwell, who has a channel on a French satellite, to produce entertainment for European commercial TV. Doubtless it will be American formats, performed by multi-national casts and dubbed into various European tongues; what Renee Goddard labelled 'Euro-pudding'. If European public-service TV is folding up as much as it seems to be, it needs a confident and principled Prix Italia to uphold quality and standards.

What we get instead, when we finally come to discuss Channel Four membership in mid-afternoon, is indecisiveness. The BBC contingent, headed by a polished full-time diplomat, plays cleverly on the fears of the smaller countries. 'We should defer a decision,' says the BBC man. 'Important principles of the Prix Italia regulations are at stake. Channel Four's application shouldn't be considered separately from pending applications from Bulgaria, Iceland and Home Box Office.'

Eckart explodes. 'People round this table are worried about the consequences of admitting Channel Four,' he says. 'I think they should be
even more worried about the consequences of not admitting them.' But
most delegates are still doubtful and suspicious.

At this point Ian Macintyre, Head of BBC Radio Three, makes a
seven-minute speech, which his colleague diplomats must find devastating. 'I run Radio Three,' he says, 'which has many things in common
with Channel Four. I'm distressed at the niggling, ungenerous line which
I'm hearing from my BBC colleagues. We all seem to be saying that
Channel Four is talented and fresh and deserves to join and that we're
prepared to give it every assistance short of actual help.'

After a diplomatic break on the pretext that our three-hour argument
has exhausted the interpreters, Paul Bonner's proposal that our membership be agreed in principle is accepted. The general assembly of members
will be asked to confirm it at this autumn's Prix Italia. It means that
British independents won't have an entry again this year, and it leaves
time for the BBC to plot.

We stumble out into the cold dusk air and thank Ian Macintyre for his
speech. Later, away from his colleagues, he says he'd not been consulted
beforehand – 'although I think BBC television had' – and regretted
that the BBC was displaying a Maginot mentality because it was so
fearful of what the Peacock Report on its future financing might
recommend.

WEEK 13 *March 24–29*

In the trays of paper awaiting my return are two reviews of the new *Voices*
series: an acrid one from Peter Kemp in the *TLS*, and one by Peter
Ackroyd in *The Times*, puzzled about why he's interested in the programme and why it leaves him hungry. Kemp makes great play with
Michael Ignatieff's physical and verbal mannerisms, as have a number
of the reviewers, especially about his large and eloquently gesturing
hands. What a cruel displayer of physical characteristics the television
camera is. And how quickly yesterday's intolerable quirks and foibles
become today's loved idiosyncrasies. Alistair Burnet, the authoritarian
uncle; Terry Wogan, the ever-boyish apple of mum's eye; Esther Rantzen,
St Joan of the consumer society. Making fun of such characterisations is
one of the staple themes of post-Clive James TV writing (and he has a
camera persona too – the clued-up wisecracker from somewhere between
Melbourne and Manhattan). The whole thing says something about the
way we admit TV personalities into our familiarity or cast them as

the people we love to hate. Channel Four has so far created very few
such stock characters, and then mostly for the young audience who like
their heroes and villains in vivid colours – Jools Holland, Keith Allen,
Paula Yates and the synthetic Max Headroom! Erving Goffmann
should be still with us to talk about the presentation of self in everyday
television.

As for Michael Ignatieff, he's taken the task of chairing and helping
to shape this new series of *Voices* very seriously; he is concerned about
his role as 'traffic cop' for each debate and his wish to intervene in
his own right. I think he's made a very good start. So does the BBC,
who are trying to poach him to chair their reply to *Voices*, *Thinking
Aloud*.

Voices can be illuminating, or it can be full of impenetrable jargon at a
dizzying level of abstraction. This makes me want to do the television
equivalent of turning back the page to reread the last six paragraphs,
which of course I can do with the help of a video recorder. I imagine
that many of the people who watch *Voices* are doing so, too. Each show
draws about 200,000 viewers, a tiny audience by television standards but
enormous compared with the readership of the serious weeklies.

I grab Frank McGettigan, our head of personnel and industrial relations, next morning to talk about my future. Frank is a football-playing,
joshing ex-Fleet Street manager, who gets along well with national union
officials and has a deep well of moral indignation. 'Look Michael,' Frank
says, 'Jeremy has said repeatedly that the whole of the commissioning
group will be changed over ten years. You can't do anything about that.
However it's applied, it's a very important shield between Jeremy and
the board. If the board don't feel they have this sanction of a limited
duration contract, they would interfere much more when they disagree
with editorial policy.' I will be talking to Jeremy tomorrow about my
future, I tell Frank, and I'd like his advice. 'Get in there and argue your
own case. Everybody else will.'

After lunch, I sit down with Fiona Maddocks, my music assistant, to
look at the fine-cut of Central TV's documentary about Jeffrey Tate, the
disabled conductor. He comes over as a forthright coaxer of music from
his performers, energy crackling out of the cage of his bent body. He
defines opera as a struggle with limits: 'the most extravagant, excessive
force of expression, ordered and controlled within tight measures and
structures'.

Next day I get in to see Jeremy. It's the first time I've seen him since
Tamara's death a fortnight ago. His window-sill is full of condolence

cards. In the bright sun streaming through his windows, his eyes look bruised.

I give him my usual typed agenda for our routine meetings but say that I want to talk to him about my future. I make what I hope is a clear presentation of my situation, saying that I have eighteen months to go in my contract, that television isn't absolutely overflowing with opportunities for someone who specialises in the arts, and that to return to the live arts when they are on their knees because of cutbacks looks a bit dodgy. 'I have the impression you'll be snapped up before the end of this year by someone else, probably abroad,' he says. 'Look, Michael, at the moment I'm leaving at the end of 1988, and I want to make sure that I've replaced a number of the editors before I go. I don't want to have to sit on the sidelines and watch my successor getting it all wrong. You've made a good impact and had a much-noticed success with your arts policy. And that's not something I could say to every editor. When editors do leave Channel Four, I don't want just the unsuccessful ones to go. I want to establish the principle of change. Sooner or later I have to give someone else a chance to do the arts with a different emphasis.'

He asks questions about some of my long-term projects – *The Impressionists*, in particular – and then says he has a meeting later that day about the company's future structure and will give serious consideration to what I've said. We move on to the business of the moment. I have such a need for recognition; I feel exhilarated and acknowledged, although I've been given absolutely no assurances. At the end of an hour, I ask him what he's going to be doing over Easter. He says he's going to do all the touristy things – films and football matches – with his son. I can feel him feeling Tamara's absence in advance.

Lunch in Liz Forgan's office, salads from Cranks. 'Hello, culture king!' Liz greets me, brightly. Yesterday Jeremy got agreement from our board to appoint Liz deputy controller, with three editors working under her. She's earned the promotion. As commissioning editor for actuality, she bore the brunt of all the criticism about partiality in current affairs, whether from the IBA or from our own chairman, Edmund Dell. With the early brash tabloid *Friday Alternative*, the signposted impartialities of *Diverse Reports*, the *causes célèbres* about MI5 and Ponting, our account-ability programme *Right to Reply*, the now-confident *Channel Four News* and her invention of the television equivalent of letters to the editor, the *Video Box*, Liz has enlarged television journalism.

She talks about her expectations and apprehensions for the new job. I tell her about my conversation that morning with Jeremy. We discuss whether our news is doing enough to chart the inroads that government policy is making on the funding of the arts, higher education and technological research. Liz has more time than many for Neil Kinnock, but fears that the fight against the militants in his own party will knock the stuffing out of him. She's scathing about David Owen's opportunism. 'But in general,' she says, 'the political life is a recipe for bringing out the vanity, venality and less admirable characteristics of almost every human being I've met.'

I talk to Liz about Venice, the way people circulate in Venice. 'You hardly ever meet anyone else's eyes, because the narrow streets are so crowded and you are concentrating too much on weaving your way through to gaze at any oncoming person. Perhaps the only time that you do meet people's eyes is when you are coming in to a landing stage. You look out from the approaching boat at the eyes of all the people looking out at you, waiting to get on. One face I remember in particular: an ill-shaven old man with dark eyes, wearing a beret and an old mac, holding a plastic carrier.'

That's the kind of thing, I tell Liz, that made Venice such a haunting place for me; that, and knowing that the tides are lapping and beating against ephemeral structures. 'Not at all,' says Liz, 'what makes it such a moving and inspiring place for me is that in spite of all the erosion and decay, the city survives as a human defiance of nature.' It's a conversation between an English optimist and a Jewish doubter.

WEEK 14 *March 31–April 6*

'I wish I was a writer. Words are so much more suggestive than film. The camera is always so particular, so specific.' I am with film-maker David Perlov in Tel Aviv, on the fourteenth floor of a tower block above cheap boutiques and fast-food joints on the corner of King Saul Street and Ibn Gvirol Boulevard. I have come to Israel to look at the rough edit of *Diary*, a film diary he has been keeping since May 1973. Jeremy gave him enough money to finish a one-hour episode, and asked me to be his commissioning editor for the whole thing.

The film is now to be in five episodes running from the Yom Kippur war in 1973 to the beginning of the invasion of Lebanon in 1982. You could say equally that it's about ten years in the life of David, his wife and two daughters. Or you could say that it's a description of the three cities that matter most to him: São Paulo (he was born in Brazil, son of a conjuror, descended from a long line of rabbis); Paris, where he arrived in the early sixties, became projectionist at the Cinémathèque and got

the itch to make movies; and Tel Aviv where he has lived since he came
to Israel twenty-five years ago.

David looks like a Giacometti sculpture, like Giacometti himself, his
body like a bone pared down by the wind, deep lines etched either side
of his mouth, blue eyes. He has committed himself to an act of cinematic
truth-telling about the threads between one man's life and his country,
his countries. I can't think of any equivalent in film. Perhaps the nearest
thing is in poetry, Robert Lowell's *Life Studies.* Like Lowell, Perlov is
subject to periodic depressions.

He closes the blinds and screens the fourth episode for Orna and me.
Sitting among David's lithographs and art books we are plunged into the
chaos of the Lebanese invasion only four years ago. Tanks, guns, young
men ducking and weaving through the ruins of houses to avoid snipers,
images snatched off the television screen, wheedled out of the archives,
stretchers whizzed down hospital corridors by wide-eyed soldiers, a
huddle of surgeons round an operating table, a Syrian prisoner of war
patched up and kept under guard, a burned Israeli soldier gingerly
lowering himself into a metal bath.

The film is full of counterpoints, oases of personal life set against
public catastrophe. Perlov films his daughter and her friends dancing
against the big black empty space of an open window and the night
beyond. By its duration and placing he makes the sequence more than
literal. 'Yes,' he says, 'I can sometimes manage to put shots together so
that they add up to something like the memory of something that
happened.'

The projector stops and David opens the blinds. He looks vulnerable
in the daylight. I tell him that he's finding a way to make film do what
poetry and painting do, moving it away from journalism or fiction.

I tell him about this book. There are obvious parallels between his film
diary and this journal. How can a journal or a diary become more than
an accumulation of events and anecdotes? And what is the dividing line
between admitting the properly personal and the unacceptably private?
The domestic material in *Diary* is essential, although it needs tightening.
'I suppose it is trying to remind people of the ordinary humanness of
life,' says David. 'So much here has become ideological and political.'

Over the next three days I view six hours of his diary in various stages
of edit. The last film is a return to his origins, reaching back to childhood
and parents and his original language, Portuguese, filmed in the Brazilian
cities where he grew up.

I ask David what he feels himself to be most, Brazilian or Israeli. 'For nature, Brazil. Israel for ethics,' he says. 'And in Tel Aviv, I feel the human presence more strongly. Because it's such an ugly city, people stand out from it more clearly. In Brazil, they melt into nature.'

After he'd shown me episode one today, he said he needed to sleep for an hour. 'I was so anxious you wouldn't think it was a proper start to the film, that nobody would want to go on watching.' While he took his siesta, his wife Mira and I had lunch at a café downstairs they call 'The Jew' because it's the only one run by an Ashkenazi, an old Pole amidst the pizza and sandwich joints run by Moroccans. A roly-poly Polish mama built like a telephone kiosk serves us borscht, stuffed peppers, pickles, roast chicken and coffee at dizzying speed. Get the food down you, there may be a pogrom around the corner.

That was lunchtime. This evening David launches into an excited monologue about the Jews' lack of visual sensibility. 'They are a culture of words. When they view my films they do it like this' – he turns his head sideways to an imaginary screen, pointing his ear instead of his eye to it – 'so they can talk to each other without needing to look. They'd be quite happy with the information on the soundtrack, they don't need the pictures. Jewish culture is a culture of books and language. Meanings, not perceptions. That's why we have almost no painters.'

What about Chagall, I say. 'Jewish, but he learned from icon paintings.' Modigliani? 'A Sephardic Jew, they're special.' Soutine? 'That's something real now. The world of the *shtetl*, he accepted it.'

Next day I ring David up to say goodbye. At the end of our conversation, he says, 'Michael, can I ask you a question? What were the colours of the sweater you were wearing at dinner the other night? I'm normally very good at remembering those things, but I was drunk and excited and I can't.' Turquoise, navy and ochre, I tell Perlov, the Jew with the thinking eye.

SPRING MEETS BOSCH · INVITES 13, 23B

Prosody knows more about time than a human being would like to reckon with.

Joseph Brodsky, 'The Keening Muse'

The time that pulsates through the blood vessels of the film . . . A real picture, faithfully recording on film the time which flows beyond the edges of the frame, lives within time if time lives within it.

Andrei Tarkovsky, Sculpting in Time

ROUGHCUTS AND SEQUENCES

Stevo Wants A Video Show

A bull-necked young man, Stevo, who manages, produces and promotes post-punk bands, enters the office. He is wearing a black T-shirt, black cowboy boots, a sort of new-wave Max Miller check suit.

STEVO: I run the best fucking bands in Britain. Cabaret Voltaire. Test Department – they do industrial percussion. Soft Cell. Neubaten. The The.

MK: The what?

STEVO: The The. My label's called Some Bizarre. If you don't know this music, I'm gonna send you a box of records which will be the best fucking present you ever had. And I've got the best fucking TV show you'll ever see. Drama, video art, music, films made by the bands themselves. You'll get ratings. Innovation? I can give Channel Four all the innovation it wants. Greek singer, for example. She wears twenty contact microphones round her body, like necklaces, she's an opera singer, it's just pure unaccompanied transformed voice. It'll drive your viewers crazy!

A Nudge From The North

David Boulton, Granada Television's Head of Regional Features, sits in the office.

DAVID: I understand what you're trying to do with the cuts. But there's a danger that the Channel's arts output is concentrating only on the metropolitan or cosmopolitan world. It's important that people should know what's going on in the northwest, for example. Our regional arts magazine this year is covering the new generation of Liverpool poets; a young director doing a new Irish play at the Manchester Royal Exchange; a black organist from Oldham; Asian music from Bolton.

Ignatieff Leaps In

Udi Eichler, David Herman and Michael Ignatieff in the office. They have just recorded George Steiner and Bruno Bettelheim for the new Voices *series on Freud. Steiner attacked the Freudian inroads on the personal life, Bettelheim got Steiner to concede that he might be rationalising buried feelings. Udi has complained about the late and erratic slot for* Voices, *and questioned the reality of Channel Four's commitment to serious argument and talk.*

IGNATIEFF: I've been feeling for a long time that for all the good things that *Voices* has done in opening up British television to European and American thinkers and writers, it's time now to bring *Voices* back home, as it were, by doing a show about what's happening in British culture itself. I think this culture is going through an extraordinarily interesting moment, and as both an insider and an outsider, I'm fascinated by the anger and energy – not all of it verbal – at many different levels of society. British culture now is so *promiscuous* – there are thrusts, insights, passions coming from the world of music, from politics, from the north, the young, the actors and writers and film-makers and directors, as well as the recognised intellectuals and thinkers and academics. We could make something less decorous than *Voices*, more serious than *Wogan*. And then we could take on some really important themes that don't seem to be getting talked about: the deep Americanisation of our culture, and how we are turning our past and our cultural identity into a kind of museum, perhaps in reaction to that uniformity. And these things could take off from anything – a new book, a political event, a film, a football match.

Why Granada Television May Make Feature Films

Mike Wooller, who used to run Goldcrest Television until Goldcrest exploded and now works for Granada, comes into the office. He has read, and likes, the Shostakovich *script. If Granada decide to create a film production wing he says he'd be interested in trying to put it together.*

MIKE: But it's taking longer than I thought for them to act on my ideas. For the past month the Granada board has been fighting off takeover bids from Ladbroke, and then from Rank. The whole affair has concentrated Granada's top minds wonderfully. They realise that as long as people know they're sitting on a cash mountain – mostly from Granda TV rentals – they'll be the object of takeover bids. They've got to get that money back into production.

An Outing To Bracknell Arts Centre For An Adrian Henri Painting Retro-
spective

*Pool-players in the bar of the Chelsea Arts Club prod the bottoms of an animated
gathering of the Adrian Henri Friends, Lovers and Supporters Club. Patrick
Hughes, painter of solid-state rainbows and connoisseur of paradoxes, herds the
party into 'the chara', lamenting the absence of a crate of Newcastle Brown for
the journey. People drink white wine in plastic glasses as the sunset begins to
mellow along the M4.*

*From Edward Lucie-Smith's catalogue introduction: 'Adrian Henri and the
British cultural establishment have pursued an interesting but not always
completely cordial dialogue since the early 1960s . . . a figure who is both
provincial and international, but not metropolitan . . . one of the first people in
England to see that Modernism proposed a totally different approach to culture
than the one then being taken in London . . . a continuity which united painting
and sculpture to literature, literature to theatrical performance, theatrical performance to music, music to painting and sculpture.'*

The coach arrives at Bracknell. Occupants spill out and inspect the paintings.
The Entry of Christ into Liverpool, *a homage to Ensor, with its soft-focus
Union Jack and Colman's Mustard sign, its bemused King Ubu/Henri figure,
its local heroes and heroines. Liverpool girl's voice: 'That's me wearing the silk
scarf, next to Brian Patten.' Icons of the city: a white pigeon spreadeagled on
the kind of black door they make into temporary fences round building sites,
butcher's best cuts and the pick of the greengrocer floating in the white canvas
space. The latest paintings: gardens, fields and hedgerows, edges of a wood at
dusk, petals and leaves still glimmering.*

*Vignette of Adrian with Allen Ginsberg, both in white, two unlikely cricketers
waiting to hold up the tail of the batting.*

*A deeply authentic jazz group with a euphonium plays King Oliver numbers.
Three performance artists wearing King Kong masks apply drumsticks to ironing
boards and kitchenware, while 8mm film plays over them. Adrian Henri,
extremely drunk like everyone else, growls* St James' Infirmary *with the band.*

LIVERPOOL WOMAN'S VOICE: He kept saying, I'll have you before
you're sixteen. Then it was, I'll have you before you're twenty-one. Now
it's, I'll have you before you're forty. I must be his oldest girlfriend.

Next Day, Samuel Beckett's Eightieth Birthday: Tom Phillips's Studio

TOM: Yes, it's lovely, that Liverpool Bohemia. I used to go up there a
lot. But I don't know how much real work people get done. They're too

busy living the life to concentrate on doing the words or the pictures.

The doorbell rings, the rhythm's broken. Tom grunts, purses his lips, sighs, screws up his eyes, grits his teeth, puffs, moans, growls.

TOM: It's never any good for me when a picture starts to go too well too soon. You always have to pay the price, I do anyway. It's a moral question: holding on to what you think works, because it's precious, instead of looking for something better. You find yourself fiddling with mistakes, trying to correct them, when really the whole thing's in error.

Silence. The light falls from the street. Sound of transistor radios, Saturday morning car-cleaning.

TOM: You know, the most remarkable thing about a head is that the distance from the top of the head to the eyes is the same as from the eyes to the chin. Only we don't see it like that psychologically, because the information we really want about a face is all in the triangle between the eyes and the mouth. So you have to re-map it psychologically, to reflect our actual perception.

Tom sips coffee, mixes paint, grimaces, mutters, grunts.

TOM: Ingres used to paint all his women's eyes half as large again.

Tom's eyes, large blue eyes, stripping away, staring harder and harder.

TOM: At this very moment I don't have too much confidence in my capability. It will be better next time.

Close-up of Tom Phillips's print of the bristly back of Samuel Beckett's head, on studio wall. Its motto reads: NO MATTER. TRY AGAIN. FAIL AGAIN. FAIL BETTER.

Transmission Of 'Sinfonietta' Series

Images from the monitor: the London Sinfonietta playing Schoenberg's Pierrot Lunaire *wearing expressionist animal masks; then space-suited, playing Messiaen's* Couleurs de la Cité Céleste *in high-tech gleaming white architecture; playing Webern's* Five Pieces for Orchestra. *As each brief movement starts, the lighting shifts. Nothing else changes.*

MK: Andy Park commissioned these programmes when he was commissioning editor, Music. They bear his humour, swiftness and high spirits. Now he's left, to go back to Glasgow, BBC Scotland. I miss him:

Channel Four doesn't have too many people around who can span
Schoenberg and Phil Spector, Messiaen and Max Headroom. Nor anyone
who went down the pit at fifteen or taught himself piano after studying
at Glasgow Art School, 'because I had been trained to make sense of
visual marks, and I got my fingers to play them'.

Viewing 'State Of The Art' Assembly

*Film images on a viewing-theatre screen. Sound of Leon Golub using a meat
cleaver to scrape paint flat and press it down into the canvas grain cuts across
the babble and image flurry of a television newsroom transmitting edited images
of Mandela, Shcharansky, a demonstration of police riot-control equipment.
Shots of Golub's mercenaries and torturers, giant-sized, paper-thin and blotch-
skinned, as if skimmed and strained by their profession. In the Berwick Street
viewing theatre, Geoff Dunlop, the film's director, warns the four other people
in the room of the stage the film has reached.*

GEOFF: You're watching the roughest of rough assemblies from the episode dealing with politics and representation. It's running almost three
hours and will come down to an hour. So I ask you to adjust your pulse rate
and look at the film patiently, imagining its possible proportions and
shapes.

*Everyone in the room – producer, director, editor, writer – looks tired. They are
editing six hours of film against the clock.*

MK: I wonder how any art image can hold its own against the ceaseless flood
of the TV newsroom. Is Andy Warhol's Mao Tse-Tung, a cosmeticised
banner, any more effective or memorable than Golub's ghost interrogators
or Victor Burgin's surgical photographs and texts?

Libya

*Images on the monitor of American spokesmen, Air Force bases in Suffolk, aerial
photographs of bombed buildings in Tripoli.*

MK: At lunchtime in Tottenham Street I bump into the poet, Dannie Abse,
both of us carrying the midday *Evening Standard* with big black headlines.
'What right do they think they have to take off from *their* country?' says
Dannie. I walk down Tottenham Street imagining a Libyan terrorist re-
prisal bomb right here and now, the blast-wave of hot air on my skin,
eardrums punctured.

Alan Fountain sits in his office looking at the lunchtime news, floored.

ALAN: Nicaragua next.

TV monitor in Charlotte Street office. Title on screen: CNN NEWS BY SATEL-LITE. Jump cuts of a fast-moving, rolling news with silver-haired reassuring deep-voiced American anchormen.

MK: It feels more realistic somehow to hear an American commentator with footage of their bases at Lakenheath and Mildenhall. I keep the CNN on all afternoon, my eyes flickering to the screen over the shoulders of whoever I'm talking to. It all makes real work feel utterly insignificant: the next film of *State of the Art*, about gender and the male gaze in art; Annette Morreau's plans for the Contemporary Music Network; people urging me to do a programme on the last remaining Yiddish poets, or the history of the Royal Shakespeare Theatre. If the Mafia can poison the coffee of a man in an Italian prison who knows too much, surely the CIA could have destabilised Gaddafi without bombs? Or is it theatrics for the media, for government via the media?

Lunch With Eduardo

The Scottish-Italian sculptor Eduardo Paolozzi, with the face of a heavyweight champ and the appetite of a Rabelaisian giant, eats fish in a Charlotte Street restaurant. In Tottenham Court Road Underground his mural mosaics of jazz saxophones, high-tech circuitry and futurist architecture snake across the walls.

EDUARDO: I'm getting letters saying the advertisements are intruding on the art.

In a display at the Museum of Mankind, he sets a Mexican Day of the Dead carnival skeleton wearing a black tie and tails in a showcase next to a rusty transistor radio turned into a tribal fetish object. A cigar-box balsa-wood model of an aeroplane from Africa goes next to one of his own stratified, bisected bronze heads.

EDUARDO: I've spent the morning on my self-portrait. I'm casting each segment of my body separately, and hooking them together in odd combinations. The world's going mad, and I want to get that dislocation into my work.

Marlee, Eduardo's assistant, takes his gigantic, sausage-shaped hand into hers.

MARLEE: But in the sculpture you've still given yourself fine hands, slim fingers.

A Public Conversation With Primo Levi At The ICA

Primo Levi, author of two memoirs about being in Auschwitz and The Periodic
Table, *in which chemical elements trigger autobiographical stories, is catlike and
slight, with a gentle face framed in strong grey hair. He doesn't look sixty-seven.
He speaks about his latest book, a novel.*

PRIMO LEVI: I had to overcome an inhibition about inventing stories about
events I hadn't experienced myself. What made me do so was my need to
challenge the legend that Jews in Europe accepted their fate passively and
never fought back. Having been both a prisoner in Auschwitz and a partisan,
I know that's not true. I researched and read about the Yiddish world of
East Europe – as an Italian Jew I had only become aware of it in Auschwitz
– and I wrote the novel over a year. It was a wonderful feeling, inventing
characters, finding a language for them. Making them go where I wanted,
not be there when I didn't want them, I was omnipotent. It's very amazing
to be God.

MK: Your books grow out of the Jewish European experience of being the
underdog . . .

LEVI: I was never an underdog.

MK: But you were in Auschwitz . . .

LEVI: The ones below me were the underdogs. I kept my human abilities.
I never sank that far. Underdogs lost the capacity to speak, to articulate. An
underdog would never be likely to write anything.

MK: But you have the knowledge of what being an underdog means. Other
writers don't.

LEVI: Perhaps. Just before I started writing *The Periodic Table* I read Cesare
Pavese's diaries, and he writes there, a few days before he commits suicide,
that he has known success and failure, so now he is an adult. If he'd only
known success, he'd still be a child. Maybe that's why *The Periodic Table*
has stories of both success and failure.

MK: You've retired from being an industrial chemist, and can write full-
time. What's the difference between struggling with language and struggling with the chemical elements?

LEVI: Language is more difficult. It knows more than you do. Chemical
elements are just brute matter, however big they may be. With chemistry,
you can sometimes have the sensation of winning.

Walking Through Soho To A Cutting Room

Track past the wholesale rag-trade joints, the second-hand reggae and blues stores, the sex shops, the Armenian restaurant, the buttons and trimmings supplier, the dispenser of catering equipment and utensils, up several flights of stairs.

MK: It may wind up in Cannes, where the world's television mighty and hopefuls are headed this week for MIP, the Marché International des Programmes; breast-beating full-page ads in the trade press, parties and screenings, commercial and libidinous encounters in hotels, all the fun of the fair. But for programme-makers like ours, it all starts here, in tiny cramped rooms in the thick of the city, above the retailers and the whores' calling cards.

Viewing 'State Of The Art' Assembly

Film images on a viewing-theatre screen. Douglas Cramer, producer of Dynasty, The Colbys *and California's most important contemporary art collector, speaks to camera. On set with his dancing girls, he wears no tie and Italian knitwear; for the interview he's conservative, grey houndstooth sports jacket, grey knitted wool tie, grey moustache.*

CRAMER: I need escape from my work, and I find it in discussing art with dealers, and in helping the Los Angeles Museum of Contemporary Art. I bled for that place. I see four or five hours of dailies every day, film that is rough. When I get home I want to look at something that's permanent. When I was divorced, the art collection my wife and I had built up was sold at auction at a very good moment. It fetched excellent prices. I was blessed. But don't get me wrong – I don't play art the way I play the stock market or gold.

Judith Wechsler Meets Mike Dibb About 'The Painter's World'

Judith and Peter McGhee, the Head of National programmes for WGBH Boston, in the office. Mike Dibb asks Judith to explain what she's trying to do in her latest film about capturing movement and time in painting. She talks steadily and passionately for five minutes.

DIBB: There you are! The animation and vividness of the way you explain it is ten times more alive than the commentary you've put on the film. Look, Judith, the films belong to you. But I think I can help you find ways of drawing in people rather than lecturing them, using living speech rather than narration.

A Restaurant – Peter Greenaway, Tom Phillips, MK

Greenaway explains why he hasn't been available for A TV Dante as promised: his next feature film is having teething troubles. Phillips looks glum. Greenaway takes the blame and promises to deliver what he's promised within the next six weeks.

MK: I'm worried about the broken impetus of your programme. Dante's *Inferno* is only worth doing for television if it communicates what being in hell is like. Primo Levi's account of Auschwitz is Dantean: it holds the worst there can be in a steady gaze. What would be a waste of time would be some tricksy exercise in deconstructing a classic which forgot the poem's human and tragic dimension.

A Videotape Of Peter Brook's Workshops

On the TV monitor, videotape rushes of a six-day open workshop in Paris the week before, in which Peter Brook and his actors explored and explained how he makes theatre. Images of Brook quietly speaking to his company and the audience, about silence, sound, body, text, gesture. He speaks carefully, paintakingly, each phrase a step along a tightrope.

BROOK: To begin, you must create a space, interior or exterior, which is as empty as possible. You must always return to the necessity of having nothing at all to begin with. In the void, anything can become an event . . . Faithfulness to one's own concentration – that's the deep source of any inspiration. Faithfulness to one's partner, to whom one must adapt. Faithfulness to the audience, to whom the actor must open himself, or else he becomes its enemy . . . Make specific the idea that everything is possible, no matter what impurity of styles it entails. Make the invisible appear from the visible: if something abnormal is to come forth, what is normal must exist first. Then you heighten it. That's where theatricality comes in. You must make something strong so that the invisible fills our space.

Tom Phillips's Studio: Portrait Sitting

Tom's blue eyes, staring intensely. It seems to be going better this time.

MK: My last sitting for a month. Tom's off to Crete, to research a commission for the Imperial War Museum. And then I'll be in New York for the Museum of Broadcasting season. Meanwhile, this oasis, this accumulation of time in a South London room.

After two hours, I stretch and come round to Tom's side of the canvas. We both look at it.

MK: The forehead's very good, old dome. Mouth's not right. But I look so bloody soulful, Tom.

TOM: Well Mike, if you *will* shoulder the entire burden of your race unaided . . .

Dinner With Anita Brookner

We collect Claire Bloom and Philip Roth first; I've arranged the dinner so that Anita can meet Philip. He opens the door to us in the middle of a manic shtick. Anna Steiger, Claire's daughter, has just returned from a week in Rome, most of it spent in nightclubs.

PHILIP (*in fortissimo, in the agonised voice of a betrayed Jewish paterfamilias*): My daughter, the goy-lover! My daughter, the pork-eater! All week she spends with a blond Norwegian! How can you sit there in front of this good woman from Israel, who's suffered for our race! I'll tell you what I'm going to do! I'm going to throw myself out of the window right now! And your suitcase full of clothes to attract the goyim, I'll throw that out too!

And he picks up the case which bursts open, spilling clothes. We buckle it together, goaded by Philip into hysterical laughter. I remember his definition of the novelist as impersonator, ventriloquist.

ROTH: I enjoyed that. It must be fun being a Jewish patriarch, entitled to throw a big act like that.

We lose our way in Anita's square, one of those places off the Fulham Road where the numbers aren't sequential – and anyway, I've written it down wrong, so we turn up half an hour late. But Anita seems quite composed, and we sit down for a drink in her incredibly tidy flat, books piled neatly – Schnitzer on top of Plato – on dust-free tables. Anita says she's been thinking of giving up teaching art history at the Courtauld, but I don't believe her: she clearly loves her students and the activity of teaching. She has the swift responses of someone who spends a lot of time alone. On her walls are what look like French nineteenth-century engravings, tiny images, deep blacks. Manet's Baudelaire portrait, she tells me later, Fantin-Latour's attempts to allegorise Berlioz – 'a failure'. The conversation comes round to Emily Dickinson, whom Claire is playing in a television programme, and I suddenly see Anita as a cross between Emily Dickinson, a threshold life producing works of fierce power, and George Eliot, fearsomely intelligent and concerned.

We walk round to her French restaurant. Soon she and Philip are locked in writers' talk, comparing their working days (Philip delays starting his as long as he can, then does full office hours every day), the pleasures of editing your material once it's there, being Jewish in England or America (she feels she'll never belong to the English Club, he feels he has no need to belong to the American equivalent, if there is one). There is careful-feeling appreciation of early or recent books, guarded sharing.

Next day Philip says he's impressed by the severity of her judgement on her work. I get the sense he finds it a bit unnerving. Philip has given me a memoir of Bernard Malamud which he wrote after Malamud's death last month. Although Brookner and Malamud are worlds apart, in some ways Philip's words on him apply to her: 'His was a need so harsh that it makes one ache even to consider the sheer size of it.'

Lunch With Farrukh Dhondy, Multicultural Commissioning Editor

Farrukh in his office, engrossed in City Limits, *whose cover story is his thriller serial,* King of the Ghetto, *starting this week. Walking through Soho to a restaurant, Farrukh even more elated and exuberant than usual.*

FARRUKH: I'd written first drafts of two of the four episodes when I got the job at Channel Four. I had to get the other two done in a fortnight, before I got swamped by the job. It's all come at the right moment – Hanif opened up the subject of Bengalis in the East End with *My Beautiful Laundrette*. I think popular forms of TV are better for political theatre than theatre itself. Political theatre has become too predictable, address-ing obvious audiences – although David Edgar's *Maydays* went further than blaming the bosses, the police and the Americans, and I liked David Hare's *Map of the World* – perhaps because it bashed V. S. Naipaul.

We are eating in a Turkish restaurant.

FARRUKH: There was an ideologically correct feminist-leftist actress in *King of the Ghetto*. She was outraged by the unpredictability of her lines. She wanted to play a virtuous stereotype, like the black and Asian community officials who can't understand why I cancelled the Channel's black weekly magazine show, or why I don't keep banging home the anti-racist message, or why I'm not positively discriminating in favour of black and Asian programme-makers. Behalfism, I call it, always doing something on behalf of others, always being representative. Behalfism doesn't make good television.

Farrukh's animated, gleeful face, his supersonic speech, the bounce in his voice. Street-smart energy, good in Brixton or Broadwater Farm, irresistible at the BBC or the Labour Party.

FARRUKH: It wouldn't take much to push beyond our current party boundaries and ideological categories to some new political and cultural movement that would have the zest to sweep the country, Mike. Because Britain is *essentially* democratic, man – not just bourgeois democracy. Look at the way our secretaries shout at us!

Chernobyl

Images from the TV monitor: fuzzy Soviet newsreels of a nuclear-power plant, of people in hospital beds tended by white-coated doctors. In the office, the producer of a film about to shoot in Poland talks about her fear of being contaminated by the radioactive cloud shown in the map of Europe on the TV screen.

MK: Another event whose announcement stuns thought. We're continually terrorised. Libyan bombs, terrorist reprisals, radioactivity: a conjunction of events and an overkill of information is enough to drive you into superstition.

Superstition

Viewing theatre at Charlotte Street. Michael Clark's Hail the New Puritan *is being shown to the press. Florid creatures from London's gay subculture swirl in a nightclub scene. Like Diane Arbus photos come to life, defiantly fragile gay couples, self-promoting fashion designers, painted freaks and camp crazies have thirty seconds of camera fame each.*

MK: Looks like a medieval Dance of Death . . .

The Normal Heart

Martin Sheen on stage at the Royal Court theatre as the protagonist of Larry Kramer's play, the first about AIDS in London. Sheen has expressed interest in playing Shostakovich in the Rudkin–Palmer film. He plays a fiftyish gay writer who preaches sexual abstinence and falls in love with a man who dies of AIDS. Sheen's compact body and fierce eyes pounce and stab; he has a defencelessness in despair; he turns a social documentary into a tragic cry.

MK: Invisible breath into the air from a Soviet factory chimney; a virus killing three-quarters of its victims inside three years. Hard to avoid a gut fear that 'we're hitting the ceiling', as a historian put it in *Voices* last month.

Think-Tank About The Arts On Channel Four

Jeremy Isaacs's office, Friday morning. Jeremy, half a dozen editors, MK in a rough circle.

JEREMY: We're generally acknowledged to have done a lot for the arts, and to have done it well. But are there things we're not doing, are we doing too much of some things, not enough of others, are we getting it wrong in any important ways?

ALAN FOUNTAIN: Michael, most of your arts output is what I would call class-specific. It's based on a traditional view of history and it ignores culture in the broader sense of things most people experience for pleasure.

ROD STONEMAN: There's been an emphasis on the metropolis and on great works, which ignores all the recent thinking about masterpieces as problematical constructions.

Farrukh isn't saying anything. Does he think this is all 'seventiesspeak'? Alan makes his points, with a kind of fervour that seems to say, 'Look, I've just got these few moments to clarify this mistake in your thinking before I rush off to talk to a miners' support group or a video workshop from the northeast.' If I didn't know that he also reads poetry, I'd be tempted to classify him as a sea-green incorruptible. Alan acts as an alter ego for me, he's a haunted, charming, chain-smoking Reality Principle on legs.

MK: I agree with you that we need to talk more broadly about cultural programmes and not just arts programmes. But I do believe in differences of talent, and in disseminating great works, though there's no timeless pantheon of masterpieces. I've stressed the 'aesthetic' in my output because I'm aware that you, Alan, stress the 'agit-prop' in yours. I adjust my policy to take account of what fellow editors are up to – as we all do.

Manet X-Rayed

Manet paintings on the walls of the Courtauld galleries, flanked by x-ray photographs showing their earlier states. In Le Jambon *the x-ray shows how*

Manet added a tablecloth wrinkle under the knife blade, cut and restretched the canvas so the joint of ham has less space around it.

MK: It moves into you, like a close-up. And in the final version of *Olympia*, he added the black pussy at the girl's feet and made the bouquet held by the servant even more open and luscious. No wonder people gasped; they were used to the mythologised saccharine nudes in the Salons.

Spectators at the café-concert*: a group of small paintings.*

MK: He cut them out of larger compositions and framed them separately, to earn more money. But also to get a more modern, fragmented, composition. The framing implies activity and bustle beyond the edges, not just something quintessential within them. Painted cinematic shots. Is there a way *The Impressionists* could make film resonate like these paintings? And keep narrative and character alive too?

Language Games

Colin MacCabe, Head of the British Film Institute Production Board, puppyish and breathless, in the office, Friday.

COLIN: Mike, I've got this terrific conference – the last thing I organised at the University of Strathclyde before I came to the BFI – about *Linguistics and Literature*, with Derrida, Raymond Williams, Fredric Jameson, all the big names, doing a stocktaking. Will you videotape it for Channel Four? It's in three weeks' time. Sorry for the short notice.

Gaelic

John McGrath, telephoning from a booth in the Western Highlands, the same Friday.

JOHN: Mike, we had a terrific opening of *There is a Happy Land* last night. People still know the Gaelic songs. Please come up and see it before we start filming. We'll pick the most beautiful village of the tour.

Transatlantic

On the telephone, the same Friday, MK talks to Susan Sontag, asks her to make a speech at the opening of the Museum of Broadcasting Channel Four season. Then to Jules Feiffer, asking the same, and congratulating him on winning a Pulitzer Prize for the best political cartoons.

The Live Show Talk

Jeremy Isaacs's office, the same Friday. He pours drinks for Michael Ignatieff and MK, congratulates Ignatieff on the current Voices *series.*

JEREMY: But for the kind of live show I'm looking for, Michael, your strengths may be your worst obstacle. I can't imagine you asking the naive questions that Huw Wheldon would ask, for example, in the name of bluff common sense. Or paraphrasing what a philosopher's just said, which Bryan Magee used to do, much to the philosopher's fury. But that means things escape the viewers when they might reach them.

MICHAEL: Look, Jeremy, I am what I am, unashamedly. But talk on television is in trouble. You know the sort of show I want. What are you looking for?

JEREMY: One in which intellectuals don't have a monopoly of cleverness. This show should give viewers insights that they're incapable of articulating, about concerns that touch a nerve in everybody. Most talk on television is political debate, anecdote or hucksterism. I want this to be a riveting live event. Not only does the subject have to matter, but there should be chemistry between people – and I don't mean television as theatre of embarrassment, like the public punch-ups David Frost used to provoke. It should happen in a big studio, with the cameras moving around, shooting over shoulders. I want a show that relentlessly pursues issues and ideas in conversation, that has the feel and texture of life, not an academic discussion.

WEEKS 20–21 *May 12–26 New York*

A MONTAGE

'SINCE NOVEMBER 1982 CHANNEL FOUR IN GREAT BRITAIN HAS BEEN FULFILLING ITS MANDATE AS A GENERATOR OF INNOVATIVE AND EXPERIMENTAL PROGRAMMING. THE MUSEUM OF BROADCASTING'S NEW SEMINAR AND SCREENING SERIES ''THE ARTS ON BRITAIN'S CHANNEL FOUR: EXTENDING THE MEDIUM'' FOCUSES ON THE CHANNEL'S ACHIEVEMENTS IN NURTURING THE CONTEMPORARY ARTS...'

Seen and Heard

If I lived in London, it would be the New York light I would miss. New York light, reflected from sheets of steel and glass, coagulating in fierce brightness, New York light, luminous and metallic, scouring the skin, crisp on sidewalk and fire escape, glowing up from the Hudson glimpsed at the end of Tenth Street, lifting the morning step of the lightweight-suited traveller to the uptown subway. 'There's so much light here.' We are speaking on a bright Sunday afternoon in the cavernous dimness of a hi-tech restaurant called Greene Street, on Greene Street.

'Rodin was working in the light-catching material of dark bronze. Look at the rising and falling line of hands – a fluttering counterpoint music to the bass beat of the drapery.' A hundred well-tailored souls listen to the young art historian in the auditorium of the Metropolitan Museum rousing himself to a frenzy of metaphors, a froth of adjectives, as he celebrates *The Burghers of Calais*.

'Say, buddy, wontcha help a guy stay drunk for a month?' Grizzled fifty-year-old on a doorstep on Broadway and Spring Street.

On 57th Street another old man wearing a green sponge rubber Statue of Liberty crown and wielding a green sponge rubber Liberty torch. Advance mementoes of an anniversary not due till July.

'Say, buddy, gimme 22 cents to make a phone call to stop me having a drink.' Bearded paroxysmic flailing on crutches, on West 10th Street.

VAN GOGH CLEANERS AND LAUNDERERS

'People come to New York not for its past or for aesthetic experiences, but for the varieties of life that it affords in concentrated form': Hungarian writer George Konrad, in the 125th birthday issue of *The Nation*, out this month.

Three old blacks sitting in the sun on West 23rd Street watching a painter perilously hanging from a balcony of the Chelsea Hotel, repainting window frames. 'He sure ain't got no lifeline on his ass.'

'Godfather Two – America's Proust'

'Television,' says the raw laconic voice of the expatriate British documentary director, 'is like dropping a feather into the Grand Canyon and waiting for the echo.'

'When we signal the start of the speeches at the opening ceremony, some people will move into the auditorium, others will stay drinking at the bar. It's always the same. There are people who want to listen, and people who want to network.' The city is full of networks, grids, circuits: swift telephone connections, digitalised voices immediately tripwired telling you this number is not in service; a taxi barrelling up an avenue, sweeping along a transverse street, the plot of the city planted in anyone's head; density, compactness, proximity; jewellers, art galleries, authors' agents stacked up in zones; connections, introductions, 'working the room'. When I tell Robert Batscha, the director of the Museum of Broadcasting, that this is the first time I've heard 'network' used as a verb, he looks mildly, but only mildly, surprised.

Arguments with Oneself

Jeremy walks into the dining room at the Dorset for breakfast the morning after he arrives. Bustling, slightly pugnacious, contained in a light grey suit, he advances among the tables of shirt-sleeved businessmen who've driven in from Long Island or New Jersey and are now holding their first meeting of the day. One of them has a calculator on the tablecloth next to his bran muffin. Jeremy looks round at them, admiring: 'Where do they get all that energy?'

A few days ago he was at the Cannes Film Festival, where a film Channel Four co-produced, Andrei Tarkovsky's *The Sacrifice*, is in competition. 'Probably one of the greatest works of art since the gloomier plays of Aeschylus,' mutters Jeremy. 'It may even win the big prize.'

Jeremy asks me what he ought to be saying about keeping the Channel innovative when he addresses next week's Open Day of the Independent Programme Producers' Association. New strands of subject matter? Rotation of Channel Four editors? Taking programmes off before they decline into self-parody? 'Don't make a fetish of innovation, Jeremy, you're talking to a small percentage of genuine creative talent and a majority of entrepreneurs who just want to keep their show on the road. We're all about halfway through a curve, a trajectory, and one of the most innovative things we might do is to strengthen the threads that connect us. We must deepen what we do. It would be a loss to the Channel if the principle of rotation meant regressing to more primitive versions of the truths we started out from.'

His face is imperturbable as I speak, making my words sound like special pleading. Is it the face of a subtle Jew or a stern Scot? Jeremy Isaacs doesn't need to adopt any ideological position of pluralism, any democratic justification for the dialogue and clash of opinion which lie at the heart of Channel Four. The clash is in him, in his own psyche, between Scot and Jew, romantic and realist, connoisseur and populist, forthcoming and restrained. Argumentative is the adjective that best fits this man. Which way will he pounce next?

'In the *New York Times* interview, the girl described me as being a benevolent tyrant,' says Jeremy. 'Then she quotes me saying, better a malevolent democrat than a benevolent tyrant. The truth is I'm a pragmatic idealist. I'll do almost anything to make the Channel prosper so that it can do its proper job.'

They are queuing round the block at the Museum of Broadcasting to get into our first seminar, 'The Place of Channel Four in British Broadcasting'. All the constituencies are there – the silk-and-mohair-suited executives of the commercial networks, the floridly casual artists of SoHo and the Village, PBS producers and above all American independent film-makers and video-makers, come to learn more about this channel that gives their British counterparts something approaching a decent chance.

Before Jeremy or I can speak, Robert Batscha introduces the Director-General of the IBA, John Whitney. In an unexpected speech, he praises Channel Four as a loved and unruly member of the independent television family. Do I sense Jeremy twitching at being upstaged? When his turn comes, he launches into an account of the cultural arguments and constitutional debates – and fervent lobbying by programme-makers – which have made the Channel what it is. 'Television isn't just an industry,' he concludes, 'although it's also an industry.' We run our compilation tape, and I have about five minutes left to make a few points. I ask why in television the special relationship between Britain and America only reinforces each other's most conservative stereotypes: 'We show your soaps and your cops, you show our costume drama and our imperial nostalgia. What about each other's contemporary expression?' I wind up with a reason for bothering to get art into television at all. It's a quote from the American literary critic Kenneth Burke: 'Art may be of value purely through preventing a society from becoming too assertively, too hopelessly itself.'

'When people care more for the institution than for broadcasting it's a disaster,' says Jeremy later. His comments on this trip about the BBC have been merciless. At a lunch at WNET, New York's PBS station, he inveighs against the BBC's imperial posture and territorial imperative. 'You can't continue to expand on a falling income.' He attacks the overheads of the BBC bureaucracy, and asks our host why WNET's overheads are so high. The reply, not altogether convincing, is that it's the price of freedom from a meddlesome and politicised Washington bureaucracy.

Instinctively, Jeremy nags away at these contradictions, a natural troublemaker. Yet by the end of his week here, one of his old friends ('a little Jewish guy who used to collect money for the Abraham Lincoln Brigade when he was a kid in Chicago, and now advises IBM what to sponsor on television') said that he'd never seen Jeremy so pleased, in what he called his depressive and shrugging way, by all the recognition.

'That's all very well,' says Jeremy in a restaurant on 43rd and Broadway which tries to ape La Coupole, 'but the people who are heaping all this praise on me are precisely the people who would never employ me if I needed a job over here.'

Seen and Heard

'Let me tell you about today's specials,' says our Laurie-Anderson-cropped waitress, in her cute bow-tie and pageboy jacket and pants, one of the countless cross-dressed Buttons of the Great American Restaurant Pantomime. 'For starters we can offer you soft-shell crabs with a slightly spicy tarragon vinegar and Dijon mustard sauce. The house salad is endive, radicchio and miniature tomatoes, no the lettuce is not iceberg, ma'am. For entree, I can recommend the papillote of salmon. It comes in its own foil container with steamed fresh vegetables and a light white wine sauce, I can tell you it's delicious . . .'

The syllables tumble out, the eyes are bright, the face gleams with the wish to give pleasure. Once I wanted to make a candid camera film of America's waiters and waitresses reeling out the specials across the nation, speeding, stumbling, always smiling. 'When did spaghetti turn into pasta? When it went up from $3.50 to $12.'

New York is a food city. It's even called the Big Apple. I've been trying to raise money here for a feature-length documentary Mike Dibb would like to make, tracing twenty-four hours in the city's food-cycle, from the dawn deliveries by truck, train and boat to the late-night garbage collection and disposal. A metaphor of the cultures and codes of the metropolis, I call it, a symphony of a city. Everyone I describe it to loves the idea; most have their own food or diet story to contribute; no one will come up with even a decent slice of the $300,000 it would cost to make. On the Bowery I watch a Chinese fishmonger lift a gigantic seabass out of a glass tank and stun it on the chopping block.

Political food joke: Ronald Reagan and Nancy in a good restaurant. The waitress takes the order from Nancy. 'What will it be for starters, ma'am?' 'For starters I'd like the artichoke hearts in creamy Italian dressing.' 'Artichoke hearts in creamy Italian dressing. And for your entree?' 'I'll have the marinaded chicken stuffed with foie gras.' 'Marinaded chicken. And the vegetable?' 'He'll have the same.'

'In this city all the energy goes into work, all the sensuality into food. This is one of the last few real cappuccinos you can get here. Chinatown's eating up little Italy.'

'The audience is considerably dumber than it was. They're morons. They don't know how to behave in theatres – they can't even be quiet. The amount they eat in theatres – it's as if they were at home. They're totally corrupted by the television experience. And they expect the same television emotional results: sentimentality instead of emotion, tactile sensation and shock instead of thrill.' Sidney Lumet on 'What's wrong with Hollywood' in the spring number of *American Film*.

I'M BLIND WON'T YOU BUY A PENCIL round the neck of an upright fiftyish black man on Fifth Avenue. At his feet a red plastic drinking bowl for his guide-dog.

'Now I'm living without her I can breathe. No wonder, said my shrink, you were living under house arrest.'

Sunny American names and shopfronts: BARNEY, SAM, FORMERLY JOE'S, ROCCO'S BAKERY, RANDY, JODY. And VAN GOGH, as well as being a CLEANERS AND LAUNDERERS, is also a REMOVERS.

Jules Feiffer has won the Pulitzer Prize for twenty-five years of his editorial cartoons in the *Village Voice*. 'It's terrific when they give you a prize for being a bad boy for twenty-five years.' Dinner in his West End Avenue apartment, with a yuppie couple, and Jules and Jenny's new baby, who kisses the cold white wine bottle. 'I can't get beyond the first act of my play. It must be because I'm happy. I can't write about happiness, I need contradiction, conflict. And I've lost the belief I had in the sixties that statements can change anything. Perhaps it's having the baby, and not caring so much about the world. And also I take the mood of the times. If Reagan doesn't give a damn, nor do I.'

Sunday lunch with Susan Sontag and her son David Rieff in the Silver Palace, 'a vast Hong Kong barn' as she calls it. Diminutive waitresses wheel round institutional metal trolleys with tiny baskets of *dim sum*.

Between Susan and her son a competition in brilliance, from which at a certain point Susan retires gracefully, leaving the floor to pyrotechnic David. 'The PEN Congress? Norman wanted a party, that's why it happened . . . I'm sitting with Grass and Fuentes and I find myself talking about Colonel Cavafy . . . Czeslaw comes up and we're soon deep in sludgy Polish metaphysics . . .' The allusions ricochet, the dropped names resound. I ask Susan, who has urged me to view a film by a depressed Frenchman and referred to a letter from a downcast Israeli novelist, how many people in need she has around her. 'My first novel, someone reminded me, was called *The Benefactor*.' David picks up the theme of being a writer with a conscience, and turns it into a comic shtick: 'Dr Gordimer, Dr Gordimer, please hurry to Ward C. Human rights violation in Ward C. Dr Gordimer to human rights violation in Ward C.'

Jazzband under the trees in Central Park, Saturday afternoon. Trombone and vocals, tenor and alto, electric guitar, bass, bongos and drums, and later the most beautiful long-necked blonde girl on trumpet. The sun beats down through the leaves, two black girls weave to the beat, a hat full of coins goes round, the singer grunts 'Going to Chicago' and the blues sidle in and tears prick my eyes for the full-heartedness of it all.

TV, Money, Culture, Democracy

Next day, a seminar with the six British independent programme-makers – John Wyver, Mike Dibb, Gina Newson, Jeremy Marre, Jane Thorburn, Udi Eichler – who talk, to an audience largely composed of American independents, about what it's like making programmes for Channel Four. Mike Dibb's account of leaving the BBC and what he's trying to do is, like everything he does, quiet and lucid. 'I was at the BBC for nineteen years,' he says. 'I left because I wanted to do a series about time, which was rejected by the BBC. At that same moment Channel Four came into existence, and the idea was enthusiastically received. I'd characterise the atmosphere at the BBC when I left as a kind of freedom with indifference. I moved to a freedom with enthusiasm, but with infinitely less resources. No doubt that the experience is quite a shock: to exchange the largesse of the BBC's resources, where there's always something at the end of a phone, for a situation where you have to calculate the cost of the drawing pins as well as everything else.

'*About Time*, the series I made for Channel Four, has no commentary.

That makes it very difficult to show in America because you seem to need hosts to introduce and explain, and this works against the heart of what I'm trying to do. I approach films not with a thesis I want to prove but with questions I want to ask. And the process of making the film is the process of giving possible, tentative answers to some of those questions.

'In film you have an extraordinary possibility of bringing together worlds which normally are kept separate. You can place within the same film the experience of a steel worker and of a theoretical physicist. You can talk about the moon landing and you can juxtapose that with 'Moon River' or the 'Moonlight Sonata'. You can confront menstrual dreams with the dreams of advertising, the poetry of everyday speech with written poetry. You can bring different worlds to bear on each other: the monastic orders of St Benedict with the industrial production line; or a woman talking about quantum physics as a context for her own recent giving birth to a child. These are the ways in which film is so expressive and why commentary, rather than helping to explain ideas, actually enfeebles the poetic possibilities which such a method gives rise to.'

A PBS executive at a meeting next day: 'We just taped *Churchill*, the first of two one-man shows performed by Robert Hardy. We're going to pair it with an Eisenhower show. We got them funded by General Dynamics, which makes its money through contracts with the Pentagon – the F-16 rifle, the Abraham Tank. We showed them the promotional copy: 'Eisenhower and Churchill, two famous war heroes of the twentieth century'. They said, 'Could you cut the word war?'

WEEK 21 *May 26 London*

While I've been away my *Dance on Four* season has opened with the Michael Clark–Charles Atlas film, *Hail the New Puritan*. Predictably, since it contains a cross-section of London's more bizarre underworld freaks, a number of bare bottoms and a T-shirt with a graphic sexual invitation, it has attracted complaints: twenty-five calls objecting to the obscenity and a letter saying why does Michael Clark have to spoil his wonderful dancing by descending into the decadent underworld. But among those calls are a handful that thank us for doing something so unusual and, as one telephoner says, 'unsanitised'. At our Programme Review Mike Bolland says it's a good example of the uncategorisable programmes which Channel Four ought to be doing: a fusion of dance, documentary and improvised drama. I believe it manages unexpectedly to express both the hopelessness and defiant carnival of young people in Britain – or at least in London – now.

The other programme that's begun while I've been away is *Open the Box*, Michael Jackson's six-part series about television itself. Last week Chris Rawlence's film watched people watching television, using video-tapes made by a camera inside a TV set. This week Gina Newson's film examines how television constructs the idea of 'ordinary' people. An old couple who have been burgled three times are interviewed for a documentary about victims. The producer of the game show *The Price is Right* whips up a studio audience to a frenzy of merriment and tells them that they are helping to make 'people's television'. The documentary director says most interviews are like one-night stands: 'immediate inti-macy but no real exchange of emotion'.

The French government announced the privatisation of TFI, the first and most popular television channel, while I was away. In protest, the three public-service channels immediately went on a one-day strike. The new Minister of Culture and Communications, Jean-Pierre Léotard, tried to calm the storm by saying that he would be in-stalling real competition with two commercial channels competing against two public-service channels. The climate under the Chirac government is getting nastier, with political infighting and unleashed police imposition of law and order, and there are some gruesome tycoons licking their lips at the prospect of owning a national television channel.

Justin Dukes, our managing director, tells me that he is clearing his decks in anticipation of the Peacock Report on the financing of the BBC – and thus the rest of British broadcasting. Justin, who came to Channel Four from the world of newspapers, is a rapid, committed and effective manager, who has built a firm framework for the creative people at the Channel, and challenged many practices in commercial television. There have been rumours that one of Peacock's recommendations might be to separate Channel Four from the ITV subscription and ask us to sell our own advertising. Other than dogma, I can't see any good reason for this now. The links that we have with the ITV companies, although full of what John Whitney would call 'abrasiveness', now make financial sense. Our share of the total commercial television audience now matches the percentage of total advertising revenue which the ITV companies provide as our budget.

'Welcome to the damp glamour of Scotland,' says John McGrath. We are driving four hours from Edinburgh to the Western Highlands, where I have come to see John's 7:84 company perform *There is a Happy Land*, a show telling in songs and stories the history of the Highlands from pre-Christianity and the clan chiefs to absentee landlords and NATO bases. The show is playing one-night stands in small village halls, touring its own cyclorama, lights and sound system for the six-piece band Ossian, a vocalist and two narrators. The songs are in Gaelic. John has already filmed the performance, and will add extra shooting – landscape, faces, historical documents – to make three programmes.

It is raining, of course, but the place is spectacular: mists across sheets of water; a blue rim of hills, space to see the swoop and weave of flocks of herons; stags, hinds, seals; giant hills shouldering down to the road; mossy slopes stained with rich rained-in colours – peat-brown, brown-green, pressed purple. And everywhere Blackface sheep and lambs with black noses and feet. But listening to John as we drive, I soon learn to suspect the picturesque. 'These are the sheep whose owners deported thousands of people off this land. And even now that the crofters have some protection, nothing's easy. There's been so much rain the past year that it's washed the goodness out of the earth. The grass is thin and lambs are dying this spring.'

We arrive at Dornie, a village of fifty houses and a ruined castle on the arm of a loch. I watch a performance in the village hall, crammed to capacity with an audience of all ages. Perhaps it's because I'm still suffering from jet-lag, but the performance seems over-insistent, nudgingly populist. Late dinner in the little hotel with a group of exhausted actors, musicians and stage crew, who have just struck their set and lights.

Next afternoon we climb a single-track windy road through muffling mist. Out the other side and down to Applecross, a strip of houses along the edge of absolutely silent, steely water. In the pub, a babble of hearty voices. Three big, broad, ruddy chaps are sticking two bottles of Scotch into a plastic carrier, before they go home to watch the World Cup, which is already coming out of the pub's television. Well, there are three members of the populace who won't be coming to see John's people's theatre.

I'm wrong. They turn up at the hall, which is again packed, a bit late and having obviously started in on the Scotch. They mutter loudly to each other throughout the show. But when the modern Gaelic songs come at the end – about being exiled in Canada and longing for home, about the rocket bases in the Highlands – they are the ones who know the tunes and the words. And, from what I overhear, one of them is taping the World Cup. So much for people who say that television is killing live theatre and people's culture. It depends how deep its roots stick.

Tonight's show is swift, vivid, light and all the more telling. If this is the tone of the performance that John has filmed, we could have the basis of something remarkable. And, although it's cost more to shoot it out here, it needed to be done: there's definitely a sense of contact tonight between the stage and the people whose history it is telling. The edge of the pipes and swirl of the fiddles, the keening laments and lullabies, feisty jigs and skipping dances, bardic visions and cheeky anecdotes about legendary land raids – all these reach out to their own audience, and could speak beyond that.

After the show I help pack all the stuff in the van and we drive back through the mist. Next day John and Liz, his actress wife who is the show's main narrator, drive me back to Edinburgh and then drive on a further hour to Glasgow where she will perform in a benefit meeting in memory of the fiftieth anniversary of the Spanish Civil War. 'All the Glasgow Stalinists will be there, of course,' says Liz, 'and they'll mostly be men.' I've known John and Liz since we were all students at Oxford and Liz played Molly Bloom in an adaptation of *Ulysses* which John directed, and in which I played 'stately plump Buck Mulligan'. Their commitment to this work in Scotland is staggering. I ask John whether he misses London, which they left five years ago. 'I miss the intellectual stimulus, but you get a lot in its place: political solidarity, passion, and this kind of beauty and roots,' he says, looking out at the gigantic hills. When we get back to Edinburgh the trees and the sky seem too small.

WEEK 23 *Monday, June 2*

Jeremy, his tiredness showing, stands up in front of a full house of independent programme-makers and a sprinkling of ITV producers in the horseshoe-shaped lecture theatre of the Royal Institution. It is open day for IPPA, the Independent Programme Producers' Association, and Jeremy is delivering a report to the troops. The last such open day was a year before we went on air and, speaking for over an hour, he summarises achievements, looks at problems, tries to point ahead.

'We have succeeded, thanks to the efforts and talents of many people in this room. Had we not succeeded, you might not be sitting here. We have succeeded because we had three important things: a clear brief, a comparatively free hand, and a guaranteed income. I am in the most enviable position of any broadcaster: I know what money I have to spend for the coming year.

'Have we changed direction in order to succeed? Well, look at the programmes on the first night of Channel Four and ask yourself whether we haven't continued as we began. The first programme on Channel Four was *Countdown*, a French game show adapted by Yorkshire Television. Then we started in with our twice-weekly soap, *Brookside*. Then we had the first edition of *Channel Four News*, and pretty disastrous it was. But it was different: we said no royalty, no individual crime, no natural disasters. Now *Channel Four News* is watched by 800,000 people on average: that's an audience we can ride with. Then we had a very strong *Film on Four*. *Film on Four*, as well as taking an important part in major international films such as *Paris, Texas* and Andrei Tarkovsky's *The Sacrifice*, has stuck to its original intention: to be specific about British modes of thinking and feeling. We had a film by the Comic Strip, a new generation of comedians whose work appeals to the young and works well on film. And we had *In the Pink*, a late-night feminist cabaret.

'I also want to mention *Voices* in this context. This programme, now in its fifth series, counts as a zero-rated programme in terms of audience measurement. That means it's seen by around 250,000 people. Channel Four needs such zero-rated programmes, and will continue to do them.'

He moves on through education, sport, popular music, fiction and the choice of foreign movies which test the IBA's definitions of acceptable taste. 'It's as if we've shifted into a new era,' he says. 'Once broadcasters used to want to reach everybody with everything. The family was the measure of the level of any programme, and the general took precedence over the particular. One of the things that used to madden me at ITV controllers' meetings was programme directors saying, "I went to the cinema last night and saw a wonderful movie. What a pity we can't put it on television."'

Next day lunch at the British Council. Two back-bench Tory MPs who have never seen the point of the British Council have been invited. Sir John Burgh, the British Council's director, trenchantly presents the strong points of the Council's work, and invites comments. The Tory MP across the table says if there's a demand for this stuff it will create a market. I reply that the need for the arts is not like the demand for roads or hospitals. People don't know they have a need for the arts until they start to taste them and acquire the appetite. It's a latent need, hard to measure or predict. Of course, it's difficult to make hard-headed arguments for something that is a latent need. But isn't it the responsibility of elected politicians who call themselves civilised to allow for the possibility that people will discover these needs, and make sure that opportunities are put in their path? Or do we leave everything to market forces?

Two days later, at a meeting of the Lyric Theatre Hammersmith board, there is a replay of the same argument. This time it involves the new Labour Council of Hammersmith, who will be represented on our board from next month. The leader of its Leisure and Recreations Committee has published an interview in the local freebie paper saying that the theatre is elitist, should cater for all tastes and should give back the interest on the money that the council has granted it. For the Tories, the arbiter is the free market and supply-side demand; for these socialists, it's a demagogic idea of what the populace wants. Philistinism is common to both.

WEEK 24 *June 9–13*

'So we start in tight on Lena Horne, almost whispering "Stormy Weather" with just a double bass – beautiful Lenny Bush,' says John Scoffield, dapper Head of Light Entertainment for Central TV; 'and we slowly crab round still keeping in close, and we come round, and we come round and WHAM!! Suddenly there's a whole forty-piece big band blowing its heart out and we're right up her arse and your hair's standing on end. That's what I call an entertainment special, using a studio properly. That's what you don't get nowadays.' And my glee in hearing things told that way – like my pleasure in jazz – reminds me how much of a showman I am at heart.

Angus Gibson, a gangly, boyish and threadbare South African, comes into the office. He would have had with him a black writer and actor from Soweto, but when they arrived at London airport his friend had to go back; the police had just killed his brother in a riot. Angus has been making a living doing commercials and directing drama for South African television. Getting more and more frustrated by the compromises, he and a group of friends – black, white and coloured – decided to use theatre as the only way left to talk about South Africa. They started a company and celebrated their tenth anniversary this year with a show called *Sophiatown*. Sophiatown was a suburb west of Johannesburg, originally developed for the white and privileged. When the town council put the sewage facilities next door, the developer began to sell off the houses in Sophiatown to non-whites, and soon the place became a vibrant mixture of raffish elements: shebeens, whores, criminal gangs, show business, jazz, gangsters, the Church, *Drum* magazine and the African National Congress. In 1955 the government removed the inhabitants and razed Sophiatown after a bitter campaign of resistance.

Angus wants to do a film about the play, the theatre and memories of Sophiatown itself. I will read the material he's left me and respond rapidly. I have a feeling that whatever I send him will be opened and scrutinised.

Down to Bristol to see Peter Stein's production of Verdi's *Otello* for the Welsh National Opera. The star of the production is the chorus, exemplifying Peter Stein's mellowed Marxist belief that Verdi's opera, like Greek tragedy, is based on 'the tension between the hero and the collectivity'. Condensed into a picture frame about one-third of the available proscenium space, the chorus swirls, shifts, vanishes and re-groups like the inhabitants of a huge, crowded Veronese painting. When only Otello and Desdemona are on stage, Lucio Fanti's set looks like a desolate De Chirico. It has all the narrative excitement of nineteenth-century pictorialism and yet is utterly surreal and modern: when the double doors at the back of the set open there are huge photographic blow-ups of waves, as conceptual as anything in Magritte. It's a piece of alert modern theatre, grounded in a sense of history; a fusion of stage imagery, music, and packed emotion.

Two days looking at the rough cuts of *State of the Art*, with all the team and Wibke von Bonin, our co-producer from WDR in Cologne. Geoff Dunlop, the director, has reached the point where he's trying to float a nimbus of ideas and context around the presentations of the three or four artists in each of his six films. In the first film he has set himself the difficult task of making postmodernism tangible. Futuristic and technological images, architecture that quotes from past styles, the blithe juxtaposition of trivial and serious, high and low, float past on a bed of still-undigested quotations from Lyotard, Raymond Williams, Fredric Jameson, Baudrillard and the artists themselves. Of course the words are not yet integrated into a web of sound, but one can begin to see the 'choric' function that these episodes could have, if they are well edited and delivered. They will certainly challenge – and thus initially irritate –

viewers used to an authoritative guide in art films, such as Kenneth Clark or Robert Hughes.

The series will be subtitled 'Ideas and Images in the 1980s'. Some of the artists come across with full-blooded visual images as well as fluent ideas, whereas others have less telling images and are chiefly there for the sake of their ideas, sometimes expressed in tortuous artspeak. The series will be a survey of symptoms as well as achievements. The kind of talk I like best in the films is when an artist is trying to say the unsayable as precisely as possible: Anthony Gormley, whose cast-lead bodies make powerful screen images, talking about the 'tribal aspect of making sculpture' or the body 'as a house for spirit and matter during a brief sojourn'. Or Howard Hodgkin: 'Being an artist is like being given a life sentence in an open prison – but of a very comfortable kind.'

I walk down to the ICA with Wibke at lunchtime to see Helen Chadwick's installation *On Mutability*. She has filled two of the lofty well-proportioned Nash rooms, the first with a pool in which float pale blue xeroxes of her own naked body and of sensuous imagery – Leda's swan, a lamb, froth, resplendent golden spheres like planets on the water's surface. On the walls are computer printouts of sinuous classical columns. At the top of each one is a blown-up photo of the artist crying. In the adjoining room is a tall column of thick perspex packed with decaying refuse. It looks extremely beautiful – stripes of colour gradually declining to a bubbling dark brown. It is also a potent image, of decay and change. But why is the most sensuous thing in *On Mutability* not the pale blue photostats of the body ecstatic, but the rich mulch? Does Helen Chadwick mean to say that art defers to nature?

A breakfast meeting with Siobhan Davies, Ian Spink, Peter Mumford and Terry Braun, about *Dancelines*, the six-week exploratory workshop for new television dance, which starts in the autumn. The meeting is in Sue Davies's kitchen, full of bicycles, her husband's big photographs of nude dancers and her two-month-old baby crawling all over her as we talk. I formulate what I hope the exercise will explore. It should be a set of tensions: between the live gesture captured in real time and segments edited into a montage, between documentary and shaped material, between dance's purity of movement and television's indiscriminate imagery and reference. I would like it to be as vivid as sport on television, but more predestined.

WEEK 25 *June 16–22*

At Alan Fountain's suggestion, a group of editors meet to discuss what Channel Four might do in 1988 to mark the twentieth anniversary of 1968. 'I was eleven in 1968, and wearing blue serge knickers to school,' says Cresta Norris, our assistant editor for current affairs. Normally, I think television is too obsessed with anniversaries, but this one feels different. Something of the spirit of 1968 – mistrust of monolithic meanings and institutions, a wider idea of culture and identity – presides over Channel Four (although it's also possible to read it as an example of anti-corporatist Toryism, splitting up bureaucracies and encouraging small businesses). There's another sense, an unashamedly personal one, in which 1968 is an anniversary worth marking for many of us round the table. Many of our generation, who were in their twenties in 1968, now hold key positions in television, publishing, the arts and journalism. Apart from wanting to remember one's political and sexual coming of age, there's a need to decipher what happened then, for people in their twenties today. A bunch of old farts talking about the days of barricades and hope might only increase their guarded scepticism, but a set of programmes that retold history, sifted out mythology and measured consequences – while communicating the elation and giddy sense of possibility many of us felt – might not go amiss.

As well as giving a comprehensive narrative, whatever we decide to do must be international – Paris, but also Prague, Chicago, West Germany, Ireland and Vietnam. It could trace a number of brief lives – Régis Debray perhaps, but also a French car-worker who joined the May '68 students. And from a cultural point of view (perhaps the most lasting, since the political gains seem to have been reversed in France, Britain and America) there might be programmes tracing political theatre and politics as theatre, and the reinterpretation of Freud through Marcuse: the liberation of instinct for better and, in the case of drugs, probably for worse.

Alan and I will write a paper for Jeremy, proposing a week-long event in May 1988 moving, as Alan says, from recreation of the experience to its analysis. With a flash of Grouchomarxism, Alan says we must kick out the Friday night news and fill it with stories that would have happened in May 1968. Agincourt talk . . .

Next day, I finally see Harrison Birtwistle's new opera, *The Mask of Orpheus*, at the Coliseum. I've commissioned a profile of Harry containing extracts of the opera, to introduce a four-programme Birtwistle festival.

The Mask of Orpheus opened while I was in America, and has been greeted with extravagant superlatives. Since I first met Harry in the mid-seventies at the National Theatre, he's been talking about it, trying to finish it and get it on, first at Glyndebourne, then at Covent Garden, finally at English National Opera.

The first act sets the motifs: Orpheus and Eurydice, each played by three masked performers as humans, heroes and myths; three levels of sound, voice, orchestra and an enveloping, sweeping, sometimes cataclysmic electronic tape. Everything is miked, so there's a great ocean of sound, controlled from the back of the stalls.

Because of the overall amplification, the sound universe of the piece has an impersonal formality which gives the whole work a choric quality even when soloists are singing or speaking. Your ears are working overtime to identify strata of sounds and their origins. It's like being an aural archaeologist.

It is in the second act – Orpheus's descent into the underworld to get Eurydice, and his loss of her on his return – that Birtwistle's musical and theatrical designs cohere most memorably. For almost an hour, great surges of percussion, seismic waves of layered sound sweep over you as Orpheus fights his way down through inferno's arches, finds his woman, fights upwards, loses her. The music batters against the roof and walls of the Coliseum, a mammoth cry, something at once elemental, ancestral and utterly modern.

Next morning, returning to the Coliseum for the filming of extracts, I have coffee with Harry. He's pleased, but his manner is as wary as ever. He's also as dapper as ever, in an equally undemonstrative way: a lightweight sky-blue jacket already rumpled, matching his eyes.

'I've written a thematic opera,' he says, 'in which initial elements are repeated, refracted, distorted, transformed, dreamed. That's why I chose mythology, whose stories do that anyway, and not an ordinary subject or story. I wanted the theatre to speak the way the music speaks.'

We talk about the music of his contemporaries. 'The trouble with Philip Glass's music is that it's completely interchangeable. You can lift bits from one work into another without anyone noticing.' He doesn't think much of current musical fashion. 'Minimalism will be utterly forgotten. It will scarcely rate a footnote in the history books.' We talk about the film Andrew Snell is making with and about him. He's going to compose a piece specially for it, rehearse it in front of the cameras, and extend it out across the film. That will make the film more a musical object in itself, less a documentary about music.

Seven German opera houses have asked about the rights to do their own productions of *The Mask of Orpheus*. Good for Harry, and maybe good for us too: now I might be able to get money from German TV or a German producer into the Birtwistle programmes, whose budgets are tight.

On Saturday morning, to Tom's for the portrait. He's been in a Bordeaux wine chateau all week, making drawings – delicate pen miniatures of vine-filled horizontals, a sudden steeple, a snaky tree above the chateau cornice – to pay for his bed and eminently satisfactory board.

'The best time is between six o'clock and dinnertime,' says Tom. 'The sun is just as low as at dawn, but things have collected something during the day. It's magic. Probably very unscientific.'

'Not really,' I say. 'The gathered heat makes the air vibrate, or something.'

'Maybe.' He starts to size up again, checking with the canvas.

'Listen, Tom, I've got an important announcement. My beard. I've decided to let it grow out, the way you see it now.'

'Very important.' Tom has a beard too, fuller than mine has been. 'You've decided to stop being the clipped, efficient arts administrator.'

'Well, I don't know if it's that. When I saw myself in your painting with my beard trimmed right back, I thought I looked like – what was it you said – a "sad Venetian ghetto Jew, who hasn't had time to shave".'

'So it's goodbye to the *shtetl*?'

'Well, maybe we're saying the same thing. The *shtetl* boy would want to become the acknowledged, efficient arts administrator.'

We work through the morning – well, Tom does and I chatter, except when the radio tells us India lose three wickets in the Test. At the end of the morning, they're 131 for 7, the mouth on my portrait has moved up half an inch, and Tom has realised there's something wrong with my right shoulder.

We're going to have lunch with Eduardo Paolozzi, one of Tom's fellow Academicians. We pick him up in his studio off the Fulham Road, crammed with plaster-cast body segments, paperbacks, torn-out images, a cast of a Mexican god-statue, African masks. Shy at first, Eduardo moves around his studio, and begins talking with a flood of reminiscence, scholarship, gifts – plaster models of a public statue, envelopes of handpicked postcards which he's prepared for us. At his local Italian restaurant, feted by the padrone and talking Italian, he mellows, and we talk about what it's like starting out as a peasant. Which is what Eduardo still thinks he is: a tough, sceptical, resourceful, equipped artist-peasant.

WEEK 26 *June 22–27*

The riggers are watching England v. Argentina from Mexico City on a monitor in the outside broadcast van. One screen showing our lads in the World Cup heat is flanked by five screens of sweating opera singers. The outside broadcast unit is parked behind the Coliseum where the camera rehearsal for English National Opera's production of Dvořák's *Rusalka* is happening on a hot Sunday night. Derek Bailey and his team and David Pountney, who staged *Rusalka*, crouch over their wall of monitors, Derek finger-snapping for cuts, muttering alterations to the script as good shots appear by serendipity, or bad shots materialise that looked good on paper. What a real-time, five-camera recording may lose in accuracy it gains in performance drive. After an hour and a half in the van, I emerge blinking and hear the disgruntled riggers swearing to revenge England's football defeat by 'giving the Argies another Falklands hiding'.

Julian Bond and Chris Rawlence come in next day to discuss *The Impressionists*, whose final first-draft script Julian has just sent to be typed. 'It moves too slowly through the first episodes,' murmurs Julian, and within half an hour we've agreed that if the dramatic core of the series is to be the struggle to see a changing world in a modern way, and if Cézanne and Monet are the most tenacious seekers of this new seeing, then the whole narrative structure needs to be folded back on itself, with a new hundred-minute first episode built around Cézanne and Monet as contrasted old men recalling the myths and realities of Impressionism's beginnings. This would enable us to condense the material of the first three episodes, which now seem bio-picaresque: maverick young people gathering in Paris to outface the artistic and social obscurantism of the Second Empire. It also helps us be more elliptical, which is truer to impressionism – and cheaper.

We need to find a producer who will nurse the scripts through the rewrite, make a budget, and help the production company and Channel Four raise money. The series can't cost less than £2.5 million. We hope to get Germany, Italy, Austria, Switzerland and France to join in. And next week I'm seeing the man from IBM who decides about putting money into television. Will we be able to stick to something that makes dramatic and art-historical sense, or will international co-production take the edge off it?

Next day Marina Warner, Gina Newson and I sit on the grass in Gordon Square, talking to Diane Wolkstein about the Sumerian myth of Inanna, the first recorded goddess in history. Diane has come over from New York, where she is the city's 'official storyteller'. A New York independent producer sent me the book of Inanna's stories and hymns which Diane had translated with Samuel Noah Kramer, the 80-year-old doyen of Sumerian studies in America.

Diane has just braved the air-conditioned chill of the Channel Four studio to perform highlights of the whole Inanna story to the three of us. Hard to cast the proper spell in that technological space, but she succeeded in communicating something both ancient and immediate. Especially when Inanna lists the ambiguous attributes of civilisation which her father has granted her:

> He gave me the art of the hero
> He gave me the art of power
> He gave me the art of treachery
> He gave me the art of straightforwardness
> He gave me the plundering of cities

I'm interested because I'm looking for something more resonant than contemporary art, less in need of shock reinterpretation than the familiar classics, something coming from a pre-print culture that might have an affinity with television if one could find an appropriate form for it.

Gina listens quietly, Marina asks questions and draws parallels between the cult of Inanna and the Virgin Mary. I wanted Gina and Marina to meet Diane because I sensed common ground between their films on the mythologies and images of women, and this story, this storyteller. I see that Gina is half-intrigued, half-wary, especially about whether Diane's heightened performance style would work for the camera. And Diane too is wary; she doesn't want her storytelling swamped by film tricks. As we walk back, Marina points out the Courtauld Institute Library and sings its praises. 'It's an open-stack library, you know. Aby Warburg, who founded it, believed in what he called the good neighbour policy: what you are looking for is probably not in the book you know about, but in its neighbour on the shelves.'

That strikes me as one of the best ways of defining and defending public-service broadcasting. There are leaks already this week of the

Peacock Report, which is supposedly advocating a gradual shift to 'electronic publishing', where viewers would call up only the programmes
they wanted, and pay for them by credit card. That would do away with
broadcasting's equivalent of Warburg's 'good neighbour policy'. There
would be little chance of viewers stumbling across something they didn't
know they wanted until they'd had a taste of it, as is still possible in
mixed-schedule public broadcasting. It would happen less, if at all, in
targeted 'narrow-casting'.

At the *Rusalka* recording that evening, I see the good neighbour policy
in action in ENO's large, festive and avid audience. Peter Jonas, their
managing director, says it's been their best season yet, with near-capacity
houses for Janáček's *Katya Kabanova* and Busoni's *Doctor Faust*, neither
of which are familiar pieces. It must be the effect of their proximity in
the repertoire to loved favourites like *The Merry Widow*, *The Bartered Bride*
and *Fledermaus*. The *Rusalka* recording goes well, there are very few
mishaps and retakes. I think the Freudian imagery which Pountney and
his designer Lazarides have grafted on to Dvořák's fairy tale will work
vividly on screen.

Programme Review meeting discusses *Open the Box*, whose episode about
Crossroads got an audience of 3 million, crowning a series which has
gathered a lot of attention. I think it's worked because the best of the
films translated analysis into sharp and enjoyable documentary; some of
my colleagues thought the programmes were too long on entertainment
and too short on thought, especially the final one, a mosaic about sex and
violence on TV. Farrukh makes the telling point that *Open the Box* feels
like the consensual thinking of a professional elite, tolerantly anatomising
its own professional practices. 'It's symptomatic of a pernicious orthodoxy
that I sometimes suspect around the Channel,' he says. 'You know, a
badge of courage for blacks and feminists. And media analysts . . .'

Lunch, at Justin Dukes's invitation, with Frank Dunlop, director of the
Edinburgh Festival, at Bertorelli's, the old room in the back, untouched by
the brasserification of the front half. Justin has invited me and Stephen
Phillips, Channel Four's arts reporter, to talk to Frank about this year's
Edinburgh Festival. Advance bookings are down, due to American fear
of flying to terrorist- and fallout-infested Europe. Frank is in fine fettle,
laying about the new Edinburgh council with glee: 'They don't have
enough to do, so they invent things, like changing the names of streets.
There must be twenty Mandela Groves across Scotland now, and there's
a Mandela Room and a Mandela Throne in the Council House. I said,

I'll lead a bunch of mercenaries to spring Mandela from jail, but I'm not going to a meeting in any Mandela Room. And after all the talk, you wind up getting £600,000 from the city towards a £3 million budget.'

The talk moves to the nature of festivals in general. Los Angeles Arts Festival has been given a million dollars from the Inner City Fund; a proposed New York Festival is getting $2.8 million from American Express in seed money alone. If things go on at this rate, says Frank, culture – or at least arts festivals – will wind up as a mere pretext for filling hotels, developing real estate and promoting credit cards.

Peter Brook rings from Paris. He's leaving for South Africa, in search of actors for the English-language *Mahabharata*. 'It didn't seem the right time to cancel the trip, despite the violence and the bombs. The Market Theatre in Johannesburg will be looking after me, and will know what's happening.' South Africa's going to explode, it's already begun, but this time there's no belief that the struggle itself will forge new values, as we told ourselves it would in other wars of independence: Algeria, Vietnam. Of course, we were over-idealistic then.

Seeing the final performance of *The Mask of Orpheus* with all this in mind makes me reflect on Harry Birtwistle's comment, 'There are many ways of being political.' Not only does the ferocity of sound as Orpheus descends into the underworld seem the very music of modern carnage; the implacable repetition in different registers of Orpheus's fate – suicide by hanging, dismemberment and beheading by crazed women – seems a metaphor for the doomed reiterations of today's politics: violent injustice overturned by vengeful counter-violence, the revolution devouring its own children again and again.

Next day, when I meet Stewart Purvis, editor of *Channel Four News*, which has been putting out penetrating daily stories from South Africa despite all the obstacles placed in its path, I say that arts stories in *Channel Four News* shouldn't just be light relief, icing on the bitter pill, previews of new films or shows, investigations into arts funding, obituaries of the mighty dead or profiles of rising talents; they should also show art and artists measuring up to the extremes of our world, in Africa, Ireland, Eastern Europe, finding images and stories about what's happening that go deeper into the individual and social psyche than journalism can.

SUMMER 1850: WHEAS 27 · 37

No poem is ever written for its story-line's sake only, just as no life is lived for the sake of an obituary.

Joseph Brodsky, 'The Keening Muse'

There is no rewind button on the BETAMAX of life.

Nam June Paik 'La Vie, Satellites, One Meeting – One Life'

I pass most of the weekend reading Robert Hewison's acute book on British art and society in the sixties, *Too Much*. Hard to suppress an inappropriately nostalgic reaction that 'they're playing our tune'. But hard too not to go along with Howard Brenton's feelings: 'It was defeated. A generation dreaming of a beautiful utopia was kicked – kicked awake and not dead. I've got to believe not kicked dead. May 1968 gave me a desperation I still have.'

But reading Hewison also reminds me what a wayward path I followed through the sixties, even by the standards of those shape-shifting times. I believed in institutions, such as theatres for the widest audience, as well as in the counter-culture which subverted institutions; my allegiances were to the classics as much as to the avant-garde; I wanted political and social change but, as a 'rootless cosmopolitan' Jew, I was also sceptical about the price of political passion and righteousness.

Most of the people I enjoy working with now, whether or not we belong to the same generation, have negotiated their own version of that path, preserving their distance from British pieties. But the terrain has changed so much. The week offers many illustrations of how the utopian sixties have become the disabused, disjointed, eighties:

Take Your Desires for Realities
Against the railings of the Tavistock Square unemployment office, which I drive past every day to Channel Four, a queue waits. There are never less than twenty people. The men stare longingly at two young girls walking past in ankle warmers and bright T-shirts on their way to class at the London School of Contemporary Dance nearby.

In the Beginning was the Corporation
'They're hot to trot,' Mike Dann whispers to me at the end of a meeting with the man who decides what TV programmes IBM will underwrite. Mike started out as a Chicago kid selling a communist newspaper supporting the Republicans during the Spanish Civil War, became head

of programmes for CBS television, and now counsels IBM. Or rather
IBM Europe – 'a hemisphere which stretches from Greenland to Africa,'
he says. What IBM may be hot to trot about is *The Painter's World*, a
series on European painting. Their sponsorship could mean a million
dollars to cover the production, a book, an exhibition, promotion for the
whole package. 'It's instructive, beautiful, and it's not controversial,' says
the IBM man.

The Consciousness Industry

I get a telex from Unitel, the German producers of opera and music
films, offering to put £100,000 into our two Harrison Birtwistle programmes. They will undoubtedly exact their price, urging me to buy or
co-produce their programmes to the tune of much more than £100,000.
In cultural television, which has a limited world market, there are definitely no free lunches.

Murdoch's Revenge

The *Sunday Times* has gone to town about the money that Peter Hall and
Trevor Nunn have earned through transfers or co-productions with the
commercial theatre. It *is* troubling, and perhaps neither the National nor
the Royal Shakespeare are currently at their best. I doubt that Roger Planchon at the Théâtre National Populaire or Peter Stein at Berlin's Schau-
buhne – two comparable, and arguably even more talented directors of
European publicly funded theatres – have made that kind of money from
commercial exploitation. But neither have their theatres been as underfunded as the RSC and the National, forcing them into closer collusion with
Broadway and the West End than is healthy for a public theatre.

There's a fevered and predictable follow-up in Fleet Street all week,
pandering to envy and philistinism. What Arnold Wesker called the
Lilliputian spirit of the newshounds is given full rein. So I write a letter
to the *Guardian* suggesting that the vendetta against Peter Hall just might
have something to do with the gleeful caricature of a Murdoch-like figure
in David Hare and Howard Brenton's play *Pravda*, which is the runaway
success of the National's season. It was only a matter of time before
Murdoch got his revenge – and since his newspaper is no friend of public
funding for the arts, it must have seemed a good idea to clobber Trevor
Nunn at the same time.

The Peacock Report on the financing of the BBC is published. What is
salutary about Peacock is that he articulates so clearly the hard-nosed

belief of the times that there is nothing, television included, that cannot be assimilated into an economic, technological, individualistic, marketed and thus 'libertarian' view of reality.

There are many human needs which can be predicted and manipulated, but there are also needs which are invisible until they are awakened. And the label 'consumer sovereignty' doesn't fit, the act of consumption doesn't describe, such needs. Like so many concepts of the eighties, it's an opaque overlay, a tidy blueprint covering an unruly garden.

My own area of television – the arts, or TV aspiring to become an art itself – pinpoints the limitations of Peacockish common sense, enshrined in the Report's minimalist definition of the public-service ideal as 'any major modification of purely commercial provision resulting from public policy'. To anyone who grew up with the concept of a common culture, shared but not cheapened, the barefaced shift of emphasis in this definition – the idea of the public realm as an aberration from the commercial norm – is breathtaking.

Believers in the public-service ethos, indeed in public as opposed to corporate or commercial reality, have been backed into a corner by neo-conservative political economists. Richard Francis, who stood up to the BBC governors over the *Real Lives* row and was sacked as managing director of BBC Radio for his pains, writes in the *Sunday Times* that 'there is something infinite' about public-service broadcasting, that it is 'a comprehensive concept'. Neither term would stand up to the scalpel of free-market ideologues. What a pity that in the same week as Peacock, the financial rewards that Peter Hall and Trevor Nunn have earned from productions originated in the subsidised theatre will seem to many to have blurred the distinction between non-commercial and commercial.

Europe's television and newspapers are full of the flotillas and fireworks of America's celebration of the Statue of Liberty centenary. Andy Warhol sidles into London for a show of his portraits, and unerringly puts his finger on the blur between media and reality: 'We were just at the Statue of Liberty celebrations. The sun was out. It was a perfect day. The Fourth of July. We were in a boat with millions of people and it felt like we were in a TV movie. Not even a real movie, but a TV movie.'

WEEK 28 *July 7–11*

Michael Dibb and Peter Fuller talk through their feature-length documentary *Naturally Creative*. I have read Peter's outline of the film's ideas which he first formulated in his essay 'Art and Biology'. There he makes the case that human nature is inherently creative, and has symbolic and imaginative capacities beyond the reach of even the most gifted kitten or chimpanzee. His case rests on recent work in evolutionary biology and the psychoanalytical insights of D. W. Winnicott into what goes on between the baby, the breast, the mother and the doll. These connections are part of Peter's determined search for a view of art that is less reductive than much Marxist writing, or the flights into minimalism and conceptualism of many modernist critics – and radical artists.

Michael and Peter's collaboration began at the BBC and they have made four films together. There is a fluent collaboration between them, just as there was between Mike and John Berger on *Ways of Seeing*; in fact Peter Fuller extends and prolongs many points of inquiry which Berger began. But I don't want the shorthand between them to become a comfortable complicity and I say so. 'The Peacock Report has proposed a definition of human nature which conforms to the free-market/consumer-satisfaction model,' I say. 'Surely your film should be polemical in its own way about people's natural creative needs?'

Mike's sensuous realisation of the ideas that Peter formulates and provokes could give rise to something irrefutable: a picture of imagination as something rooted biologically and psychologically in human beings, whether as makers or receivers. If he pulls it off, the film could be a small, oblique act of resistance speaking to aspects of the viewer that shriller, more ideological, arguments don't reach.

Jeremy comes to Programme Review next day. He does so on average every other week, and there's an inevitable, almost pantomime ritual: at around 11 a.m., the door of our boardroom opens and the heads of fifteen commissioning editors and presentation, press and marketing people swivel to see if it's him. On the receiving end of all these gazes, Jeremy infallibly makes the same gestures: pause on the threshold, beetle brows, eyes sweeping the assembly like a belligerent biped. If body language ever means anything, this, especially his thrust lip, does; but what? It's like a self-mocking mime of a stern father. He knows he himself has sown the seeds of the mischief he must now control.

I talked about the words 'paternal' and 'paternalism' yesterday when I had a working picnic with David Rose. Prompted by a scathing reference to paternalism in the *Guardian*, I said to David, 'What's the alternative? Infantilism? Or simply learning to be better fathers?' The reference was to Jeremy: we'd been discussing what he was going to do in 1988, after his current contract ends. There's been press speculation about his going to the BBC as Director-General; David was saying that if he went, his successor might radically alter Channel Four, especially if, as Peacock mentions, it were to sell its own advertising and compete for audiences with ITV. Then the Channel might seek a very different kind of father-figure.

This morning, Jeremy continues the ritual entrance, padding slowly round the circumference of the table, a cross between a louring tiger and a tracking camera. As always, he signals to Liz Forgan not to interrupt what's going on, which is an assessment of last Friday's five-hour rock-and-roll show, *Eurotube*, a live hook-up with Europe. The question for all such shows is how can they follow the immense excitement of Live Aid, which went out on air a year ago this week. By all accounts *Eurotube* did pretty well, with a strong British line-up, good live production and no really appalling Euro-bands, although a Norwegian group called Leather Nun had to be seen to be believed.

Jeremy moves into the discussion, turning to next year's plans and possibilities. There will be more money, because ITV's revenues are buoyant. Some of that new money will be used to fund new subject areas – science, money, media, Scotland – and extra hours; but the crucial question is, since we are doing well by building on popular elements – the afternoon game show *Countdown*, American comedy, strong movies and purchased mini-series – can we in future marginally improve our performance by relying more on programmes that we have initiated?

He sounds like a man with a renewed appetite for his job. Perhaps his three weeks off in Sicily have helped him begin to get over Tamara's death. Certainly the lower lip juts less tensely than usual.

In the evening, I turn up to a board meeting of the Lyric Theatre Hammersmith, the first to include new Labour local councillors. Four council representatives come to the board meeting. They have hitherto refused the theatre's offers to brief them on policy, background and finance. This meeting is their chance to find out, and to question. It doesn't go too badly, although when Peter James, the theatre's director, talks about successful transfers to the West End which have brought the Lyric revenue, you can sense the councillors thinking, why is the local borough providing 75 per cent funding if these glamorous theatre-folk can make money in the West End?

A more serious skirmish comes when a solemn young man attacks the artistic policy for not being local enough, not reflecting the multi-cultural mix of the inner city, and not making enough efforts to attract the community. 'Why can't it be more like the Albany at Deptford?' he asks. Because the building, an ornate Frank Matcham Victorian auditorium, doesn't lend itself easily to populist knees-up shows or agit-prop, I find myself saying. Local resident members weigh in with figures and statistics about Hammersmith's loyalty and love for the theatre. Maybe it will ease up as we all get to know each other.

Other words and images of the week: David Perlov phones from Israel to say that the studio where he'd been editing his film has been taken over by a Cannon Films feature, and no one will pay him any attention, so his *Diary* will be delivered late . . . Tony Palmer, gleeful in a MOSTLY MOZART T-shirt, thinks he may have found the rest of the money for the Shostakovich film, from a Swiss bank . . . Sensuous, tender nudes, mostly by Man Ray, in *L'Amour Fou: Photography and Surrealism*, at the Hayward. Do they exalt or exploit women? Or exploit them by an inhuman exaltation? . . . David Graham, director of Diverse Production, whom I visit down in Hammersmith, wants to put Machiavelli's *Discorsi* on screen as if they were contemporary party politicals . . . Mark Morris, wunderkind of American dance as Michael Clark is of ours, flailing his long limbs to Vivaldi like a demented postmodern pierrot in an American dance programme I'll show next year. Talking to Melvyn Bragg, whom I phone after hearing he collapsed from overdoing things. 'What are you going to do less of?' I ask. 'Favours for people,' he says.

WEEK 29 *July 14–20*

We transmit Gina Newson's and Marina Warner's film *Imaginary Women*. It was inspired by Marina's book *Monuments and Maidens*, which asks why most statues of women are naked or thinly robed and represent abstract virtues – Liberty, Justice, Industry, Harvest – while most statues of men are dressed and represent real, named people. Gina's film examines how the female body has been used to symbolise lofty abstractions, and how a new generation of women artists is changing these preconceptions. The form of the film is subtle and fluid: a collage of goddesses pedestalled in railway buffets or gentlemen's clubs, publicity logos with Boadicean warriors, cartoons and classical heroines wittily woven together. Then it moves into a dinner party, hosted by Marina, where six women – a pop singer, a fashion designer, three artists and a choreographer – discuss women's symbolic inheritance and show how they're altering it in their work.

The dinner party is compelling watching – gazes of avid attention or barely concealed dislike, Toyah Wilcox's flaring orange hair and swift personal insights, Katharine Hamnett wearing a cheeky crumpled version of the white hat an outfield cricketer might use to avoid sunstroke and recalling how she got herself photographed with Mrs Thatcher wearing a T-shirt with the slogan 58% DON'T WANT PERSHING; Susan Hiller's multi-syllabic analyses and inquiring nods and hums to see if class is keeping up with her, and Marina Warner at the top of the table, bright-eyed, clear-voiced, searching. The table talk doesn't entirely avoid knee-jerk counter-rhetoric, but perhaps that's inevitable when former victims reassert themselves.

The men who have spoken to me about the film found it 'compelling', but also partial – although that may also be due to the unfamiliarity of a television programme that sets out its partiality clearly rather than slipping its prejudices in as if they were part of nature. Udi Eichler, the producer of *Voices*, asked how you could deal with this subject without considering the long period of a child's dependence on the breast: 'Of course the child is going to invest the mother with lofty virtues and goddess-like stature.'

All in all, it's done what I hoped: set some questions about our collective unconscious into orbit, in a form which is engaging and intricate. Next week we repeat Gina and Marina's dissection of the legends and mythology surrounding Joan of Arc. Together with the film biography of Lee Miller – first Man Ray's model and mistress, then a forceful photographer in her own right – I hope that these programmes, grouped under the title *Picturing Women*, have kept alive an undogmatic feminist inquiry.

Channel Four has given me a different working relationship with women. When Sue Crockford joined the Channel as assistant education editor, she greeted me with a cheery one-liner worthy of Posy Simmonds: 'Oh, I know all about you! Your ex-wife and I were in the same consciousness-raising group.' And I remember early on in the Channel, how pleased and faintly bewildered I was by what seemed after the National Theatre like an extraordinary number of talented women in positions of real power: Naomi Sargant, Senior Commissioning Editor, Education; Liz Forgan, Commissioning Editor, Actuality; Carol Haslam, Commissioning Editor, Documentaries; Sue Stoessl, Head of Marketing, and many others. At the National when I was there, casting director was the highest any woman reached in the creative team. And even there, her authority over actors was only borrowed from the director, almost invariably a man, towards whom she played a traditional mothering, providing role. I was so struck by the difference when I came to Charlotte Street that I must have gone around in a kind of daze of delight. Sue Stoessl, whose wits were sharpened in the bullish world of ITV competitiveness, brought me up short one day: 'Michael, you're unbelievable. You're so deferential to women here. We only have to open our mouths and you're ready to see our point of view.' Since when, Sue and I have had one or two solid arguments about how the Channel is marketed, and I've come down to earth . . .

I go to a screening of Andrei Tarkovsky's *The Sacrifice*, a film I've been eagerly awaiting since I met the wiry Russian director in David Rose's office just after he'd decided to stay in the West. What draws me to artists like Tarkovsky and Yuri Lyubimov (who directed Dostoevsky's *The Possessed* for us last year) – and to that pantheon of torn and triumphant Russian poets and poetesses at the start of this century – is an elemental vision, a determination to see through surfaces to the heart. Ultimate concerns, a spirituality that has been tempered by the bitterest trials the twentieth century can offer, a sense of big wheels turning, deep voices amid the shrillness.

Tarkovsky's films arrested me with this visionary quality, realised in specific cinematic terms, slow, steady camera explorations, lighting that suggests secrets as well as clarity. And above all, a sense of charged time. Time loaded with human intention and searching, film time that makes no concessions but offers a confrontation that can speak to an audience as more than spectators. The other masters of this kind of film are Bergman and Antonioni; in the theatre, Ibsen has the same unwavering penetration.

The Sacrifice, a two-and-a-half-hour film shot on a remote Swedish island, feels like Ibsen, the Ibsen who knew the tragedy of conscience and consciousness, and also believed in trolls and spells.

I recognise Tarkovsky's familiar trademarks: a sustained choreography of long takes on still and moving groups in a room, on a shore; the eruption of grainy images of memory or the unconscious into the flow of the present; a soundtrack full of the noises of nature – rain, waves, wind, distant human or animal cries – suddenly pierced by magnified roars which may be sonic booms or a seismic catastrophe, the outbreak of war or the end of time.

Two sequences crack open resistance. Shortly after the television announces a state of emergency, the professor's wife, played by Susan Fleetwood, a lightning-conductor actress I've known since we were both at the Royal Shakespeare in the sixties, has hysterics. Whether it's from fear of dying, or an explosion of all the dissatisfactions and unhappiness of her marriage, it's hard to say. What you can't take your mind off is the extremity of what's going on in real, unscissored time: this woman on the floor, legs bared and thrashing, mouth torn open by howls, bottomless sobs. It goes on for much longer than conventional drama would allow.

And then the climactic sequence when the protagonist sets his house on fire. It's in long shot, like that poem of Auden's about Icarus falling into the sea, far away, beyond calm fields. The house catches fire quickly, the sound of cracking flames and crashing beams is deafening, magnified to mean more than what it literally is. The professor sits on the ground, watching his home burn down. From the woods his wife and daughter and the family doctor, her lover, come running. Then an ambulance; the interns chasing the professor across the field, mad as King Lear, wearing a Japanese robe because he's come to think the truth is Japanese. Across the path of the chase cycles a black-clad servant girl who has the powers of a witch. And all this is one sustained shot, panning and tracking and finally pulling back to the flaring skeleton of the house tumbling down on itself, then cut, silence. It's objectively real, before your very eyes, at the same time it transcends common-sense reality. It's a film-maker doing what Artaud said all artists should do, 'signalling through the flames'.

'The little monkey wouldn't stop crawling all over my camera,' Sven Nykvist, Tarkovsky's cinematographer, told David Rose when he went over the shoot (*The Sacrifice* is co-produced by Channel Four, as are *A Room with a View, Letter to Brezhnev*). What will happen to it when it's crammed into a tiny television screen? Will the camera explorations just look ponderous, because television feeds the appetite for rapidity? Will the dynamic range of its sound, from distant tracery to massive concussion, be squashed up by domestic receiver speakers?

A week ago, a mime artist, dancer and choreographer in an outrageous suit delivered a videotape of his Anne Frank ballet to our front desk, insisting that he wouldn't leave until my secretary had personally taken it from his hands. The tape had been preceded by several voluble letters, all copied to Jeremy Isaacs, saying that the ballet had the blessing of Anne Frank's father, had successfully been staged across three continents, represented an investment of lifeblood, commitment and personal savings, and had to be shown on Channel Four to alert British viewers to the Holocaust and the dangers of racism. Several more letters and phone calls followed. Jeremy asked me to watch it sooner rather than later.

Yesterday I did so. Yiddish folk dance played by a souped-up symphony orchestra reveals the young Anne dancing blithely with her girlfriends in the garden, shot in rigid long shot in a black-walled studio. Choreography not bad, but the thing seems to be taking place far away, at the end of a long tunnel. Ominous beat of drums, and a goose-stepping Nazi enters, melodramatically circling the innocent children . . . I fast-forward, select other passages, find them no better, write the man a gentle but firm letter, saying it must have been effective on stage but wouldn't be immediate on television, so I must regretfully say no. I add, since I know he won't take this quietly, that this is my final decision. And I copy the letter to Jeremy.

I don't have long to wait. Two days later, a two-page letter arrives, equating my 'final decision' with Hitler's 'Final Solution', accusing me and Jeremy of failing in our duty as British Jews, sniping at other recent dance on the Channel, saying that the Israeli government is considering showing his ballet on Holocaust Remembrance Day . . . Copied to Jeremy, of course.

Next day, annoyance wakes me at 5.30 am. Lying there I devise a letter of reply as the birds start up, and dictate it when I get into the office. It says that he can scarcely accuse me or Jeremy Isaacs of ignoring the Holocaust when we are going to screen Claude Lanzmann's nine-hour documentary *Shoah*, a devastating and comprehensive description of the concentration camps. Perhaps he'll stop now. But there will be other besiegers. We are open to all comers . . .

In a Kennington church hall the next day I hear the first run-through with orchestra of Harry Birtwistle's opera *Yan Tan Tethera*, which we'll record in the autumn. I relish the sounds he squeezes from the London Sinfonietta's nuclear ensemble: sheets of sustained strings, reverberations of bells, angular cries of oboe and flute, plucked harp-song, darkness and glitter. And across this, the bare simplicity of a piper playing a penny whistle and gambolling around the stage between the two protagonists, a displaced northern shepherd and his southern counterpart. Harry has such firmness of purpose, pressing his material – counting rhymes, spells, reincarnations, a masked chorus of sheep – to deliver everything in it, like a coral structure. He sits next to me during the run, scribbling on his score. When I enthuse, especially about a riveting young soprano, he mutters, 'The sheep are still a mess.'

On Saturday in Tom's studio, two new huge chalk drawings of my fellow sitter, Iris Murdoch, like giant African masks. Since our last sitting Tom has spent ten days in Zimbabwe, on a jury to choose an African artist for a painting prize. He talks happily about the great space, the horizontality of the landscape, the way European nags and worries drop away. And about how direct Africans are compared with Indians, he says. He was fined for speeding by a traffic policeman who, when asked for a receipt, said, 'The fine's for me. No receipt. It's cheaper with me than with my uncle the judge.'

Tom seems happy with the top of my head now. 'The problem has been that you have so many flickering expressions I'm in danger of falling between two stools if I try to get them all in, some kind of generalised El Greco.' My old sadness in repose, which makes people ask me what's the matter. Now he's going to paint out my mouth and jaw and start again. Says he'll finish by Christmas, 'when you stop writing your book'.

WEEK 30 *Saturday, July 26–Monday, July 21*

Let me try telling this week in reverse for a change. So that it's like a piece of video rewind. If this book's about television, maybe the writing should do some of the things TV and video do. Reading it will probably feel a lot like watching television: some continuities, a lot of channel-hopping, and this rewind.

Saturday evening towards dusk, I'm sitting in my garden. I've just finished reading my friend Jerome Charyn's *Metropolis: New York as Myth, Marketplace and Magical Land*, a book that I've picked up at every free moment over the past fortnight. Jerome writes like a polyglot Isaac Babel whose home pitch is not Odessa but Ellis Island. His prose is peppered with the vernacular of Jews (he calls Mayor Ed Koch 'the golem'), Chinese, Italians, Irish, blacks and Hispanics. His book digs beneath the self-promotional legends of New York, its simulations and hypes; it is a memorial to immigrant energies. It reminds me of my own allegiances to displacement, my disposition to be the outsider.

Jerome sees the Chinese and Asian Americans as today's equivalent of poor Jews knocking at America's doors. 'But will they grow invisible? Another generation of ghost shadows? Or will they learn to shout and scream, like the Jews? . . . Like the Irish before us, and the Italians, we scraped our character upon the surface of the City, and inside its bowels.'

Back to Saturday morning, I'm lying in bed dizzy from hay fever and hangover, and the phone rings and it's Colin Leventhal calling to discuss the week. Chatter about comings and goings in the Channel; it's a summer of exits, replacements and re-allocations. Then at the end, with a mischievous giggle, Colin says that he's started putting together a group to get one of the ITV franchises. They come up again in 1990. What kind of television landscape will we have then? And under what government? And if it's Labour, would Jeremy be asked to be Director-General of the BBC, and would he want to do it? In an interview in *Broadcast* this week, he says he doesn't envisage being asked to do it, but if he was, 'one would have to think about it very, very seriously'.

Late Friday night, sitting round the marble-topped counter of a fish restaurant inappropriately tucked into a sidestreet near Smithfield. We're having dinner after the wedding of Erica Bolton to Robert Hewison. With Jane Quinn, Erica publicises our dance seasons and other arts programmes. The reception takes place in Middle Temple Hall. Beneath lofty portraits of red-robed judges, a multitude of Erica's aunts, capable society women with smart hair, mingle with critics, novelists, actors, comics. Michael Clark and his brigade of punkish dancers practise falls on the parquet floor.

Before that, a glimpse of *Yan Tan Tethera* at the Queen Elizabeth Hall, the first rehearsal on stage, singers cursing and frowning as they leave the security of the rehearsal room. Before that, a long telephone conversation with Peter Brook, just back from South Africa and Nigeria, looking for actors for the English-speaking *Mahabharata*. 'When you arrive, if you're white there's no problem – unless you're carrying a TV camera. And for a long time, everything looks normal. No tanks on the streets, no soldiers. The first sign is that all the blacks you see on the streets look depressed. None of that effervescence you get from blacks elsewhere. It reminds you of the Bowery . . . The whole situation's like Nazi Germany, everyone watches everyone else. I asked John and Winston, the black actors in *Woza Albert*, to come for a talk. They came to my hotel but they insisted on coming at eleven o'clock, not for lunch, as I'd invited them. When we met, they wanted a cup of tea, and nothing else, not even a biscuit. The reason is that all the servants in the hotel are black, and they would have been accused of "wining and dining" with the white enemy if they'd eaten a meal with me . . .'

Two hours earlier, the event that has capped this day, this week. I'm in Jeremy's office with Colin, discussing opera films we plan to make over the next three years, and how we will work with Peter Hall when we do *La Traviata* from Glyndebourne next year. Jeremy asks Colin to step out for a few minutes. 'I've decided you shall have another contract after the end of this one,' he says. 'That will be it, no more after that. Two things I must say to you, Michael. Keep a tight hand on the administrative side of things. I don't want any more last-minute programme commissioning forms. And don't commission anything beyond

1990. We'll have a long handover period, with your successor working by your side. After that, we shouldn't tie his or her hands.'

Then there's a lot of muttering. I mutter thank you, and say how pleased I am. He mutters, 'Well, you're good at what you do,' and raises his eyebrows like a quizzical Santa opening his sack of gifts for a second.

Faster rewind, it's still only Friday. Two French vidéastes, who will do a monthly magazine, *Video-Plaisir*, for Canal Plus, want to buy from or co-produce with us. Haunting underwater ballet they show me, swimming to Mahler ... My colleague David Benedictus, our commissioning editor for drama series, slumped in a chair in my office, eyes downcast. He's just seen Jeremy and been told that his contract won't be renewed after next autumn. 'How am I going to live through this year, knowing that everything I'm initiating will be for someone else?'

Back through Thursday. Walking down Cork Street to St James's Park to read scripts on a deckchair. Victor Willing's mysterious chalk drawings in Bernard Jacobson's gallery: masks, discarded clothing, cubes, De Chirico emptiness. Bernard says these may be his last works; muscular dystrophy has immobilised him ... Waiting for a taxi in the ICA entrance hall. Bill McAlister gives me a catalogue of their Colin Self exhibition. I remember Colin Self from the sixties, his astringent image of a US airbase in Norfolk, rockets in their silos and a fearsome guard-dog snarling. At the end of the sixties he withdrew to make 'localist art'. In his catalogue, he quotes Van Gogh's letter about paying for paint out of money meant for food, and comments, 'Dear 400,000? unemployed Great Britain artists of 1986 – it has not changed at all, has it? I've done all mine on £40.92 pence per week supplementary benefit. God protect the Welfare State. Yours truly, Colin.'

Speed back through Wednesday into Tuesday: Jeremy asks me to a state-of-the-nation weekly conversation show, provide ten weeks of starting next April, up to two hours long, and live television. Much depends on the choice of topics and presenter. I suggest John Lloyd, the Scot who's just left the *Financial Times* to edit the *New Statesman*, and whom I know from the time he edited *Ink*, the short-lived alternative weekly paper in the expiring sixties. Someone who spans politics and culture and a Scot to boot.

Monday morning, back at the top of the week, and I'm in Kew Gardens having an outdoor theatrical event explained to me. Called *Deadwood*, it's a kind of modernist environmental masque, a promenade with ecological concerns. 'Then we come into this dell,' explains Hilary Westlake, who has devised and directed the piece for Lumiere and Son Theatre

Company, 'and we see the ants at play over there, and these European explorers in safari suits are leading us along, explaining the rainforests, telling travellers' tales . . .' We walk through ticketed trees, labelled bushes. 'From that branch one of our more athletic actors will give us his ape.'

WEEK 31 *July 28–August 1*

When things go wrong they tend to do so in clusters, epidemics of misfortune. But the converse can also be true. This week has had a high pollen-count of pleasure which is a blessing, since the real pollen-count has regularly reduced me to a sneezing and wheezing machine and kept me awake last night, clutching Anita Brookner's latest novel, *A Misalliance*, for comfort. If that's the right word for a book with a protagonist of almost extra-terrestrial loneliness, who moves in on surrounding human beings like a member of an alien species. Once again, the situation is devastating, and the prose picks over the characters like an elegantly wielded scalpel. It's as if you're inside the skin of one of those peripheral figures in a Hitchcock film who turns out to be a pathological killer in the last reel.

My morning muzziness is pierced and brightened by a call from John Drummond, BBC Radio's Controller of Music. He has persuaded the Director-General of the BBC to agree to a stereo sound simulcast on Radio Three of Harrison Birtwistle's opera *Yan Tan Tethera* when we transmit it on Channel Four next year. This is a great scoop, the first such cooperation between the BBC and a broadcaster from a rival system. But, as John says, it was a question of honour; the BBC originally commissioned the work for television, and then cancelled it when BBC Managing Director Bill Cotton decided it was expendable at a time of financial constraint. I then nipped in and got a year's option from Harry to present the work on Channel Four. 'It was the least we could do to get the egg off our faces,' says John. I can imagine him – flamboyant, voluble, persistent – persuading Alasdair Milne that it had to be done.

Next day, another buzz of pleasure. I'm in Andrew Snell's cutting room, having spent the morning painstakingly listing projects for my 1987–88 budget submission to Jeremy. I'm looking at rushes of the Birtwistle profile: Harry conducting the Grimethorpe Colliery Band, then a group from the London Sinfonietta in a ritornello he's written especially for the film, then Harry revisiting the house in Accrington where he was born and looking positively boyish when he talks about the quarry and its elemental rocks he could see from his window, and the giant power station that intruded into his countryside, precursor of all the violent intrusions into the natural wave-forms of his music. The phone rings. It's Harry for me from a call-box. A few exchanges, then a muttered announcement: 'Mike, Tony and I have decided we'd like to dedicate *Yan Tan Tethera* to you.'

I can hardly say how pleased and proud I am. When you've spent most of your working life helping the talent of artists to come to full fruition, it's a true reward when artists you regard as among the best acknowledge that you have some special gift as an encourager, a sustainer, an eliciter, a fellow spirit. In the course of the day I tell half a dozen people about it. Chuffed – an appropriately northern word – really is the best way to describe what I feel.

In the evening, a very different kind of music at the Queen Elizabeth Hall. Loose Tubes, a 21-piece big band, average age twenty-four, play one of the best jazz concerts I've ever heard. A wiry young keyboard player called Django Bates, wearing Indian trousers, a dinner jacket, no shirt and a knitted skullcap, is the mover and shaker behind this gangling, goonish, but wonderfully organised amalgam. Loose Tubes is the musical offspring of jazz composer Graham Collier, but their appetite and disciplined eclecticism belong utterly to their own generation. The pieces, all composed by Django or other band members, echo Mingus, Frank Zappa, Spike Jones and his City Slickers, gospel, African townships, Captain Beefheart, Stravinsky and Varese. The ensemble riffs and tempo changes are hair-raising, the solos full-throated and humorous. One moment you're swept up in some vertiginous wind-tunnel of sound, then you're ambling or chugging along with some offhand virtuoso soloist. Switch again, and suddenly they're putting words to a be-bop melodic tune. Lambert, Hendricks and Ross have been here before, you say, and then you realise there are twenty of them doing it in swift, impeccable unison.

I come out of it scrubbed over with music, tingling and skipping along the South Bank. 'Musical therapy,' murmurs my companion David Benedictus. David is more than usually preoccupied tonight. Moving from the self-sufficiency of being a writer into the hornet's nest of commissioning television drama series – where everyone comes to you with the rights to some fictional masterpiece that will make a wildly popular series and needs only £200,000 an hour from Channel Four – can't have been easy.

This is turning out to be the summer in which commissioning editors confer about the future. I squeeze lunch with Alan Fountain, commissioning editor for independent film and video, and like me one of the first wave of editors. It's squeezed because Alan is fifteen minutes late. Characteristic: he always gives the impression of being pressured and rushed, as if the serious outside world of strikes, demonstrations, and the disenfranchised were bearing in on him, making him ration his time with his Charlotte Street colleagues. Although that's probably how any outside observer would see most of us; our body language through most of the day signals 'do not trouble me, I'm packing in more than I can deal with'.

Alan is the living incarnation of Gramsci's dictum 'pessimism of the intellect, optimism of the will'. I've scarcely had a conversation with him that hasn't started with his sounding off about how impossible it all is, how the Channel is betraying its mission, how everything is beyond recall. And at the same time he gets through a prodigious amount of work, sustains a network of regional film and video workshops, keeps the door open to the third world, women, gays, structuralist film-makers, late Jean-Luc Godard, miners, neighbourhood oral history. All the unfulfilled minorities and groups the Channel is required to articulate. His weekly programme *The Eleventh Hour* and its companion, *People to People*, represent the grass-roots instinct of Channel Four at its purest. At the same time Alan is determined not to be the sole repository and alibi of the Channel's conscience, so he snipes at the rest of us, Thersites-like.

This morning he is, naturally, fuming. He's just come from Programme Review, where his film about police violence, *May the Force Be With You*, was discussed. I saw it on Royal Wedding Day evening and thought it was a model of its kind: acknowledging in its form its partisan position, that of the victims of law-and-order machinery as it's now applied – blacks, anti-racists and strikers. By using archive footage of police brutality with a heavily ironic soundtrack (Barbra Streisand singing *The Way We Were*) and by signalling clearly its use of dramatic reconstruction, it made no bones about its allegiances. This morning's discussion apparently failed to register any of that. 'Trouble is,' says Alan, 'that the Channel's dominated by journalists. They couldn't see a formal innovation if it came up and bit them. So we never have that discussion. Everyone around that table accepts the norms of television journalism.'

As we settle into lunch, and I find out he hasn't heard anything about the renewal of his contract and is saying that he can't make up his mind whether or not he wants to stay, a whole style of living and arguing comes across, clear and heartfelt and pugnacious on behalf of those who are less privileged than him or me. 'Accountability,' he says, 'real accountability with teeth, the kind the IBA never exerts when the ITV companies infringe the terms of their franchises – that's what every institution needs, whether it's a television channel, a political party or the country. When I go to programme review discussions, I feel I'm speaking for all the unrepresented people outside the room.'

Jeremy met Alan when they were both sitting on the BFI Production Board, and he recognised – and argued with – a coherent and consequent grass-roots democrat. Hiring him for Channel Four was another example of Jeremy picking specific individuals for their track record and fitness for a labelled job. But he and Jeremy have continued their arguments. 'I told Jeremy that I wanted the Channel to create and pay for a committee to whom I would be accountable. He said he wasn't going to have that as long as he was here. And of course he can always fall back on reminding me that without him I wouldn't be here in the first place.'

But Alan clings to his committee idea, even if he concedes that in the area of culture and artistic innovation Zhdanov's shadow lies across such thinking. 'Five years ago I would have tied someone like you down to such a committee. Now I can see it wouldn't work. People like you need manoeuvrability. But you should still need to justify your policy every two years.' Which is, I think, what I'm obliged to do by our short-term contract system, only my work isn't assessed by a representative committee, whatever that would be for the arts . . .

While I find Alan a magnetic person, with an attractive aura of worry and concern and an inspiring political ethic that goes back to the Levellers, I'm troubled by his prescriptions for political behaviour, especially about securing the future of Channel Four. He reproaches Jeremy for failing to provide a written policy and firm administrative structures that would tie the hands of his successor. All that we have instead, says Alan, is the Broadcasting Act and its generalities – 'distinctive service', 'innovation', 'minority interests and groups'. Alan thinks that's too loose; Jeremy's successor could subvert the purposes of the Channel, change its character.

'But Alan, Jeremy doesn't think that way for two reasons. Don't forget he did Greek and Latin at Oxford; democracy for him is rooted in ancient Greece. And then he's a Jew, suspicious of charters and structures.'

'I think he keeps it vague for a much less noble reason. He likes running things himself.'

'Maybe. But isn't there a danger of building in too many safeguards against takeover and subversion? That's a bunker mentality. So what happens if someone takes over Channel Four and runs it in a way you or I would disagree with? How long does a disaster last? And what is a historical success? When they asked Mao Tse-Tung whether the French Revolution had been a success, he said it was too soon to say.'

Glimpses of the rushes of the rest of the week. Lunch with Iris Murdoch, her respect for the pessimism of the Frankfurt school against the authoritarian optimism of Sartre; she's been writing a new introduction to her *Sartre: Romantic Rationalist*, and is more than ever suspicious of his attempts to 'totalise' explanations of history and individuals within a scientistic Marxism with a vanguard leadership. 'It leaves out morality.'

Morality, shaping a high crafted piece of theatrical carpentry, is what makes Brian Clark's *The Petition*, opening at the Lyttelton, so stirring. John Mills and Rosemary Harris, as a retired general and his anti-nuclear petition-signing wife, plunge through one hundred hyper-naturalistic minutes, stage time and real time coinciding, and put a burning glass on their marriage and her imminent death by cancer as well as on the conflagration that may swallow us all. Brian's bold directness is allied to traditional theatrical skills. After the warmth of the first-night reception he stands in the NT foyer, happily bemused. 'It was only Peter Hall's direction that made me realise how much of my father I'd put into the character of the general. Nothing in common superficially between a nonconformist Christian socialist blacksmith and career army officer, except that they both had an idea of duty and service.'

I sit in Michael Nyman's sunny attic, as he and Chris Rawlence take me through the words and music of their opera of Oliver Sacks's *The Man Who Mistook His Wife for a Hat*, about a music professor who can only recognise faces and objects when a thread of humming or singing – a melodic narrative – sustains his outline of reality. A psychological parable against reductionism, which should become even more resonant in its musical and dramatic realisation, first at the ICA, then on screen.

Walking back through Grosvenor Square, there's Melvyn Bragg under a tree, having his picture taken for the jacket of his next novel. He looks rested after his recent illness and holiday in Cumbria. But when I tell him I'll be in Channel Four until December 1989, his instant reaction is to plug his celebration of the French Revolution in July 1989. Maybe he didn't realise that I might have left next year. Or maybe it's just good old metropolitan automatism. I might have done the same to someone else, equally unthinkingly.

Fiona Maddocks, on her last day as my music assistant editor before she leaves to work on the arts page of the *Independent*, talks about what it was like running *Comment*, our daily opinion slot right after the news, which she did before she came to me. 'I got tired of having old men at my feet, wanting my body or three minutes on television.' I'll miss Fiona's commitment to musical standards, her boundless charm with programme-makers, her scurrying off at the end of the day with her fiddle case to play trios, her ability to send me up rotten.

WEEK 32 *August 3–8*

It pours down all Sunday, fierce heavy sheets of hot summer rain. I put on the first cassette of *Shoah*, Claude Lanzmann's nine-hour documentary about the Holocaust. I've had it on my shelf for over a month, scared to sit down and watch, even though I've already seen the first two hours in a Paris cinema which led me to chase up Lanzmann and make sure we got it for the Channel. Now I watch it again from the start. Lanzmann has the same Dostoevskian fervour on screen, interrogating leathery Polish peasants, as he had when I met him. He needed that megalomaniac determination to push him through the ten years of its making.

Telling documentary details: the luxuriance of the Polish forests in the spring sunshine now, voices recalling the ovens and mass graves then, behind those trees, beneath this grass. The slit-throat gesture Poles mimed at the railway stations to Jews inside the cattle trucks, warning them they were travelling to their deaths. Six people demonstrate it: some make it look desperate and tragic, others, a cruel mockery.

Next morning in a cutting room I look at a rough assembly of John McGrath's shoot of the concert of Gaelic songs and stories. It starts out a bit antiquarian, but steadily gains power. We talk about the film's structure and the next phase of shooting – landscapes, artefacts, faces of today's Highlands. The music is lyrical, humorous, defiant.

At the end of the day, farewell drinks for Fiona Maddocks. As well as colleagues, lots of musicians who have worked with Fiona turn up: Harry Birtwistle, Paul Crossley, Michael Vyner. In reply to tributes, Fiona makes a good speech, revealing that she's given Jeremy a pitch-pipe and encouraged him to sing, but with little effect. And she charts my musical rise and fall from the days when I used to jog with Monteverdi or Messiaen on the Walkman to my current reprehensible craze for 'New Age' Japanese yuppie music.

In the evening to the Bolshoi at Covent Garden. *The Golden Age* is magnificent kitsch, reminiscent of mass gymnastics and Red Square march-pasts in its heroic vein, gleefully aping American musicals in its depiction of Westernised decadence. There is a gangster's moll performance worthy of Cyd Charisse or Zizi Jeanmaire. The score is by Shostakovich, and Orna and I have an interval drink with Tony Palmer, who hopes to shoot his Shostakovich film next year. I talk about the nightmare fortissimos of mass exuberance in Shostakovich's music: like sweat on the inside of the skull. 'His music is always on the edge of hysteria,' says Tony.

Next day I look at the finished print of the second film of *State of the Art*, about value and how it's constructed in the art world. Now that the film has its aura of intersecting quotations and commentary, its ironic account of the tensions and complicities between museums, collectors, self-promoting artists and critics is sharper than ever. This film is the most accessible and journalistic of the series. Will viewers accept its oblique references and absence of a reassuring narrator signposting what they should think and see? It's not just a stylistic eccentricity, I think, but a genuine response to a fragmented and contradictory world, seized before it's been labelled for the textbooks. .

Next day I have lunch with Renee Goddard. She asks for a rapid survey of who's doing well and who not so well with the Channel. Renee, who has the tough wit of her Berlin childhood, calls one of my colleagues 'an organisational rabbit'.

Alan Fountain and I see Jeremy to discuss our proposal for a cluster of programmes to mark the twentieth anniversary of May 1968. Jeremy is sceptical about the value or relevance of commemorating something that effectively passed Britain by. By strict current affairs and political criteria, he's right. But without getting sentimental about it, 1968 in its broadest meanings was more than politics in the traditional sense. By the end of our discussion, Alan and I have breached his resistance somewhat. Jeremy still maintains that the British working class was unaffected by the events in Paris and Prague, and he's still against what he calls 'wallowing', but he acknowledges that its effect on what Alan calls 'a fracture of the middle class' is worth examining, along with its reassessment of Freud and its risky identification of politics with theatre.

In 1968 Jeremy would have been in his late thirties, and Alan and I in our late twenties. A decade at that stage of life makes a big difference. Afterwards Alan catches me and murmurs, 'That must be the first time that relevance to the working class was a criterion in deciding whether we do a Channel Four programme.'

At Thursday's Programme Review meeting John Ranelagh hammers away at Liz Forgan and what he sees as the Channel's tendency to a leftish consensus. John's way of arguing is to disrupt his opponent's flow of thought. I call it terroristic; he retorts that its abruptness is televisual. I persevere, and say that he's in danger of settling into a mathematical reckoning, counting screen time for political positions rather than looking at the tenor and form of each programme. We're required to provide a distinctive service. When most television and newspapers succeed in disguising their prejudices as the status quo, what's wrong with a counter-pamphlet that signals in its form that it is a partisan corrective? Isn't he underestimating viewers' ability to distinguish a polemic from a supposedly neutral description? This debate will run and run. It's important we discuss it properly inside the Channel, otherwise we'll be the victims of nervous nannies within the IBA or fundamentalist backbenchers.

In the afternoon to Tony Palmer's house, to deliver what he calls my 'seminar' on his Shostakovich film, which means trying to get to the bottom of how he intends to cast, design and shoot it. He's still reeling from having had dinner the night before with Mrs Shostakovich, in London with the Bolshoi. She asked through the interpreter whether he was planning to make a 'truthful' film about her husband. When Tony said he was, she looked sad. It became clear why when he delivered her back to her hotel and she asked him up to her room. 'There were two KGB heavies,' says Tony, 'and they made it clear that there was no question of her cooperating with an anti-Soviet film. She rushed into the bathroom crying. She hardly stopped crying till I left.' I tell Tony that we don't need her cooperation, since he's making drama not documentary, and that the fact that the BBC is making a Shostakovich documentary with the cooperation of Soviet television means that it won't be able to say things he and Rudkin will say. But he's worried about the competition.

From him to the Queen Elizabeth Hall for the premiere of Harrison Birtwistle's *Yan Tan Tethera*, which Channel Four is co-producing with Opera Factory and the London Sinfonietta, and which will be videotaped next month. From the barest material – a folk-tale contest between a northern and a southern shepherd involving a magic hill, a devilish piper and the incantatory counting of flocks of sheep – Harry and his librettist Tony Harrison have made a hundred-minute work. Their 'mechanical pastoral' has the power of a ballad and the sophistication of a Swiss timepiece. Its symmetries and subtly altered repetitions show Harry's fascination with circular and linear time. Sometimes time appears to

stand still, immobilised by a slowing musical pulse, soaring vocal and
woodwind lines, a wash of dark bass sounds; sometimes it accelerates,
splintered short phrases and jagged musical exclamations whipped along
in an overwhelming frenzy. It has a sly humour, not just because it is the
only opera in which a female chorus, masked and crawling on all fours,
plays two flocks of sheep. It has glints of inexplicable, ancient mystery –
buried treasure, a magic cave, charmed sarsen stones. Omar Ibrahim
sings the role of the northern shepherd with valley-spanning power and
a Yorkshire accent. And there's once again a perfect fit between the
chosen story and the compositional process, so that events and characters
are held fast in a structure that is both musical and narrative. It is,
literally, spellbinding.

Farewell lunch next day for Ann Harris, our chief co-production
executive. Another bright woman leaving the Channel, in the wake of
Carol Haslam, who's gone to the satellite service Superchannel, and
Carole Myer, who's now distributing cinema films for a clutch of prestigious British producers. Liz Forgan tells me at Ann's lunch that it's
sexist to talk about the number of bright attractive women in Channel
Four; it means that other women I worked with previously were neither
bright nor attractive. I tell her I don't mean that; what I mean is that so
few women were allowed any scope or authority at all when I was at the
National Theatre, apart from the casting director and leading actresses.

Ann has evolved from a BBC-trained salesperson, and a mum who
joined Channel Four wanting a three-day-a-week job, to a capable and,
yes, attractive executive. 'A talented deal-maker,' mutters her erstwhile
boss, Colin Leventhal.

WEEKS 33–34 *August 11–20*

Cosi Fan Tutte by David Freeman's Opera Factory, to a packed Queen
Elizabeth Hall. He's set it on a beach, with Fiordiligi, Dorabella and
Despina in swimwear so you can't tell to begin with who's mistress, who
servant. Everyone is constantly changing clothes, which is realistic for a
beach and metaphorical for Mozart's comedy of love disguises. There is
laughter worthy of Ayckbourn, and the tears and quickened heartbeat of
real feeling. Most of the audience look as if they've never seen an
opera before; the rest are opera buffs (including the administrators of
Glyndebourne and the Royal Opera House) come along to see what this
young upstart approach, with its bikinis and punk wigs and modern body
language and cheap ticket prices, is all about.

Next night, back again for a second look at *Yan Tan Tethera* with

Ebbehard Scheele, the German producer who has said he will buy
into the production. At second hearing, there are even more subtleties
in the instrumental music that swells into the action, becomes the
action.

Scheele's contribution to this, and to other Channel Four programmes
including Andrew Snell's portrait of Harry Birtwistle and Norman
Swallow's biography of Prokofiev, is a quid pro quo for our own investment in three of his 35mm opera films – Debussy's *Pelléas et Mélisande*,
Britten's *Billy Budd* and Tippett's *Midsummer Marriage*. We meet to
negotiate the deal, which Colin Leventhal conducts with gravity and
stately pace. Global figures are quoted, extra projects mentioned.
Ebbehard will report back to his boss, Leo Kirch, one of Europe's media
magnates. We appear to have embarked upon a co-production.

Next day I get a call from LA SEPT in Paris, inviting me to join a
working group for the French television cultural service along with Pierre
Boulez, the theatre director Roger Planchon, various members of the
Collège de France and the editor of *Libération*. I'm pleased, both on my
own account and for Channel Four, whose example will influence the
way the French decide how to run cultural television. When I tell Jeremy
about these developments he's pleased, but sceptical: 'Will it produce
new kinds of television programmes, Michael?'

I'm persuaded to appear on *Right to Reply*, our weekly programme in
which viewers can tax programme-makers or television executives for
putting on programmes they find offensive. My task is to defend *Sym-
phonie Fantastique: Anima*, an Austrian film based on Berlioz's music,
against viewers who complained it degraded women. I find myself in the
studio opposite a young woman who tells me that she is a performance
artist, recently graduated from Leeds Polytechnic, currently engaged in
'sound-work'. She makes the feminist case against the film, reducing it
to its literal elements and ignoring its style and its message.

'There are no real women in the film,' says the young woman. 'No,' I
reply, 'it's about images and fantasies that divide the sexes; its final
sentence says that it's all been about a male image of women, not about
reality.' 'It stereotypes women,' she says. 'Stereotypes are in the mind of
the beholder,' I reply, a touch glibly. 'If only it showed some of the
sensitivity about women and their representation displayed by Channel
Four's recent series *Picturing Women*,' she says; and I forget to tell her
that the male chauvinist monster across the table was also responsible
for commissioning the ideologically correct *Picturing Women*.

I'm genuinely bewildered by her vehemence and the outrage of other viewers. Does dogma blind the senses? Is anything unfamiliar in form always initially rejected as offensive?

What bewilders me even more after the weekend is the logbook of viewers' calls after my appearance. Was I really 'arrogant and opinionated'? I thought I was polite and firm. Is any TV person who appears on television automatically invested with the trappings of irresponsible power? Well, you can't hold a position in this business – even the artsy end of it – and expect sympathy.

Would a warning in the *TV Times* and at the start of the film, as my interlocutor wanted, have helped, or would it have been a perverse come-on? We are now about to insert a graphic warning device on films which might offend: an eye in a traffic-warning triangle with the legend 'Special Discretion Required'. I'm torn about the whole thing. TV does walk into your privacy, it's true, and things can be sprung on you without your choice or preparation. But censorship is a contagious virus.

This partly conditioned indignation shrinks into perspective over the weekend when I watch 'Prisoner of Consciousness', a documentary in the new science series *Equinox*, which John Ranelagh commissioned. It's about Clive Wearing, a musician and conductor specialising in seventeenth-century music. Eighteen months ago a virus that attacks one in a million people destroyed parts of his brain and all of his memory. Only when he's playing or conducting music does this man who feels like a living dead person see, hear, taste, touch, recognise. If his wife has been absent for more than ten minutes, he greets her with the grateful sobs of a man reunited with his beloved after a lifetime's separation. His wife explains to Jonathan Miller that when Clive was really ill, he would play a piece of music, come to the repeat marks, forget he'd played it once, go back to the beginning, and could theoretically have gone on playing it for ever.

Jonathan is self-effacingly attentive to both Clive and his wife, makes some helpful analogies between computer retrieval and memory, and reminds her that Clive's comparatively undamaged right half of the brain is the bit that is musical. But that's only the beginning of an explanation of why the abstract continuities of music should soothe away his distress, momentarily.

A working Sunday in the Channel Four studio, where Andrew Snell is taping an interview with Harrison Birtwistle for his film profile. The morning is a conversation with fellow composer Nigel Osborne. Nigel's sensitive intelligence and knowledge puts Harry at his ease, and he opens up in a way I've rarely seen. His feeling for music and theatre was nourished, he says, by playing clarinet for *Mother Goose* and *Jack and the Beanstalk* at the Leeds Empire: 'I know all about vamp till ready and playing for the tabs.' Perhaps this early panto knowhow explains his wish to rescue fairy tales and folk stories from childishness in *Down by the Greenwood Side, Yan Tan Tethera*, and his forthcoming Royal Opera House commission about Jack and the beanstalk.

Harry's ideas go working away in my head all night, and wake me at 6.30 am on Monday. I get up in a kind of alert daze, and put on a tape of one of the forthcoming series of *Voices*. It's about whether psychoanalysis is a science or deals with some other kind of truth. An American antagonist attacks the untestability of psychoanalysis; a French analyst, severely clamping a pipe and refusing eye contact with his interlocutor, rises to a convincing defence; a cuddly historian of science rebuts the attack by saying that it's based on an outdated idea of what is scientific. Lying there with sunshine and birdsong streaming through the garden window, and a dramatic exchange of ideas and expressive body language on the screen, I hope it will feel as good to viewers when it goes out late at night.

Three aspects of the interconnections between money, art, film and television over the next two days. Colin Tweedie, the voluble head of the Association of Business Sponsorship for the Arts, talks about the gentleman-amateur types who dole out sponsorship for the arts for many British businesses. Most British sponsorship of the arts still works on the basis of philanthropy and a chance to mingle with the stars, instead of being part of a marketing and promotional plan, as American corporations see it. There are obvious dangers in that policy, of course; but if this government really believes the private sector should play an increasing part, says Colin Tweedie, it needs educating to do it better than this. He also gossips gleefully about how Margaret Thatcher keeps putting down Richard Luce, her current arts minister, saying how inferior he is to his predecessor, Lord Gowrie.

'The reason why the City is so reluctant to invest in intellectual property rather than goods and services is that so much subjective judgement is required,' says a merchant banker next day to me and Colin Leventhal. We've been invited to meet one of their American clients, who has made millions in the rag trade, manufactures in Hong Kong, has a Chinese-American wife, and wants to produce documentaries about Chinese culture. Another kind of amateur. Soon the talk moves on to the City's fears about investment in films. It's the size of investment –

£10 million and up – and the sheer unpredictability of cinema that alarms them. We talk about low-budget Channel Four films which cost less than £2 million. Surely that kind of modest venture would be a reasonable risk, asks Colin. Our hosts are noncommittal. On the walls of the dining room are twenty exquisite Moghul Indian miniatures. 'We got them when we bought up a bank in Hong Kong.'

The third example of the transactions of money and television is the continuing debate this week about whether Channel Four should sell its own advertising, an option canvassed in the Peacock Report. Justin Dukes, our managing director, tells me he has commissioned research so that our board can take a view on the matter. Already muscles are being flexed in the *Guardian* this week, with huffing-and-puffing threats from David Elstein, formerly an independent and now programme controller of Thames, 'to blow Channel Four out of the water' if we were to compete with ITV for advertising, and spirited replies from key independents like Michael Darlow and Phil Redmond, who makes *Brookside*, saying the independents could make most programmes better and cheaper than the ITV 'factories'.

To the Tricycle Theatre in Kilburn to see *Born in the RSA*, the play from the Market Theatre Johannesburg which Barney Simon and his multi-racial cast researched and wrote together in a month last year. Dealing with the traumas of the first South African state of emergency – the radicalisation of young blacks, a white police informer shopping his girlfriend, solitary confinement, interrogations – it has the immediacy of a living newspaper, and the conviction of being made and performed by people who are up to their necks in the reality they are putting on stage. Mary McMurray will tape *Born in the RSA* for me next month. It must retain some stylisation if it is to reach people as the timelessness of a current situation.

Its mirror image would be Aeschylus' *Oresteia*, which we are repeating over three successive Sundays. When we first put out Aeschylus' trilogy, in the early months of the Channel, many people found it unsuitable for television. Too unnaturalistic, they said. Now I'm pleased to hear from Adrian Metcalfe, commissioning editor for sport, and even from Orna, who originally thought it was just my obsession with theatre, how powerfully the story and rhythms and language and, above all, the masked choruses work. Orna is a great circumscriber and editor of my tendencies to artistic obfuscation and plain bullshit. She's clever as a pin, quick on the draw and more direct than I am; without her I would be in danger of becoming an untethered balloon. If she comes round to liking something I'm responsible for, it means a lot to me.

WEEKS 34–35 *August 21–25*

The Edinburgh International (though it's pretty parochial or Anglo-American most years) Television Festival is an annual family huddle; a bear-pit for groundlings to attack principal players; a platform for unions, independents, academics, politicos; a hothouse of ideas, some (as they say) seminal, others hot air. I can't imagine anything like it taking place in America, or in any European country. It's an expression of the spirit that produced the British tradition of broadcasting inquiries – Beveridge, Pilkington, Annan and now Peacock – and the cultural gravity of Richard Hoggart, Raymond Williams, the Arts Council when Roy Shaw was Secretary-General, and all their predecessors in thinking about class, industry, culture and democracy. It's also Dionysiac and showbiz in a way Lord Reith, the original Scottish patriarch of the BBC, would scarcely have approved. But this suits its location in the thick of Edinburgh's Festival of the Arts and its proliferating fringe, neatly encapsulated this year by a local journalist who said he was getting tired of smiling wanly at young men in bowler hats with painted faces.

I'm met at Edinburgh airport by Barbara Grigor. She and her husband Murray, two of the pioneering Scottish independents, are making a film for me about the sculptor Eduardo Paolozzi, and I've come up before the TV festival to view an assemblage and to look at rushes of another film which they're producing, about Robert Burns's songs. We drive to Inverkeithing, the little Fifeshire town outside Edinburgh where they live and have their cutting room. 'James Lee, who used to run Goldcrest, called us a husband-and-wife team who live above the shop,' says Barbara. 'Well, we at least are still in business.' Murray tells me about the fringe show that has delivered the Festival's obligatory scandal, a Slovenian version of Brecht's *Baal* in which the spectators, limited to twenty-six per performance, sit with their heads thrust through holes in the stage. The action – including setting transistor radios on fire – swirls round and dangerously close to their faces. 'It tells you what totalitarianism must be like, and makes you glad you missed it,' says Murray. Edinburgh's fire brigade is inspecting the show, so I may have missed its last performance.

A six-plate Steenbeck editing table is waiting in the stables of the Grigors' sixteenth-century stone house. Out of the attic window I see shipyards and sea. On the screen Paolozzi's hands are tearing illustrations out of books, cutting round outlines, slicing, sawing, sticking. Here he is in the Munich Glyptotek, drawing Greek statue heads and torsos, a bunched stubby body among the antique heroes with their chipped marble faces as battered as his own. Here he is interrogating art critics and curators among a display of early aeroplanes, seen through a case containing a Mexican Day of the Dead skeleton in evening dress, an African fetish sculpture of an aeroplane, and one of his own stratified cut-up bronze heads; a Surrealist *bricoleur* in the age of information technology. The film, already full of good things, will need to find a rigorous yet freely associative form, like Paolozzi's art itself.

Tim Neat, director of the Robert Burns film, joins us and we look at rushes of Serge Hovey, the American whose research and arrangements launched a new edition of Burns's songs and triggered the film. He is gradually dying of multiple sclerosis. He can no longer speak. His wife points to letters on a board, and he clamps his teeth for yes. He runs a computer by nudging it with his elbow. Jean Redpath, Scottish folksinger, sits on his bed in California and sings to him. Through the letter-board, he corrects her.

Tim's film will have to use tact and skill to handle such devastating material without voyeurism. But there's a story to tell of the determination of mind over matter, as well as the retrieval of classic words and music buried under sentimental and chauvinistic accretions. Tim puts on specimens of his other shooting, including the Burri Man, the Scottish version of the fertility god, the Green Man: a splay-legged arms-spread figure entirely covered with sticky burrs, and crowned with a hat made of flowers. He is being helped down a village street, a folk hero and a sci-fi apparition. Behind him is the nineteenth-century iron tracery of the Forth Bridge.

Next morning, a screening of John McGrath's three-part drama series for us, *Blood Red Roses*, condensed into a two and a half hour single film. John calls it 'a domestic epic'; it follows the life of a woman from rebellious childhood in the 1950s through trades-union militancy to a resistance both personal and political in 1980s' Glasgow. It began as a play for John's 7:84 theatre company, performed to working-class audiences across Scotland. The first third is irresistible, the forging of an indomitable nature; I find the middle part, charting the heroine's leadership of a strike and its effects on her marriage, more stagey; but the third part, when she's blacklisted, unemployed, husbandless and still fighting, puts a believable defiant heroine on the screen, resisting Thatcherite fragmentation with a muted strength that has roots in her whole life. Nobody before this has made a TV miniseries about a militant woman.

Television drama is the subject of the MacTaggart Lecture, which opens the Television Festival. It's given by Troy Kennedy-Martin, who co-wrote the pioneering police series *Z Cars* with John McGrath twenty years ago, and has written this year's BBC series *Edge of Darkness*, using the elliptical conventions of the film noir to deal with the labyrinth of secrecy surrounding nuclear energy. Troy was the first to articulate the case against television naturalism, in an article which appeared in the theatre magazine *Encore* in the early sixties, when I was one of its editors. Now, in the age of video-clips and commercials, he returns to the attack, calling for 'micro-dramas', condensed 'shards' of story and image, made in clusters, scheduled rapidly so that they have the urgency of their subject matter, and repeated immediately, because they have the kind of density that bears more than one viewing.

Troy wants an oppositional drama that will respond to the realities of unemployment, for example, by 'deconstructing' the reality imposed by news and current affairs. 'We need quicker feedback,' he says, quoting the eighteen-month production time needed for most drama series. I find this argument the most telling in his lecture. If television can fuse its 'natural' journalistic tempo with the heightened use of visual imagery, text and music, and get the results scheduled with sufficient concentration and continuity, it might come up with a form that would have the immediacy of news with the texture and gravity of a dramatic poem. The prospect makes me think more acutely about two of my own projects – Greenaway and Phillips's *A TV Dante* and Richard Eyre's version of Tony Harrison's poem 'V' – although neither has the immediate actuality which Troy is seeking.

Next morning, in the chapel-like atmosphere of the Queen's Hall, I listen to a brilliant Hungarian soprano, Adrienne Csengery, performing a song cycle about solitude, love and its bittersweet aftermath by her countryman György Kurtág. The compression of the music, the sharp sound-clusters between voice and instruments; the virtuosity of the solo voice, drawing out bright wires of sound; the fifteen musical haikus with which the work ends, becoming steadily sparser and weightier – if television could find a form that had this concentration and continual metamorphosis . . . But music is ultimately unparaphrasable. And that is why all other art aspires to its condition.

That afternoon a Television Festival debate, 'Are the Independents Working?', brings together two figureheads of the television duopoly –

Bill Cotton, managing director of BBC Television, and Paul Fox, chief executive of Yorkshire Television – two trades-union officials, and a chairman who is involved with the campaign to get 25 per cent of BBC and ITV output made by independent programme-makers. It's a slagging match. Bill Cotton uses the condescending metaphor of a prefabricated bungalow – the independents – contrasted with the solid-built mansion of the BBC. Paul Fox reminds the audience in Big Daddy style that 'we're not prepared to be jostled out of the way unless there's some advantage for us.' And Tony Hearn, general secretary of the British Entertainments Trade Association, comes on in fine worker-hero style, attacking the producers and directors in the audience as a pampered elite compared with the commissionaires, cloakroom attendants and tea-ladies among his membership who would face redundancy if the independents 'dismantled' (a word which Bill Cotton uses too) the BBC. He is promptly reminded that trades-union general secretaries are also members of a privileged elite.

It's an uneasy occasion, full of hands unwilling to grasp nettles, shadowed by the spectre of free-market competition via direct-broadcast satellite intrusion, multi-national media moguls and deregulation. The best of the independents perform well, though. Nicholas Fraser attacks the 'aggressive negativism' of Fox and Cotton. Philip Whitehead sharpens the distinction between freelance employment by the duopoly – 'short-term seasonal labour' and a sustained independent foothold in British broadcasting – 'having a small freeholding on the slopes of the system'. David Graham reminds the BBC of its vulnerability as 'a low-wage, low-tech institution' in a time of unprecedented competition for British television. But I come away thinking that British institutional inertia, the conservatism that has in many ways preserved some of the best qualities and continuities of our culture, may be too trapped in the coils of its own traditions to confront the Murdochs, Maxwells, Berlusconis, Ted Turners and other buccaneers of a global, homogenised, profit-seeking media industry.

Sunday afternoon's session is about the Peacock Report, and will give the BBC, ITV and the independents a chance to argue their fierce disagreements. Before the debate I walk down Cowgate, turning into the alleys and closes whose gaunt walls instantly conjure up the eighteenth-century Edinburgh of David Hume and Adam Smith, who has become the patron saint of today's orthodoxies of free market and consumer power.

Against a backdrop of lichened tombs below Calton Hill old men are playing bowls on an Astroturf green. With time in hand I cross over to the New Town. I go into the Scottish Portrait Gallery's exhibition about Fox Talbot, David Octavius Hill and the Adamson brothers, pioneers of photography. 'Photography has already enabled us to hand down to future ages a picture of the sunshine of yesterday, or a memorial of the haze of today,' wrote the *Athenaeum* in February 1845, drawing on the accents of Sir Thomas Browne's elegy 'Urne Buriall' to express a new sense of the poignancy of the passing moment and the miracle of its capture. John Logie Baird – another Scottish image pioneer – must have felt the same. I walk round the quiet Sunday lunchtime gallery, scrutinising these sepia traces, this preserved time. A Reverend Candish posing stiffly for the exposure, his arm supported, a strut firming up his back. An unknown woman, hands folded, long frowning eyebrows. Young Scots blades with names like Nevil Story-Maskelyne dressing up as Ossian, as Delacroix Arabs or as monks out of Victorian narrative painting. Other arts give any new medium its models to begin with. Fox Talbot, who thought photography 'the pencil of nature', had two favourite still-life subjects: a marble bust of Patroclus and a child's rocking horse. Photography starts to come into its own when the documentary impulse begins: snatched, blurred figures of Highland fusiliers, a surreal image of Nelson's column under construction.

The hall is packed for the post-Peacock debate. Peacock makes a long and pugnacious speech, delivered with brisk, at times almost testy, conviction. Behind his orotund periods, you sense the contentment of a true believer who has accumulated evidence for his faith. He shakes his head a lot when criticisms are made from the audience, while they are being made, as if to say, 'But can't you see, it's so simple, it's staring you in the face.' But as the debate proceeds, nursed along by Brenda Maddox in a slightly 'we-experts-know-best' way, as important ideas are compressed into rubbed-smooth tokens of argument, it's hard to avoid the feeling that it's becoming a professional ritual. At one point Professor Peacock labels all the television professionals present as 'vested interests'.

It's left to Philip Whitehead, speaking with the experience of having been a member of the Annan Committee, a Labour MP and now an independent programme-maker, to bring the discussion down from diagrams to likelihoods. 'There's a lack of workable hinge between the Peacock Report's analyses and its proposals. But it ignores what the free market has already done. Look at Rupert Murdoch's Sky Channel, pumping out multi-national schlock across Europe, think about the press

baron Hersant in France, likely to get a French privatised channel and
a share of the satellite. These men are already planning the internationalis-
ation of television, based on lowest-common-denominator programmes.
And they have privileged relationships with national governments –
Berlusconi with Craxi, Murdoch with Hawke. And I've specifically mentioned only socialist governments.'

His alternative to Peacock is 'a regulatory body which would lease
space on a common grid, paid for out of public resource'. Regulation –
a dirty word among today's libertarians – would preserve the 'universality
of provision' that Whitehead sees as the bedrock of public service. But
he doesn't have a convincing solution for the satellite dish at the bottom
of the garden competing with his common grid and its services, other than
a wishful reference to a forthcoming meeting of European broadcasting
ministers to discuss encrypting satellite signals. 'Encrypting': another
code word for the new fraternity of experts. Soon we'll need a linguistic
surgeon to take a scalpel to the new media language, the way Molière
operated on the mystifying jargon of seventeenth-century doctors.

We already need another kind of language expert, someone who will
revitalise the discourse of public service in terms that cannot be dismantled by free-market ironheads.

'Consumer preference is all very well,' I say from the floor, 'but what
about needs that people didn't know they had until something is put in
their path that makes them aware? "Cultural heritage", which Professor
Peacock says should be sustained by a small element of public funding
in his ideal consumer market, is an embattled definition, separating the
arts from the world now; preserving such a heritage would be a defensive
posture.' The Professor retorts that consumers don't have to be automata.
But if the education system doesn't equip them and advertising fools
them, where is the counter-force? I take the day's last shuttle out of
Edinburgh and get home, realising that I've not been to either of the
Festival's key theatre performances, Lorca by a Spanish company, Euri-
pides by the Japanese, both reputedly marvellous. I am getting too
wrapped up in TV.

Next day I have a drink with the Russian poet Joseph Brodsky, who
has come over to London for a few weeks from New York, where he
lives. I have been rereading his poetry, in which the gravity and glitter of
Pushkin and Auden combine, and delighting in his newly published
collection of essays, *Less Than One*. In one essay he says that a choice of
metre can be a moral and not just a technical matter.

His worktable, in a room in a friend's house, looks out over damp luxuriant Hampstead gardens. A bottle of Bushmill's – 'the only whisky that doesn't hurt your throat' – stands next to the typewriter, in which there's a poem in Russian with erasures and additions. A couch, a couple of armchairs, lamps, bookshelves; otherwise the room has a provisional air, because the house around it is being renovated and there are bare boards beneath our feet. But it's appropriate for a displaced person. Sentenced as a 'social parasite' when he was in Russia, Brodsky has been an involuntary exile since 1972. He writes most movingly about places that resemble his native Leningrad: Venice, Istanbul, outposts of empire at the sea's edge. 'Space to me,' writes this nomad, 'is both lesser and less dear than time. Not because it is lesser but because it is a thing, while time is an idea about a thing.' I heard from Susan Sontag that he almost died this year, after a second heart attack. He's not supposed to smoke or drink.

He pours us whisky. He's ginger-haired, freckled, aquiline, Jewish, with a high, thin, fast voice, constantly making amendments and revisions to his sentences, as to his poems. You have the sense of simultaneous meanings coming into his head, like incoming flights on different runways at once. We talk about scraps and acquaintances to start with. The conversation takes off when we get to Dante; I've mentioned the video version of Canto Five of the *Inferno*. Brodsky gets very excited, as if I've hit a bull's-eye of poetry. Stands up. More whisky. 'There are maybe only five, six great poets. Homer, Virgil, Ovid, Dante, Shakespeare . . . all right, reluctantly, Baudelaire. Dante, especially in the *Paradiso*, is for me the greatest. I first read him when I was sixteen, in a translation by a man from Georgia who had passed the whole war translating the *Commedia*. I would like to do Dante for the screen, to bring this great poetry to many people. It would have to be done on a spiral, with actors speaking the text on a rising spiral. Because Dante is a mixture of Western space – the horizontal – and Christian time, moving up towards paradise – the vertical. Dante affects everyone in poetry. Auden's line "They died as men before their bodies died," you know . . .'

His voice puffs and speeds and hums and generates, his hands sketch, they reach after his thoughts, the room darkens. 'Poetry comes from a different order of things, it turns everything upside down.' 'So how do you live on the level of poetry, and in everyday life?' 'Life is schizophrenic.' 'Is that what the myth of Orpheus is about?' 'He knew about life's two sides. He looked back, he wanted to marry her. Poetry unfits you for other human beings. You should do a programme about the psyche of the artist.' He tries to bum a cigarette off me.

We leave the house together. He is having dinner with a Russian conductor – 'clandestinely, I'm not supposed to know him'. We make an agenda for our next meeting, before he goes back to New York. He scurries off, leaving a slipstream of urgency.

WEEK 35 *August 27–31*

Another aeroplane, with Strauss as muzak-soother; I'm on my way to Salzburg to meet music television colleagues at the International Musik Zentrum congress. The cavernous Kongressalle dwarfs the fifty participants, but all the key people are there from Germany, Austria, France, Italy, Scandinavia, America. The strong British representation features Sir Denis Forman, Granada's chairman; Brian Wenham, Managing Director of BBC Radio; and Jeremy Isaacs. Handshakes, bear-hugs, production plans exchanged, deals discussed over coffee.

In the evening I have a ticket for a new Penderecki opera, *The Black Mask*, at the Kleine Festspielhaus. New Penderecki operas aren't really what the Salzburg Festival is about.

The composer and his librettist/director Harry Kupfer have taken a Hauptmann play set in seventeenth-century Venice, and made it an allegory of a rich post-war society with guilty secrets and exploitations. The result is expressionist *Grand Guignol*, to music that makes remarkable sounds, but also descends to horror-film cliché. The Marxist message does not appear to scratch the impassive surface of *le tout Salzburg* in their black tie, hairdos and make-up, gowns and jewellery. Penderecki's opening percussion glissando is drowned by the fortissimo clatter of my neighbour's multiple bracelets as she settles her handbag.

I have supper with Jeremy and Gillian Widdicombe in a beer-house. He has been packing up his possessions before moving house. He talks about what to do with his paintings. He came across a copy of his letter of application to the Channel Four board. 'I said I would change the face of the British film industry, and that the arts would have a key place.' He also said he'd introduce new sports to British television. 'American football was the one we went for. The other week 80,000 people went to Wembley stadium to watch two British teams playing American football in a new league. And I thought, I got them there,' says Jeremy. 'And then someone in television came up and said, I hear you're going to do a season of gay programmes this autumn, please don't, don't make it impossible for me to watch Channel Four. And I thought, what prejudice. It made me want to do a gay season fifty-two weeks of the year.'

Next day at the IMZ congress there are speeches on the future of music television, the role of the producer and director. Reiner Moritz gives a crisp survey of the various genres of music on television. 'Why does the contemporary aesthetic work in mass design, but not in the mass media?' he asks, citing the lack of the music of today on television. Sir Denis Forman, claiming to be 'in the springtime of my senility', gives a witty introduction to *Man and Music*, the social history of music which Granada are making for us, full of drolleries about the drawbacks of filming players, dramatising the past, creating subjective images for music. The concert grand, he says, should be redesigned in clear plastic to suit the camera. He mentions Mozart's 'melancholy always bordering on panic'.

I take a taxi to the airport, and a plane to Paris to talk with Peter Brook about filming his theatre version of the *Mahabharata*, a work which has given me more challenges and revelations than anything else in the past decade. In the days after I first saw it in a quarry outside Avignon last summer I tried to capture its impact and meaning in words, clutching at an unseizable experience at the outer limits of theatre:

Peter Brook's *Mahabharata* is the reinsertion into the European mind of a saga like the *Iliad*, a compendium of the marvellous like *The Arabian Nights*, a collage of action and religion like the Bible. It also offers the excitement of a bumper storybook, or *Star Wars*, or the comic-strips, through which Arjuna and Krishna are purveyed to millions of Indian children today. And it is the culmination of Brook's fifteen-year-old International Centre of Theatre Creation, the anti-theatre or parallel theatre he has been running in Paris.

Fifteen times the size of the Bible, the *Mahabharata* was written in Sanskrit, but the words you hear in Avignon are French, spoken with a piquant diversity of accents matching each actor's distinctive shape, skin and race. A diminutive North African Jew as elephant-headed Ganesha, then as Krishna. Vyasa, the bard of the poem, a ginger-haired Gascon. Tiny Japanese, long-limbed loping Senegalese, pale-skinned Germans and Poles, a wide-lipped Lebanese. Over three nights a multi-cultural group of actors plays out an ancient accumulation of fantastic fables, wisdom parables and fierce physical confrontations in an arena of rock, sand, water and fire.

Brook and Jean-Claude Carrière have adapted the *Mahabharata* into three plays: *The Game of Dice, The Exile in the Forest* and *The War*. The titles describe the key scenes and actions in the combat

between two related clans which forms the heart of the *Mahabharata*:
the dice game in which Yudishthira gambles away his kingdom, his
family and himself; the wounding and healing exile in which he, his four
brothers and their shared wife learn from loss; and the culminating
battle in which multitudes die and yet the world and its inhabitants
are restored to a better order, a truer *dharma*. Brook and his company
continually come up with theatrical actions embodying the deepest vision
of the *Mahabharata*, and of Brook's idea of theatre: that reality is
deliquescent, so that there is no single way, political, psychological or
moral, to seize it; that we live in a superimposed plurality of worlds.

His staging conjures up emblems and images in the quarry which
give a flickering apprehension of reality. The stage lighting shrinks,
shifts and expands the space; the cracked rock face and standing
sheets of water are illuminated by clusters of candles and torches until
they tremble insubstantially. The costumes – vivid Kathakali colours
and dried-out sacking, cuirasses and boots suggesting feudal Tudors
and Japanese samurai, saffron and white robes against glittering sand
– open out the harmonics of the story and the national variety of the
actors.

Brook makes bamboo screens, bows and arrows and chariot-wheels
into both literal story elements and symbolic emblems of the mastery
of life or the imminence of death. This kind of theatre almost
transcends the stubborn materiality of bodies and things on a stage.

One thread guides you through the *Mahabharata*'s luxuriant forest:
the making of a good king. Like Shakespeare's history-play cycle,
this story centres on a man passing through trials and tribulations in
order to become a better monarch, of his kingdom and of himself.
This personal development, from weak goodness to a strength greater
for having been wrecked and remade, is like the journey of many
apprentice rulers in Shakespeare – Henry IV, Prince Hal becoming
Henry V, Richard II in his fruitful desolation. But here the personal is
inseparable from the public, and from the cosmic: the *Mahabharata*'s
Great Chain of Being has the limitless reverberations which Shakespeare
fully attained only in his later tragedies and romances.

'It's the age of Kali, fire swells, swept by the wind, fire pierces the
earth, destroys the underworld, wind and fire turn the world to a
crust, huge clouds appear, blue, yellow, red, water falls, water pours
down and drowns the earth, twelve years of storms, mountains tear
the water, I can't see the world any more, and then, when nothing is
left but a grey sea without man, beast, or tree, the creator drinks up the

terrible wind and falls asleep.' As Yudishthira speaks these words the silence is almost unbearable. A vision of destruction imagined two thousand years ago dredges up our worst nightmares now. Not that this *Mahabharata* tries opportunistically to plug into our fears of nuclear destruction, of man-made dismemberment of the universal fabric: it just extends its story of fratricidal war on to every possible plane.

When, on the third evening of the *Mahabharata*, the war between the Pandaras and the Kauravas breaks out and runs its bitter course, it does so on every level. The physical: tournament skills of swirling swords and clubs, straining bows and whizzing arrows, dervish warriors leaping, wheel formations slowly turning in a choreography of carnage, all the combat display we thrill to in tattoos. The magical-mystical: Krishna's devastating war-disc, and the unbeatable divine weapon Shiva bestows, whose secret mantra some strange hermit whispers in your ear. And the cosmic: war of the worlds, ultimate firestorm, everything consumed, as *dharma* pursues its path, as destiny demands.

On the eve of battle, ringed by a circle of hard-breathing soldiers weaponed to the hilt, the sky god Krishna deepens his lesson. The *Bhagavad-Gita*, separated from its story, has become the moral distillation of the *Mahabharata* for the West, its acceptable digest version. Reintegrated here into the plot of an immense saga, with dogs of war straining at the leash, Krishna's message to Arjuna, who is appalled at the massacre he will perpetrate, becomes an urgent parable, not a set of precepts.

KRISHNA: 'Matter is changeable, but I am all that you say, all that you think. Everything rests upon me, like pearls on a thread. I am the sweet smell of the earth and I am the heat of fire, I am appearance and disappearance, I am the trickery of tricksters, I am the gleam of whatever shines. All creatures fall into the night, and all are restored to the day. I have already defeated all these warriors; he who thinks he can kill, and he who thinks he can be killed are equally mistaken. Weapons cannot pierce this life that animates you, nor fire burn it, nor water dampen it, nor wind dry it out. Have no fear, and stand up, for I love you.'

Then the two armies tear each other limb from limb. War as metaphor, war as brutal reality.

Offstage, Death's voice asks: 'What is the greatest marvel?' Yudishthira replies: 'Each day death strikes around us and we live as if we were immortal beings.' A weightless black girl ecstatically

arches herself as a gazelle, like some figure from an erotic temple frieze.
A wheel whipped along by an actor to signify a chariot later becomes
the wheel of life on which its rider dies. Sounds echo around the natural
amphitheatre – blare of horn and trombone, wail of reeds,
reverberations of sitar – as transparent cloths are stretched up to
shield us from manifestations of divine glory. There are scenes of
Jacobean horror, Chekhovian tenderness; above all, reminders of those
Shakespeare parables in which cloud-capped towers dissolve and a
life becomes a scene in a play, to be replaced by another, but not lost.
Since he set up in Paris with his international theatre research group
and began to scour the world seeking clues and traces of the way
theatre can speak across cultural boundaries, Peter Brook has been a
paradoxical presence: an institution, yet constitutionally fluid; fixed and
nomadic; rooted and transitory. The *Mahabharata*, with its sprouting
perspectives and liquid structures, is a vessel which might have been
destined for his passionate detachment and for the theatre's intrinsic
'lies like truth'.

That was written in the literal and metaphysical heat of last summer.
Now, thirteen months later, I come to a Paris still largely closed and
shuttered ('our infidelity to our clients will end on September 2' says a
sign on a restaurant) to meet Peter Brook and Jean-Claude Carrière with
an American and a French producer, to decide a strategy for filming the
Mahabharata in India for cinema and television in 1988.

I wake up next morning still thinned out by fatigue, take an early walk
past the Vietnamese restaurants on the rue Dante and then the metro to
Pigalle with David Picker, the American producer, who already worked
with Peter on the film of *Marat/Sade*. Jean-Claude Carrière's house,
where we will meet Peter, is in a courtyard off the streets of sex
shows and erotic aids. It used to be a brothel and a gambling den;
Toulouse-Lautrec worked in the studio upstairs. Jean-Claude has a
wooden statue of Kama, the goddess of sexual desire, in his living room,
a human-headed horse with breasts and udders.

Peter arrives with his assistant Marie-Hélène. He sits waiting for our
meeting to start, feet crossed, hands loosely clasped, head held still, with
its blue eye-beacons lifted. A quietly alert Buddha in a state of readiness
for anything; something too of the composure of a soft-spoken Mafia
godfather.

David Picker leads our discussion, deftly laying out the key questions.
A former president of Paramount and head of production at United

Artists, David is now an independent producer. Lucien Duval, the French producer, arrives. Lucien, who made his money with the *Emmanuelle* films and was bowled over by an all-day marathon performance of the *Mahabharata*, is a chirpy operator who leans into you like a big blinking owl. I am entertained by the talk of these film people. I even believe some of it. I'm just not sure how what I saw at Avignon will be able to attract six million dollars, the budget they are discussing.

We are to meet again tonight for work and dinner at Jean-Claude's. I catch up on my sleep for an hour back at the hotel, and go for a walk towards sunset in the Jardin du Luxembourg. Sitting on a floral-pattern wrought-iron seat, watching a flaxen-haired kid beat hell out of his older brother on the tennis court, while couples stroll home down the gravel paths beneath beech trees, I pass a melancholic half hour, traveller's distress at dusk in an alien place.

Back in Pigalle, Jean-Claude opens a bottle of champagne. Peter's partner and producer of all his theatrical work, Micheline Rozan, joins us to put figures to our formula. Her caring, sharp-tongued authority and vibrant style have made both his company and their Bouffes du Nord theatre what they are: volatile, welcoming, a strong family. She plunges into our plans with characteristic vigour, testing and questioning in her resonant voice. She says I ought to see Jean-Claude's library, and he takes me upstairs for a tour. On each landing of his house is an angled mirror, as in a periscope. From the upper floors, Madame could have seen which of her esteemed clients was arriving, and alerted his favourite girl.

The walls of Jean-Claude's study are clustered with photographs of film directors with whom he's worked – Billy Wilder and above all Buñuel, for whom he wrote all the last-period screenplays, *Belle de Jour, The Discreet Charm of the Bourgeoisie, The Phantom of Liberty*. The library itself is an inner room lined with books, many leather-bound, from floor to ceiling. 'This section is for books about apocalypse and the end of the world, one of my favourite topics. Here is literature of the fantastic, a big collection. And here are my surrealist texts – manuscripts and first editions. Here's a manuscript of the only text André Breton wrote about the cinema. And here's Jarry's *Ubu Roi*, given to me by Buñuel. Over here is poetry. I'm very interested in French sixteenth- and seventeenth-century poetry. Do you realise there was virtually no French poetry worth talking about between Racine and the Romantics?'

Downstairs over dinner we talk about how Jean-Claude will shape nine hours of stage play into a film of less than three hours. The transvestites are out on the Place Pigalle as we try to find a taxi afterwards. The talk, the wine, the week spent in four countries keep me whirling inside and I don't get to sleep until 3 am.

WEEKS 36–37 *September 1–11*

I wake up back home on Monday morning deaf in my left ear from too much airline cabin compression. My hands shake when I try to write the week's entry. 'No, I'm not going to write my memoirs,' Jeremy said the other night. 'Michael's doing the honest thing, catching it as it happens.' But at times like this, I feel less like a camera, more like a breathless sprinter. Or if a camera, then one with a motorised shutter, buzzing and spitting as it snaps. The French for a snap is *instantané*. And for a photographic print, *cliché*. Writing should get beyond either, achieve a mental depth of focus. But so many fragments keep spinning into the mind's viewfinder. Adrian Mitchell ringing up last night: 'I've just thought of a cheeky election slogan for Labour: "Glenys or Denis? You Can Tell By The Spouse Who You Want In The House".'

Two hours watching Peggy Ashcroft talking, on a tiny monitor. Derek Bailey is editing his profile of her, and needs to know from me how long it should run. Like all actors who want to conceal where their gift comes from, Dame Peg (as she was known when I worked at Stratford) has a fund of party pieces, about being at drama school with Olivier, about Lilian Baylis running the Old Vic during the twenties. She says how much she has always enjoyed playing men's parts or male disguises, from Cassius in the school play to Shen Te/Shui Ta in Brecht's *The Good Person of Setzuan*. And the way she talks about *Hedda Gabler* shows what a step forward it was for her to get beyond the 'nice-girl' parts she was afraid of getting stuck with. Her commitment to permanent companies (the Royal Shakespeare, George Devine's Royal Court) also comes across strongly.

One exchange pinpoints the precision and concentration of her work. Billington asks her about what it was like rehearsing with Samuel Beckett as Winnie in *Happy Days*, and refers to her starting the play buried up to the waist in sand. 'Earth, Michael, earth. Sand could blow away.'

While I am viewing this tape, Jeremy and Peter Hall have been talking about who should direct the television version of Peter's production of *La Traviata* at Glyndebourne next summer. Peter would like to do it himself; Jeremy would prefer that he worked with an experienced and sympathetic TV director. For Jeremy there's a lot at stake: he's pleased at having secured one opera a year from Glyndebourne (with the help of facilities and finance from TVS, the ITV station of the region), when the BBC had previously held the monopoly. For Peter, too, it matters a lot: he needs to have a few incontestable creative successes to overcome recent smears and slurs.

We talked in my office before I took him down to see Jeremy. He looked like a veteran prizefighter, said he was definitely leaving the National Theatre in 1988, asked me whether I was still enjoying this job, talked about the theatre's 'enduring ephemerality'. I took him into Jeremy's office and left the two of them together.

Tuesday morning begins with something like an act of self-censorship. In a fortnight's time I have scheduled a film about Picasso, at 9.15 pm on a Sunday. The film, by a French director, is threaded through with graphic sequences of bullfighting, bringing home the fierce Spanish culture from which Picasso sprang and the importance in his personal mythology of the bull, the Minotaur, as a figure of energy, sexuality, tragedy and death.

Colleagues who viewed the film at the Cannes Television Festival this year were disturbed by its bullfight blood and guts and thought it should be edited. But Picasso is shocking, he breaks taboos, his work is about violence as well as tenderness; the film incorporates its violent images in a sustained argument and analysis. I show it to Liz Forgan in her capacity as deputy controller. We sit in her office and look at all the bullfighting sequences. I argue for retaining all of them with an appropriate announcement at the top of the film, except perhaps one: a close-up of a picador's pike going into the bull's flesh and being rotated in a gush of blood with a fierce squelch. Although used as a metaphor for the artist's worst personal and public unhappiness, the immediacy of this close-up makes it more literal than metaphorical. The risk is that animal-loving viewers will switch off, protest and miss the rest of an excellent film. 'Anyway, Liz,' I say, 'the previous sequence makes the point fully.' 'The alibi of the censor through the ages,' says Liz. Still, we remove the shot, which lasts about twenty seconds. 'Perhaps the one thing Mary White-house has done,' says Liz, 'is to make me watch images of violence more closely.'

At the end of the afternoon I meet Jeremy to talk about my 1987–88 plans. Before we do so, I ask him what happened with Peter Hall. He sighs. 'He promised he would do a proper camera script, and listen to a producer. I gave way a bit. I said I'd think about it and let him know this week. If the meeting had happened in his office, I could have stated my position, said it was my last word, and left.' Another sigh. I want to tell him that I think he should produce it himself, with Peter directing. It doesn't seem the moment. He looks preoccupied, nods absently when I say, 'What's the big deal, anyway? In the end, it's another re-transmission from the stage, not a feature film.'

We turn to my budget for next year. I've prepared a sketch schedule, showing the programmes I'd like to get transmitted in each quarter. Jenny has written it out elegantly on a large sheet of paper. We go through it and he seems to like it. 'You should get 80–90 per cent of this on air,' he says. Then he makes a more formal speech, urging me to think during my holidays about which elements of my plans show a fresh departure, which are the formula as before. 'Perhaps it's time for less adaptations of theatre. Maybe you'll want to do more about poetry, or architecture. I know I've filled up some of your slots with a lot of good but conventional classical music, but we still need to innovate musically. When's that thing of yours about the Civil War and English music? Will Palmer get the rest of the money for Shostakovich? Maybe we should make a long-term arrangement with Opera Factory and the London Sinfonietta. To me, Michael, the two most important programmes on your list are the experimental video season and the late-night live show about the way we're going. Television art and a television event.'

Out it comes, rat-a-tat-tat, the seasoned TV ringmaster at his finger-snapping best. Except for a moment, when he seems to go vacant. What is it? 'Oh nothing, I was just thinking about my chairman.' It's as if the programme-maker in him were reluctantly dragged back to duty as the chief executive, having to argue out with his chairman and board the pros and cons of Channel Four selling its own advertising.

It's a week for scrutinising great actors. Next day I look at cut sequences of Simon Callow's profile of Charles Laughton, which will coincide with Simon's book next Christmas. Simon and I grew very close over three months in 1980, when we worked every day on Shakespeare's sonnets. He taught me a lot about the actor's existential leap into a character, about sexuality and acting, about sheer energy, about what he called 'the actor's ontological void' which requires him to become other than himself. Intimacy of the rehearsal room, painstaking seriousness, finding parallels between Shakespeare and Proust, total playfulness, all-encompassing while it lasts. 'The trouble with doing a one-man show,' said Simon one day, looking at my frown when he'd finished a run-through, 'is that you know that all the director's notes are going to be for you.'

His exploration of Charles Laughton is pursued with boldness and tenacity, one self-constructed actor trying to find out how another Humpty Dumpty put his pieces together. 'Did he give you a lot when you worked with him?' Simon asks Rex Harrison. 'He gave a lot to the camera,' replies the straightfaced, weatherbeaten star. 'When I cast him as Bottom,' says Peter Hall, 'I found out that no matter where I put him on stage he became the focal point. That huge moon-face, those great round eyes. He was an epic actor whom we lost to Hollywood.' In Hollywood Simon gazes at the collapsed cliff which once was Laughton's garden. Laughton and Brecht sat in it in 1943 translating Brecht's *Galileo*; in a poem Brecht compared their choice of words with 'the English actor's' choice of plants. As well as visiting Laughton sites and interviewing fellow actors and directors, Simon will anatomise six key Laughton roles preserved on film, probing his disguises and displays, his concealments and exposures, the progress of his talent and the homosexuality he came to accept.

Lunch with Liz Forgan, whom I've seen much more often since she was made deputy controller – not least because she's often up on our floor talking to Farrukh Dhondy and Alan Fountain, who now work directly to her. She's always respected Alan's severity of judgement and downbeat determination; now she's clearly enjoying Farrukh's exuberance. 'He's making us aware of an extraordinary community right under our noses: the British Asians. Just the kind of thing the Channel is meant to be doing.'

Liz has been through most of the thickets of argument about consensus, impartiality and balance which the Channel has traversed. She has done battle with the IBA, with our own chairman Edmund Dell (who, as a former MP, has rigid views on media and politics), and with programme-makers who confuse opinion with verifiable facts. She is still locked in argument with John Ranelagh, who thinks the distinction too often remains blurred. Her programme-makers have brought off a number of investigative scoops like Cathy Massiter's exposure of MI5 misconduct. Like me, she has no children; much of our parental instincts goes into the job.

She's concerned (as is Alan Fountain) that because Jeremy has run the Channel so much on the basis of his particular magnetism and personality, he may leave it vulnerable to an even more meddling chairman, or a very different successor. 'He doesn't have the taste for drawn-out battering arguments, so he could be eroded.'

I drive down to Limehouse Studios to catch the end of the third day of Derek Bailey's shoot of *Yan Tan Tethera*. Once again Derek is hunched across the mixing desk, calling, cajoling, warning, wheedling the shots into being. Next door, Harry Birtwistle leans over the score and the sound desk, pushing a key now and then to bring out instrumental textures. The set, embellished with extra trees and a gauze cyclorama, looks powerfully monumental. The sheep masks are forceful faces. The strength and unexpectedness of the images could bring this music to many who would otherwise pass it by.

Last weekend before Orna and I leave for our holidays. We've rented a house in Tuscany, near Lucca, where I will also attend the Prix Italia. We start packing up books, computers, maps. I look forward to aimlessness with Orna, if we can manage to unwind. We are both creatures of tigerish obsession. Saturday night to the Lyric, Hammersmith to see Glenda Jackson and Joan Plowright in Lorca's tragedy of repression *The House of Bernarda Alba*, directed by the Spanish actress Nuria Espert. Glenda Jackson is compelling, ramrod-thin, her voice growling and cutting, a female incarnation of Fascism. Joan Plowright's comic despair and mild rebellion, the warmth of her character against Glenda's tight virago, show that not all the springs of life have dried up. At the interval I'm cornered by the young producer who has been urging me to do the play on television at the end of its run. Although it's a gripping evening, I'm going to say no. Lorca's distilled, classical playwriting requires a shared space and time with an audience; on TV it would seem artificially constrained. It's the absence in television of a watertight frame, shutting out all else to squeeze the juice from a small number of ingredients. And if ever acting required unbroken time, it's Glenda's. She rides a held silence like a jazz master crossing the beat. Make one cut in that flow, one shift of shot, and her mastery, the perilous sculpting of time that pulls a theatre audience into an actor's intimacy, is diluted. Ashcroft and Laughton would understand.

The interior of the Lyric Theatre is so beautiful, Frank Matcham's ornate plush-and-plaster auditorium promising you a treat even before the curtain goes up. Its scale makes you part of an audience, yet not swamped in a mass. The stage feels close, yet grand. Is it just sentimental of me to imagine that this space is somehow ennobled by the years' accumulated intention and emotion, renewed each night, which has soaked into its walls? In any event, it's not a sentimentality that afflicts the representatives of the newly elected Labour council on the Lyric Theatre board; at the end of the last meeting, they voted that the Lyric should return to the council the interest which the council's grant has gathered, 'as a gesture of goodwill to the borough'. As if using every penny of the grant to run a precious theatre well were some kind of bad will . . .

On Sunday we throw a party in our garden, a gathering of friends before we go on holiday. Michael Ignatieff is the first to show up. Soon he's telling Yigal Lossin, whose television history of Zionism we transmit this autumn, how his great-grandfather, a Tsarist minister, framed Russia's anti-Semitic legislation. 'So my great-grandfather is in some way responsible for the creation of your country.' It turns out to be a very Russian party. Joseph Brodsky appears: he and Ignatieff, who have crossed swords in print, are soon deep in the politics of the Revolution; Janet Suzman, who once performed Tatiana in Pushkin's *Eugene Onegin* for me, hangs on Brodsky's stories about what Trotsky really did. At the end of the party Brodsky, who is returning to New York soon, inhales the smell and sight of our garden. Through the afternoon I've seen him clutch his heart several times. 'I know I will die before long, I just don't know how soon. When I come to a party like this and I meet a pretty woman, I say to myself, why bother?' But he does.

As always, a fearful flurry of last-minute problems next day before I can get out of the office. The tape of Jules Feiffer's *Grown-Ups*, scheduled in a fortnight, hasn't arrived, and its producer, one day in Los Angeles, the next in Toronto, may not own the rights to sell to us. We pull it from the schedule. Last-minute sound edits on the English National Opera's *Rusalka*, going out this week, mean it's not ready for me to see – and even more important, hear – in the two hours I'd cleared to do so. A quick gander at the introduction to *The Possessed*, however, is reassuring: Michael Billington alerts viewers that what they're about to see is not a classic adaptation, like Dickens on the BBC. What people will make of Lyubimov's phantasmagoric vision when they do see it I can't predict. I think that his expressionism is true to Dostoevsky, and that he has made Dostoevsky's political and religious prophecies about Russia urgent and disturbing.

At lunchtime on my last day, I go to the press view of Picasso's sketchbooks at the Royal Academy. The storyboard series of drawings he did hour by hour in a single day are like frozen frames of a film: you can almost sense the time in his head, the thinking in his hand. In one gleefully dislocated self-portrait at the easel he produces his hand from where his nose should be, hooks his palette round what might just as well be a big toe as a thumb, and hangs his prick from God knows where. After this past turbulent month, it's just the way I feel.

MILITARY ROAD: NEARLY 3 OR 52

The notion of 'the ecology of broadcasting' is giving way to that of 'the broadcasting market'. It is perhaps a more appropriate way to talk about audience choice and its effects, when the model is not three or four channels, but one or two dozen. The problem with markets, nevertheless, is that they can still end up telling us the price of everything and the value of nothing. Look at the way they sell paintings.

Peter Fiddick 'May Market Force Be With You'

A poem aims at human memory. Memory is usually the last to go, as if it were trying to keep a record of the going itself. A poem thus may be the last thing to leave one's drooling lips.

Joseph Brodsky 'A Child of Civilisation'

This year's Prix Italia is in Lucca, of the chunky redbrick walls. You can climb up and walk right round the city under an arch of trees, looking down into first-floor rooms, piazzas, ornamental gardens. Meadows sweep right up to the walls, a timeless sea of green. Armies with siege machines tried to scale these walls; from turrets and outposts, the defendants would have beaten them off easily.

The Prix takes place in a resplendent villa for the jury viewings and the all-important refreshment marquee, and in the city museum for the debates and prize announcements. Once again I enjoy the counterpoint between frescoed ceilings and banks of video monitors, people wearing headphones and using microphones in front of trecento Sienese saints. Alvise Zorzi, the secretary-general of the Prix Italia who is retiring this year, has made these piquant conjunctions his trademark. With fifty Italian cities competing to host the Prix Italia each year, he has not lacked ingredients.

I drive into town early and make my way to the marquee in the Villa Guinigi, buy a coffee, wait for the delegates to show up. Familiar figures drift in, a Nordic contingent, a French brigade, colleagues from ITV and BBC. The rotund Sergio Borelli, Lenin to Zorzi's Kerensky in the Prix Italia Secretariat, tells me what's been happening during the first week at Lucca. Over the past few weeks, he and I have been discussing how to get separate membership of the Prix Italia for Channel Four. Winning a Prix Italia is the ultimate accolade in this business, and as long as we can only enter programmes under the ITV umbrella, where we contend with fifteen ITV companies for the independent television entry, our work doesn't stand much chance.

This is the beginning of the final week of the Prix Italia; our membership application will be debated at the General Assembly on the last day. Orna and I have been on holiday in Tuscany for a week already, unwinding in the garden of a rented house, days in the sunshine among ripe grapes and figs, the usual intricate dreams at night as the mind learns that it no longer has to clasp or grapple. But the grappling hooks don't let go so quickly; we got as far as Genoa when I rang the office to check up, and found that the sound on the transmission of *Rusalka* had been disastrous, viewers ringing in to complain that some of it sounded as if it had been recorded in a bathroom. Was it the sound-recordist's fault, or our transmission? A post-mortem is under way. A bitter disappointment: the thing had looked wonderful on the off-line edit, with unmixed sound. English National Opera will be furious with us. The unwinding process halts for a day or so; I'm still in the sunshine, but I'm twitching.

Under the marquee, in a conspiratorial whisper that won't reach a neighbouring table of BBC people, Sergio tells me he's pessimistic about Channel Four's chances of winning separate entry. 'Alasdair Milne came out last week, gave a BBC dinner in honour of Zorzi, invited him to Ascot, and implied that the BBC would not be pleased if Channel Four got in. Then he made the supreme effort: he kissed the native on both cheeks. At the General Assembly Zorzi will nominate a new chairman who will call for another working party to study the important issues involved, and they'll defer the decision for another year. They've got it wrapped up.'

I wander over to the BBC table. They're busy discussing who their next chairman will be. Mrs Thatcher has been trying to impose Lord Young, hotfoot from privatising British Air. Guarded fraternal greetings; the solidarity of a bunch of Brits among foreigners reasserts itself over broadcasting rivalry. Dennis Marks, head BBC music producer, appears, looking white as a sheet among the suntans. He's chairing the music jury this year, as I did last. Fewer programmes have been entered this year, he says, and there's no endurance test to match last year's three-hour Korean music-theatre piece. I tell him he's got it easy. But I know that red-eyed bunker exhaustion feeling. Above our heads on a monitor a fiddler is sawing away at Paganini.

I greet my Channel Four colleagues: Renee Goddard, our European representative, and Liz Forgan, whose commission *Maids and Madams* is the documentary entry for British independent television, which Channel Four has entered under the wing of ITV. A penetrating and moving film about the black women maids of white South African housewives, it stands a good chance of getting a prize.

Over the next few days we lobby, explain, put ourselves about. Midweek Jeremy comes out to Florence, half an hour's drive away, to lecture on 'The Future of European Broadcasting'. The advance publicity describes him as '*direttore culturale della* BBC'. 'Anticipating a bit,' mutters Nick Elliott from LWT. None of us can get there to hear him, because it's the same time as our lobbying cocktail party. Many of the delegates have received both invitations. Jeremy hasn't left himself time to appear at our party, in sharp contrast to the assiduously diplomatic Alasdair Milne. We don't have our act together.

Sue Stoessl gives me a copy of his speech. The heart of it is a discussion about whether European broadcasters banding together can create a joint popular fiction series to rival *Dallas* or *Dynasty*, to compete with American series sprayed over Europe by cable. The reason for choosing popular fiction as the test case, Jeremy argues, is that since most people use television for entertainment, and all entertainment purveys social and cultural messages, why should we absorb American messages through our fictions?

The response so far has been to attempt mighty trans-European sagas, like *Marco Polo* and *Quo Vadis*, both of which we transmitted. Visually lavish, crammed with international talent, no expense spared to bring exotic times and places to the screen, they had been made in many different languages, the Italian superstar swapping Italian dialogue with the Yugoslav starlet speaking hers in Serbo-Croatian. The final Babel was post-synchronised into English, French, German or whatever language each market required.

'Our best service to each other,' concludes Jeremy, 'is to have regard to our own national culture; to serve our own viewers in their own language, with work that touches their concerns and speaks directly to them, in the idiom they know best. That done, we can exchange the results, and display them on each other's screens, again in their original language. The answer to the American import is not a synthetic construct embodying synthetic values, narrated in Americanese: it is *echt Deutsch, la vera storia.*'

Watching Italian television, both the public channels and the proliferating commercial ones, I see series, serials and movies from abroad in which John Wayne speaks in the accents of Piedmont, Charles Dance in polished Roman tones, and a police inspector in a rather good German series sounds like a Neapolitan. Only the songs in *High Society* or *On the Town* emerge from the dubbing swamp that surrounds them. Because most foreign popular drama on British television comes from America, the British have scarcely faced this problem, or tested the broadcasting article of faith that subtitling popular fiction cuts down your audiences. It will get tested this year: we've bought a high-schlock French serial, *Chateauvallon*, and we will play each weekly episode twice, subtitled and dubbed, and ask viewers what they think. Orna is girding herself to do both subtitles and dubbing.

The Prix Italia draws towards its end. This year no prize is given for music programmes, Dennis Marks and his jury finding too much 'bread-and-butter' programming among the entries. *Maids and Madams* wins second prize in the documentary section, a Canadian observational film about an industrial dispute taking the Prix Italia. It is the first time Channel Four has won a Prix Italia award in its own right. The social whirl continues apace. NBC, who have won a special prize with a tearjerker about AIDS, host what is by all accounts an epic four-hour lunch at the Antico Caffè delle Mure, and the next night Paul Bonner and Liz Forgan are submitted to the identical menu in the same place at an IBA dinner, where Liz is forced to speak French all night to the incoming Prix Italia chairman, the one we've been told will block our membership application.

He looks like a silver-haired Vincent Price, has the reputation of being a smooth-tongued operator in the councils of European broadcasting, and hasn't actually had much to do with making or transmitting programmes for years. Undoubtedly the man for a diplomatic deferral job. Do we really want to join a club like this?

The debate about Channel Four membership at the General Assembly next day, in the museum assembly hall, lasts over two hours. Delegates from some of the smaller countries have stayed on specially, just to vote for us. I sit in the back row with Liz and Renee who is simmering, behind Paul Bonner, our controller and formal spokesman, and the phalanxes of the IBA and BBC.

The chairman, speaking with the polysyllabic abstraction which is the great French bequest to the diplomatic life, and flanked by two steely-faced bureaucrats from the European Broadcasting Union, explains that the issues raised by Channel Four's application are wide-ranging and require further study. Eckart Stein, who has proposed our membership on behalf of ZDF, West Germany's second channel, calls for a vote: 'The Prix Italia needs Channel Four more than Channel Four needs the Prix Italia.'

Michael Johnson, the BBC diplomat with the faintly wearied polite manner, tries everything in the book to trip things up. Sergio Borelli, passing behind my chair, whispers, 'It's all getting too polite. Show some anger. That's what the other countries will understand.'

To raise the temperature I use the emotive word ghetto to describe the situation of independent programme-makers. Pressure builds for a vote. Lord Thomson gives the IBA's backing. Vittorio Boni, the international representative of RAI Italian television, leaps up to say that members of the Prix Italia should not be afraid of doing something simply because the BBC doesn't want it to happen. Zorzi and his chairman are looking extremely pained. It goes to a vote. The BBC abstains. It's unanimous for Channel Four admission. It feels like a victory for the street people against the clubmen.

WEEK 43 *October 20–25*

I get back from Italy, stopping off at Riverside Studios to see what the *Dancelines* people have been up to this week. The place is buzzing with activity: people rehearsing in every corner and outside, dancers using the camera, camera crew taking class with the dancers. Sets are built and painted overnight, music made to fit rough-edited video.

The *Independent* has printed my article about the tenth anniversary of the National Theatre. The NT was caught from day one in a building made for the age of cheap energy, and which cost a million pounds a year just to light and heat. So its options were narrowed from the start, and it was inevitable that it would cohabit with the commercial theatre. Of course the National has had its peaks over the past decades: *The Mysteries* and Bill Bryden's line of work in general, everything that Brenton and Hare have done, the *Oresteia, Brand, Coriolanus, Guys and Dolls*. But many productions in the past five years have lacked the danger and urgency that is the final justification for live theatre. The open question is whether a place the size of the National is condemned to create assembly-line theatre, or whether, as so often in Britain, we invented the thing that was needed, and then simply underfunded it.

At the National's tenth birthday party last week, among many familiar faces, I met Gawn Grainger again. I remember that when I arrived at the National Gawn struck me as the archetypal actor: zesty, histrionic, mercurial (he played Mercutio at Bristol Old Vic), one of Larry's band of players at the Old Vic, then a trouper in Marlowe and Beaumarchais under the Peter Hall regime on the South Bank. Gawn memorably acted Peter Handke's story about his mother's suicide for me, and later brought his passion to Brecht when I staged a show of his poems and songs at the Cottesloe. Now he's writing plays and acting, mostly on television. 'I never met an actor as crazy as you, Gawn,' I said. 'And I never met such a weird director,' he said.

But I was never really singleminded enough to take the plunge of becoming a director. Scared of becoming father to the troupe, I guess. I invented all sorts of interesting alternatives instead, but they kept me on the periphery. Where I acquired other qualities; not least the quality of many-sidedness, which I sometimes think is a synonym for superficiality. This debate inside me will run and run.

WEEK 44 *October 27–November 1*

Jeffrey Archer has resigned as Tory deputy chairman because of a sex scandal. Farrukh swings gleefully into my office and tells me that the Asian lawyer who told the press about it used to present our black current affairs programme, *Eastern Eye*. 'A nice boy from Bombay whose head has been turned by the media,' says Farrukh. Jeffrey Archer offered me a job in 1971. I'd just left the ICA and didn't know what to do next. He had an interest in a Bond Street gallery and was looking for someone to run it. I met him in the gallery, an astonishing self-propelled sparrow of a man on permanent overdrive. Although he offered me a good salary I said no. I was suffering from severe sixties aftermath, but it didn't seem the way to start the new decade.

Geoff Dunlop comes in to talk about his next project, now that *State of the Art* is finished. He wants to make a film about Bonnard, mixing documentary, drama and painting. It's prompted by a short novel by Gabriel Josipovici, *Contre-Jour*, a speculative fiction which invents a daughter for the childless Bonnard and his eczema-ridden wife, who couldn't take a bath without Bonnard drawing or painting her in it. It would explore the artist's obsessiveness and its effect on his nearest and dearest, and would be what Geoff calls a domestic epic. 'I want to deal with personal, intimate ideas now,' says Geoff. 'I feel I've done enough on the big social and cultural ideas for a while.'

We talk about it as a further attempt, this time using fictional as well as documentary means, to make a television of intuition and ideas. In New York this year Mike Dibb said that, contrary to most people's assumptions, television was very good at exploring ideas, relating them to feelings, memory, the way we live. His own work, from *Ways of Seeing* with John Berger to the *About Time* series and the film on biology and creativity which he's making for me now, is a deepening investigation of this possibility. Geoff Dunlop's films on Merce Cunningham and Talking Heads, his essay-film with Edward Said about Western ideas of Arabs, and his presentation and questioning of ideas and images in *State of the Art*, belong in this line. So do Gina Newson's films with Marina Warner, examining the symbolism of women. It's beginning to add up to a tradition, a self-aware, exploratory body of work. Only the continuities of public-service television, and the variations on it which Channel Four represents, could have started such a tradition. Its absence in American television is noticeable.

Barrie Gavin, who comes in next day to discuss his Shelley programme, is another architect of that tradition. As editor of *Omnibus* he gave Dibb, Newson and others their chances, and made films about the ideas-in-music of Pierre Boulez and Pablo Neruda's poetry-in-politics. Barrie's series with Simon Rattle about the influence of Eastern music on Western composers is currently playing on the BBC. He reels off his usual febrile collection of projects: films on Poulenc, Henze and Berio, an approach to Leonardo da Vinci through a composer inspired by him, a portrait of the visionary nature writer Richard Jefferies. I want to do something with him about the social and perceptual meanings of photography; he always uses still photographs superbly in his films.

His Shelley film sprang from hearing Paul Foot lecture on the political poetry of Shelley at the Cheltenham Literary Festival. The environment of Barrie's film will be less genteel: a disused pumping station, an image of Britain's industrial decline, in which actors will perform a montage of Shelley's revolutionary poetry, Paul Foot will explain its historical meanings, and artist Ken Sprague's banners, flags and street cartoons will link the poetry with popular history. It will be ready next autumn. Interesting to run a film in election year about the man who said poets were the unacknowledged legislators of the world. No doubt the media-watchers in Conservative Party Central Office would call it biassed.

To Manchester to see Opera North's production of *The Capture of Troy*, as they have renamed part one of Berlioz's *The Trojans*. It's the first phase of a co-production with Welsh National and Scottish Opera; the entire work will be completed next year. I'm swept up by something quite extraordinary: an epic that is as much Shakespearean as Virgilian, classical in its shapeliness and discipline, romantic in its exuberance and passion. 'Ill though I am,' wrote Berlioz, 'I am constantly at it: my score forms itself like stalactites in damp caves, almost without me knowing it.'

Cassandra, powerfully sung by Kristine Ciesinski, rides through the work, a tall woman shrouding herself in a long red winding sheet, a figure out of Racine and Cocteau. The climactic scene where she leads the Trojan women to mass suicide rather than surrender to the Greeks, set by Tim Albery in a boxlike room twenty feet above stage level, is a scenic, musical and emotional body-blow. Throughout the evening – ninety uninterrupted minutes – fusions and conjunctions between sound, image and text flesh out Berlioz's 'exotically asymmetrical' work, as Peter Conrad calls it.

One of the reasons it works so forcefully is its design. It's set among shell-scarred walls, as if after some archetypal modern war. The stage surface recalls both beach and battlefield. There are elements of ritual and ceremony which owe more to performance art than to any authentic rendering of the ancient world. In fact, the vocabulary of performance art, its immediacy and love of surrealistic stage imagery, have much to do with the vividness of this and many other good recent opera productions. Nicholas Hytner's sandbagged and barbed-wire city in his Kent Opera production of Tippett's *King Priam* (which we're putting out this month) would be another example, another treated Troy. 'It's not grand opera with big voices,' says my opera consultant Gillian Widdicombe, who saw Jessye Norman do it at Covent Garden, 'but it's another kind of real thing.' I think so too; it's a new generation coming to terms with an operatic scale of experience and expression, their sensibilities formed by the cinema, not by opera-house rituals.

David Boulton invites us to a reception at Granada after the performance. His regional arts magazine has already made a half-hour film about the making of *The Capture of Troy*; I would like them to expand it over the next year to a long documentary which would not only follow the making of *The Trojans* but also profile Opera North, Welsh National Opera and Scottish Opera, who are doing so much to awaken opera in this country. Will they be able to go on satisfying the enthusiasm they have aroused?

Opera is reaching out everywhere this week. Back in London at a reception for British arts festivals, the Welsh composer William Matthias tells a story about one viewer's response to the film of Schoenberg's *Moses and Aaron* which we put out last week. 'I was in a hotel in Cardiff, and I turned on the television and saw this marvellous film you showed. Next morning in the breakfast room there was a big Welsh farmer. "Did you see that film on the telly last night?" he said. "Wonderful! Music *and* theology!"'

Opening night at the ICA of Michael Nyman's opera *The Man Who Mistook His Wife for a Hat*. Neurology into narrative into music; music both the vehicle and the subject matter. If a composer ever wanted a pretext for a quizzical, self-referring work, it's this. And there's something strangely unsettling and unstable about the subject. The documentary reality of the original case history belies music's melodramatising powers.

The result, in the ICA's tiny, packed theatre, is troubling and moving, imperfect in this performance (the singers haven't had time to adjust their microphones), yet already something that slips under one's intellectual defences. Written in Michael's characteristic minimalist idiom, scored for piano quintet plus harp and extra cello, what seems still to surprise the composer when I talk to him afterwards is the almost Puccinian emotion the work transmits through its grids and systems. Michael's programme note tries to batten down this current in a web of definitions. Dr P. needed music, he writes, 'as lifeline, cue, clue, cure', and his case invites from the composer 'a music which may exaggerate, suggest, narrate, dislocate, illustrate, allude, connect' . . . and so on through a list of another twenty verbs.

This verbal wall reminds me of the prose catalogues of Nyman's habitual collaborator, Peter Greenaway. This opera is the first dramatic work Michael has done without Greenaway; it allows the tenderness and lyricism which is perhaps more Michael's temperament to show through. 'Greenaway asked me why I hadn't chosen a tougher story from Sacks,' says Michael afterwards. 'If he'd written the libretto you'd have seen Dr P. hang himself at the end.' I ask him why he doesn't kick away minimalism and let his own sensibility flood through. 'Then I'd just be a neo-Romantic. I need all that scaffolding.'

So does the Sacks case history. If a composer were to swathe it in Menotti-esque lyricism, it would be bathetic, although one could imagine a more dense and complex music for Sacks's fable. Predictably, music critics who abhor minimalism clobber the piece in the press. But others respond to its arresting strangeness, the spell it exerts despite its nursery ingredients. I found it a riddling work, teetering on several knife-edges, and I can't make up my mind yet whether it's artistically evasive or just elusive. Most of it will be incorporated into Chris Rawlence's film *The Real Me*, intertwined with an Oliver Sacks interview, works and words by artists Sol Lewitt and Helen Chadwick, and other investigations into the unstable contemporary self.

Just before I left for the Nyman premiere, a fattish script for the first sixteen cantos of *A TV Dante* arrived from Peter Greenaway, who was supposed to deliver it three months ago. I don't know what I can do about the project now; because Peter hadn't delivered when I had my budget meeting, Jeremy slashed the money earmarked for the programme. It's been on and off for nearly two years since the pilot of canto five was finished. Tom Phillips, whose Dante book was the inspiration for the thing, feels rejected; Sophie Balhetchet, its producer, feels betrayed. Yet everyone who sees the pilot is excited, and I know it could be a landmark in art television.

Down at Riverside Studios, *Dancelines* is coming to the boil. I watch Ian Spink directing a take for his Edward Hopper-ish piece. A girl comes into a late afternoon room, where another girl is sitting at a table, daydreaming. As hard light falls into the room through rainwashed window-panes, and water reflections play on the ceiling, she dances out a set of complex fast steps to additive rhythms. Sue Davies is agonising over her piece, in which the camera tracks past a fresco of dancers inside punctured walls. She wants to collage photographic or moving images into the gaps in the walls. 'Everyone around me is giving me ideas, too many ideas. And I'm too open to them. Perhaps having this baby' – her four-month-old baby never leaves her side all day – 'has made me more open than usual to other people's demands and needs.'

I go with Farrukh to the ICA for a public conversation between Mario Vargas Llosa and Tariq Ali about Vargas Llosa's new novel, which describes a revolutionary faction in a future Peru. Tariq attacks him for being above history, having a passive hero, writing a cynical book. Llosa replies, 'In politics I'm a moderate; an extremist in literature.'

Next day Brian Eno talks about the television screen of the future: 'It's flat, and you'll be able to hang it on the wall like a picture, get it out when you want it, put it away when you don't. People will be able to have several in a room. It will change the kind of thing they expect to see. Television will become more like painting, less like narrative.' He promises to think about an original work for our new video series.

Norman Tebbit has been putting the heat on the BBC this week; the BBC's director-general says the Tories are trying to intimidate the BBC. It's getting to feel a bit like the Inquisition, with volunteers at Conservative Party Central Office building up evidence for an Index. On the other hand Tebbit's intemperance may have offended the British sense of fair play. William Rees-Mogg's journalistic instincts are stronger than his sympathy for Mrs Thatcher; as a BBC governor and former editor of *The Times*, he rebuts Tebbit's attack. I ring Nick Fraser, who will produce *U.K. Late*, a late-night live discussion programme, this summer. 'If *U.K. Late* had been on the air this week,' I say, 'we'd probably have argued the pros and cons of investigative journalism in a democracy. But we might not have known that the Tebbit attack was coming until the day before transmission. That's the sort of show it's going to be.'

WEEK 45 *November 2–9*

Spitting Image leads off with their bovver-boy puppet of Tebbit as news-reader in a BBC *News* the way he would like to see it. Black-leather-jacketed, the skull-headed puppet reports that the government is doing better than ever, then hands over to Kate Adie, the reporter maligned by implication in the Tory onslaught. Kate Adie turns out to be the Tebbit puppet in drag wearing a blonde wig. In front of the smoking ruins of Tripoli, she reports that the children of Libya – she hauls in a crumpled dwarf infant by the ear – actually like being bombed by the Americans. This is *Spitting Image* at its outrageous best; for once the reference to television is properly satirical rather than parasitic, and the sketch has the brevity and concision of a good cartoon.

George Melly, with whom I interview Gerald Scarfe at the ICA later in the week, believes that *Spitting Image* wouldn't have happened without the animus and aerodynamic graphics of Scarfe's cartoons. The connection highlights the difference between newsprint and television. The caricaturist, as Scarfe says, is always raising his voice to surmount the visual hubbub of headlines, ads and graphics around his work. TV's moving image makes it even harder for the artist to rise beyond resemblance into free, jubilant style. Scarfe memorialised Nixon with a ski-slope nose and pendulous lips that eventually left the page altogether and became a wooden sculpture: a swooping nasal projection and hanging from it, as if about to drop on Cambodia, a bomb-shaped jaw. The metaphorical power of such a drawing or a sculpture is stronger than most images on a TV screen. But television can be made to move beyond the likeness and the literal.

After our public conversation I invite Scarfe to come and draw on the Quantel 'electronic paintbox'. I think he might be challenged by making caricatures in real time when we do our live late-night show. He says that deadlines spur him on; this would be a deadline with a vengeance, the drawing growing before your very eyes, referring to something that happened a minute ago.

I first met Gerald Scarfe in 1966 when I asked him to make giant puppets for a CND pageant in Trafalgar Square, written by Adrian Mitchell and featuring Harold Wilson, Ian Smith, Lyndon Johnson and Robin Day. In Scarfe's book, the occasion of this week's public conversation, there's a photograph of his giant puppets on their stage, the pavement in front of the National Gallery. Thirty feet tall, the puppets are being guarded by imperturbable helmeted police, standing above the bannered title of the show, THE WHORE GAME. At the end of the performance, we released hundreds of silver-foil missiles over the heads of the crowd and threw buckets of red blood at the caricature faces of world leaders. *Spitting Image* before its time?

David Hockney's producer, Michael Deakin, comes in to tie up details on the programme Hockney will make next year, taking an electronic paintbox to Japan in cherry-blossom time and making a travel sketchbook on it. A film crew will follow him around, filming him sketching and the things he sketches. 'Will David be taking a camera with him, Michael?' I ask. 'Of course, he never goes anywhere without a camera,' says Deakin. 'Then let's make the programme a reflection on the differences between three kinds of image-making – hand-drawn, still photograph, moving film.'

Another encounter with the hand-drawn video image: John Wyver joins me to watch a tape by Jaap Drupsteen, the Dutch graphic artist and video-maker whose version of Stravinsky's *The Flood* we will show next year. Jaap draws Magritte-like landscapes and architectures, uses video collage to patchwork actors, dancers, musicians and nature footage into them, and choreographs his multi-layered images to synthesized music. He would like to make two five-minute Gertrude Stein plays; he plays us a performance of the Stein texts by someone who sounds like an Amsterdam Laurie Anderson.

There's a bold graphic pattern behind the new Ayckbourn play *Woman in Mind*, which I see that night: the double vision of its central character, struck on the head by a garden rake just before the curtain rises and thereafter entering a parallel world which rebukes and eventually swamps the awful reality of her own family. White-clad smiling figures slow-motion into her autumnal garden, smother her with smiles and affection, behave like the model husband and children in glossy magazine advertisements, dissolve into yew hedges. Her real husband is an insufferable prig with a grim live-in sister, her son an emotionally lamed dropout. When Julia Mackenzie, as the protagonist, is shaken apart by her conflicting worlds at curtain-fall, like some heroic old aircraft disintegrating as it tries to go through the sound barrier, it feels like the darkest play Ayckbourn has yet written. His geometrical skills are sharper than ever, the plot joints and hairs-breadth entrances and exits give the pleasure of virtuoso dancing. But it's a round-dance of madness, the domestic Bedlam of an ordinary British family magnified to the dimensions of the stage. No wonder the actors, playing it night after night, insensibly soften its realism towards the grotesque.

Watching a roughcut next day of the film on Pirandello which Nigel Wattis is making for our *Great Writers* series, it strikes me that Ayckbourn's achievement is to bring Pirandello's concerns about illusion, reality and madness into the world of Donald McGill postcards, Giles cartoons and seaside weekly rep. *Woman in Mind* is his *Enrico IV*, *The Norman Conquests* his *Six Characters in Search of an Author*. Both he and Pirandello rest on the theatre's doubleness: a representation renewed each night, and a fiction which we accept wholeheartedly. With this doubleness they can see round the edge of reality.

One of the few film directors who makes reality problematic is Peter Greenaway, even if his last film, *A Zed and Two Noughts*, did so at the expense of believable human relationships. He succeeds in his cinematic alchemy because he thinks beyond the camera image towards the ambiguities of painting, and because he's pushed the interaction of music and image further than any of his contemporaries. Since the summer he's been immured in his favourite place, the cutting room, editing *Belly of an Architect*, the film he shot in Rome. Now that the edit is nearing completion, and he knows I'm fretting about *A TV Dante*, he rings me late at home and talks for an hour about what he and Tom Phillips would like to do with Dante over the next two years. Does he really intend to see it through? Or is he just clinging to a future project during that insecure interregnum before his film leaves the cutting room and is seen and judged?

Lunch at Jeremy's invitation with Sir Michael Tippett. Jeremy has made it a celebratory occasion, champagne in the White Tower, still a thirties haven. Sir Colin Davis is there too, for one of the things Gillian Widdicombe and I want to discuss is a plan to make a full-scale opera film of Tippett's *The Midsummer Marriage*, conducted by Colin.

Tippett sits between Jeremy and me, a tall, sprightly, dapper octogenarian, bright blue eyes, long tapering hands, a beaming smile. I ask him what he's reading, and he tells me he's had to give up reading because he's going blind. 'Only my peripheral vision works,' he says. 'I can't make out features at a distance, only blobs. It's irreversible.' Then he spellbinds Jeremy with an account of how he lost his virginity at a brutal public school in Scotland. 'I was so unhappy at that school, with the bullying and the cold showers, that a sexual scandal was a godsend. I told my parents, they whipped me out of school, threatened the headmaster with public disclosure if he didn't retire, and sent me to another, much more agreeable school. Then they moved to France, and I spent all my summer holidays there.'

He's begun a new opera, set 'somewhere and today' and 'nowhere and tomorrow', dealing with computers and orphans and family traumas. Gillian alerted me to it over the weekend, and we're now trying, together with Welsh National Opera, to outbid the BBC to commission it, ensure it is produced in America and Europe as well as in Britain, and film it for television. I've rung his publisher, stressed our commitment to his work. We have a week to make a proposition.

Benign, mischievous, wounded and mended, the composer sits in the Channel Four cinema, intently watching our television version of the Kent Opera production of *King Priam*. The god Hermes, gold-skinned and trench-coated, sings in immense close-up Tippett's paean to his art, his words liquefied by his music:

O divine music
O stream of sound
in which the states of soul
flow, surfacing and drowning,
while we sit watching from the bank
the mirrored, mirrored world within.

Back in the world of telecommunications and anger, the BBC issues its rebuttal of Norman Tebbit's charges of prejudiced reporting. Tebbit, barely pausing for breath, counter-attacks with a head-butting assertion that the BBC has sidestepped the burden of his criticisms by answering charges that were never laid. The whole business is beginning to sound like the bone-headed school bully jeeringly having the final word in a playground altercation. Tebbit's raucousness has already fortified the self-censor in every television journalist in the country.

Four hundred and eighty people have applied to be my assistant. With two colleagues, I will interview a shortlist next week. Gill Monk, our head of personnel, gives me a folder of what she considers the fifty best, and tells me that there were theatre directors, dancers and actors galore among the rejected applicants. Another sign of tough times in the live arts.

Too tired on Saturday morning even to write up this week. Orna and I wander down to the other London, Kensington and Chelsea, to look at the shops which have clustered round the Michelin building in Fulham Road. The boutique as an art-form of the eighties. A fashionable architect, Norman Foster, has transformed a garage into Katharine Hamnett's designer shop. You go in through a narrow hump-backed tunnel, new-wave muzak playing through its glass tiles. It opens out into a stunning huge space, magnified and metamorphosed by two sets of cunningly placed mirror walls. Like the Saatchi Collection, another key eighties site, it is a revamped industrial hangar, with similar struts, girders, cast-iron pillars and harsh floor. Hamnett's clothes hang from an oasis of gown-rails in the void, like a Carl André sculpture the Saatchis might exhibit. The salesgirls are almost indistinguishable from the skeletal clothes-dummies. The whole place feels like a New York SoHo Gallery – indeed the area, with its upmarket Depression-style diners populated by local yuppies, is very New York.

I read a lot of poetry over the weekend. Jeremy asked me to pick poems to be read at a memorial evening for Tamara at the Wigmore Hall next month. I choose a Scottish ballad, Donne, Hardy, Eliot, hesitate over Sorley Maclean, get sucked into Emily Dickinson's miraculous whisper:

> The Brain is just the weight of God –
> For – Heft them – Pound for Pound –
> And they will differ – if they do –
> As Syllable from Sound –

I read this mystic vision becoming breath, vowel and consonant in Joe's Diner with the yuppies on barstools knocking back Buck's Fizz, just like their flapper grandparents did.

Another reminder of immemorial British class divisions comes next day, at a Sunday morning preview of Bill Douglas's film about the Tolpuddle Martyrs, *Comrades*, which Channel Four has co-produced with the British Screen Corporation. Nearly three hours long, moving from desolate West Country fields to the sun-baked Australian gulags where the transported labourers worked out their sentences, the film has the low-key passion of an Emily Dickinson poem. But it fatally lacks her concision and proportion. Bill Douglas, who, as Jeremy said when he decided to back *Comrades*, 'wrenched out of himself' a devastating auto-biographical film, has made something overpacked and broken-backed, like a man choking on the urgency of his own utterance. In the current state of the British cinema, *Comrades* is heartbreaking: one of the only biggish–budget British films to be made this year, it spits and splutters where it should lift and soar.

Spitting, apparently, has been behind the latest skirmish between Channel Four and the IBA. Liz Forgan, back from the weekend conference of the Royal Television Society, says that Jeremy made a fierce speech attacking the IBA's regulatory cautiousness, while conceding that it was staffed by the most civilised operatives such an institution could hope to have. He referred to our famous run-ins with the Authority – the MI5 programme, the Greek Civil War film. The spitting, to which he did not refer, has occupied much valuable executive time in Charlotte Street and Brompton Road. It is Ben Elton's saliva, in a re-run episode of *Saturday Live.* Elton got carried away in one of his fiery monologues and spat at the audience. The IBA thinks that repeated saliva, no longer live, would be offensive. The theology of censorship rides again.

WEEKS 46–47 *November 10–22*

John Drummond, BBC Controller of Music and former Edinburgh Festival director, gives the first annual lecture of the Society for the Promotion of New Music. It takes place in the Chartered Accountants Hall in the City, an elegant bunker with concrete walls that look thick enough to withstand a direct hit. The place is stiff with composers, music publishers and critics. John, dapper and uppity, talks about the challenge of new music. 'The new is a problem rather than a challenge for British society,' he says, and lists the ingredients of our crisis as an overweight historical consciousness, economic uncertainty and a crippling tendency to understatement and good manners. He singles out the musical world as particularly conservative: 'We are sheltering from the present.' John's remedies: better musical education with an awareness of contemporary music, more imaginative concert-planning and marketing and a commitment by star conductors to living composers instead of the familiar repertoire. It's good swingeing stuff, with a doughty peroration attacking government philistinism – 'We judge the present by politicians, the past by artists.'

Harry Birtwistle, with whom I have dinner afterwards, has been asked to run next year's Summerscope music festival on the South Bank, and has spent the day with a knowledgeable, eccentric music critic filling out the theme of his festival. 'I want it to be about any kind of composition that isn't sonata form,' he says. 'Early music, Xenakis, the Bruckner Mass. And the other theme will be arrangements. Each concert will start with a new arrangement of the same medieval piece.' Typical Harry: subversive and rigorous. We talk about the National Theatre, where we got to know each other. He tells me that Peter Hall, who won't be staying on after the end of his contract in 1988, has decided to form a small team of actors – not big-name stars, but actors who have developed into playing leads within the National company – to do *Cymbeline, Pericles* and *The Winter's Tale.* 'The sort of thing he should have done long before,' mutters Harry, who will be working with Peter again. As we scurry away from each other in the Smithfield drizzle, he makes a wonderful Charles Laughtonesque silhouette, huddled in a capacious coat, working his way against the wind that howls through the meat-market arcades.

Next morning, my last before going to Paris, I view Judith Wechsler's latest film in her series *The Painter's World*, before meeting her later. It deals with art's attempts to come to terms with time and storytelling. A dancer performs an Isadora Duncan piece, set against Rodin's restless, glancing drawings of dancers in motion. The randomness or contingency of still photographs is contrasted with what Judith calls 'the arrested moment, stopped on its way somewhere'; the video slow-motion or freeze-frame with painting or sculpture's grasp 'not so much of the motion seen as the moment felt'. Intellectually and verbally, the half-hour film is eloquent. Visually, it's a bit crammed. I hope the collaboration with Mike Dibb, which I've made a condition of our co-producing this series, will help the films breathe and communicate by means other than assertion and illustration.

At lunch, Mike Dibb talks about his own professional relationship to time as a film-maker. 'There are two kinds of documentary director: those, like me, who live for the moment, and those who stop what they're doing if time runs out according to their pre-planned schedule.' But doesn't that make for a scramble at the end of the shoot, I ask. 'Yes, but I can't see the point of shooting if the material isn't coming alive in front of you.' It makes me realise how much of my working time I cram into tight compartments. The overload of television gives you a spurious sense of mastery if, by getting through a large number of things, you can make a tight package of your day; there's a certain ex-hilaration in miniaturising your attention, but it can become a disabling speediness.

On my way home I stop off for a drink with Anita Brookner in the bar of a hotel near the Courtauld Institute which has become our rendezvous for these occasional encounters. The format is invariable as a Racinian scene. I babble of my over-activity. She tells me of the comparative confinement of her life. This time she announces that she's been ill over the summer, finds teaching tiring after more than twenty years, and is going to give it up next year. But there's something less stoic than usual in her account. When I tell her she looks happier than I've seen her for a long time, she says, 'My lips are sealed,' and smiles quizzically. She bows out of the art-historical series I'd hoped to get her to do. She offers to let me read the manuscript of her new book. At a certain moment she announces that it's time for her to go home and exits, indomitably.

Two programmes about television and politics when I get home. The first episode of our own *The New Enlightenment* is an exposition of neo-conservatism, which it ennobles with the label 'classic liberalism'. Its verbal taunts against 'collectivists' are matched by a use of archive footage that lumps together Nazism, Communism and the Khmer Rouge as movements that inevitably lead to piles of skulls. After this scare-story opening there's a stream of pieties about the free market as the unique source of spontaneity and liberty, a caricature of Keynesian economics and closing credits stating that the programme was made with the help of a suspicious-sounding American private underwriter, the Reason Foundation. The real Enlightenment wasn't petty or intellectually shrill. But I'm sure the programme represents the views of an important minority group, even if I don't like it.

The BBC's *Television and Number Ten* is a reminder of a prelapsarian age, when leaders made out they always spoke sterling truth, for which the media were their mouthpiece, and there was nary an image-builder or camera coach in sight. The programme has rescued from oblivion a film clip in which Churchill, looking porcine, does an impatient and disgruntled camera test for this newfangled television contraption. Three decades later, his successors have been groomed to present passable soap-opera simulacra of their selves. Subject for a twenty-first-century thesis: 'Politics and Television in the 1980s, A Study in Low-Level Histrionics'.

At noon next day, in a glitter of Paris light bouncing up from the barge-laden Seine, I scurry along the Quai Voltaire on my way to the Collège de France. I have come to Paris to attend the programme committee of LA SEPT: Société d'Edition de Programmes de Télévision. It was started up in the closing days of France's socialist government in March, to provide initially a French, and subsequently a European, cultural television service. Its first director was a political nominee, Bernard Faivre d'Arcier, counsellor to Prime Minister Fabius. In the purges and upheavals of the Chirac regime he has been ousted; a new chairman, the medieval historian Georges Duby, has been installed and a programme committee set up, which includes Pierre Boulez, the director of the Museum of Modern Art at the Pompidou Centre, Giscard d'Estaing's former minister of culture, and a batch of the great and the good from French culture, science and *l'audiovisuel*.

Over lunch, in a deeply traditional restaurant near the Sorbonne, filled with distinguished-looking *recteurs*, *doyens* and *docteurs-ès-lettres*, specific projects are discussed. To film or not to film the Comédie Française *Bérénice*? *Pelléas et Mélisande* by the Opéra de Lyon? Should the first monthly show of LA SEPT on FR3 be a celebration of ten years of the Centre Pompidou and what it has meant to French and European culture?

I sit next to Boulez and remark the inscrutable, smiling precision of his voice and gestures. We talk about mutual friends: Harry Birtwistle, who composed the electronics for *The Mask of Orpheus* at Boulez's electronic studio, IRCAM; Nicholas Snowman, who used to administer the place and is now in charge of London's South Bank concert halls. 'Nicholas is getting a long way on energy and charm,' says Boulez, 'but he doesn't have enough money, and without money you cannot persuade the British orchestras to cooperate in an overall artistic plan.'

I walk across to the press conference with Boulez. It's in the main lecture hall of the Collège de France. 'It's here I give my courses,' says Boulez. What are you teaching this year, I ask. 'The Structure and the Moment,' he says. To be a student again, devouring the lucidity of a French master . . . The place is packed with journalists. What will this new bunch unveil, they must be thinking. They've had to endure so many manifestos and promises and statements of faith about the future of French television this year. That evening Orna and I go to see Roger Planchon's production of Molière's *L'Avare*. Planchon, one of Europe's greatest stage directors, has been a huge influence on me. The year after university which I spent in his theatre as observer, walk-on, bit-part actor, was an apprenticeship in drama, sexuality, good food (when I could afford it), politics (it was the vicious final year of the Algerian war), French everyday life outside Paris, the discovery of a supplementary self you acquire when you get to speak a foreign language well. It also gave me lessons in culture which have been touchstones ever since: the importance of the classics and the dangers of swamping them in the connoisseurship of an elite, the equal importance of finding a contemporary language, how all the traditional arts have to take account of the cinema and television, how being an outsider – an Ardèche peasant, in Planchon's case – may be a passport to understanding things that mainstream people will never know.

Now, twenty-five years later, Planchon tackles a Molière play for the fifth time. *L'Avare* is traditionally the portrait of a monster obsessed with money to the exclusion of all human sentiment and sympathy. I recognise the trademarks which make Planchon such a dynamic director: a pleni-tude, verging on plethora, of stage imagery and event; the brio with which phalanxes of actors hurtle on and off, as if the stage were a corrida of energy; baroque extravagance on a classical structure; socio-economic demystification of lazy theatrical convention; violence, irony, tenderness, humour. I'm torn between feeling that the production swamps Molière in an epidemic of invention and restlessness, and succumbing to its sheer force and fullness: the intricate depiction of a day in the life of a rich merchant's household, the sculptural strangeness of the scenic constructions and props, the irresistible drollery of the film actor Michel Serrault as Harpagon, a cross between Frankie Howerd and Michael Hordern. Planchon stages the unlikely coincidences and machinations of the last act as if they were a fantastic dream, a carnival of wishes against a world run by wealth and power.

Next morning another magus of the theatre arrives. Peter Brook drives Sophie Balhetchet and me out to Sèvres, to view highlights of the video record of the *Mahabharata* he and a French vidéaste have made. An urgent reason for this Paris trip is to finalise and budget the television version of the *Mahabharata*, and I have asked Sophie, an efficient and active independent producer, to do a budget and feasibility report for me.

We arrive in Sèvres, where Jean-Claude Lubtchansky, the vidéaste who taped the *Mahabharata*, lives and has his edit suite, in a house with an unruly garden. For Sophie's benefit, Peter summarises the stages we've passed through before arriving at this solution. 'After the show opened at Avignon, Michael sent a number of possible producers to see it. Joe Strick became particularly enthusiastic. His idea was to make a nine-hour film and open it as a "road-show movie", with pre-sold tickets, in a selected number of American cities, the way he'd done with his movie of *Ulysses*. We gave him the option to raise the money and lots of Hollywood studio types came over. But the money never materialised, and I came to think that the road-show movie formula had had its day.

'Our next idea was to condense it to under three hours and make a big movie, along the lines of Kurosawa's *Ran*. David Picker, the producer who helped me with the *Marat/Sade* and who's now gone to Columbia with David Puttnam, came to see the show and went overboard. Another French producer, Lucien Duval, was equally enthused. We met in the summer, and the two of them with Michael agreed to put up the money for Jean-Claude Carrière and me to write a screenplay.

'But I was worried about two problems. Jean-Claude has always said that what is strong about our *Mahabharata* is that we do it without the elephants. Where the poem talks about thousands of elephants or chariots, we have no elephants, no bows and arrows; an actor with one wheel becomes Arjuna in his chariot. How were we going to keep this powerful stylisation in a big Kurosawa-style film? We had to preserve some theatrical dimension. And by telescoping it into less than three hours we were losing one of the strongest elements in the *Mahabharata*, its inter-lacing stories, its Arabian-Nights or Chinese-boxes quality.

'All through this period we were working with Jean-Claude Lubtchan-sky on the video of the open workshops we gave at the Bouffes du Nord earlier this year, and of performances of the *Mahabharata* in our theatre. As Jean-Claude put these together with me, we began to see that the truest response to the theatrical life of the *Mahabharata* was through video. That's why our solution now is to take a tight video group along with us for the twelve weeks we will be in India in spring 1988, tape sixteen marathon performances, look at the material as we're going along, and re-shoot some episodes in locations as if they were fiction. The final edit will be a mixture of theatrical performance, documentary material of the Indian audience or aspects of the places we visit, and scenes shot as if for a feature film.'

Drawing the curtains against the bright sunlight, we look at a half-hour tape of highlights. There is the Lebanese actress binding her eyes to join her blind husband-to-be, the power of her performance amplified in close-up. There is the bow and arrow that are literal and symbolic at the same time, the mimed flight of the arrow into Bhishma's body perfectly acceptable in this convention. The very imprecision of video compared to film is an advantage here: these extracts begin to show how it could parallel the suggestiveness of the theatre.

My third reason for coming to Paris is to watch the live late talk show *Droit de Réponse* in action. Nicholas Fraser, who will produce *U.K. Late*, a live show trying to be equally argumentative, comes with me. I appeared on the show earlier this year, spluttering out my two-centime's-worth about the future of European television and the dangers of hasty privatis-ation. I thought the show, and its genially lethal host Michel Polac, terrific. It seemed a good idea to take a closer look.

Just before ten pm on Saturday night I meet Nick in the studio, which is buzzing with anticipation. This week's programme is a Revue de Presse, a confrontation of eight journalists from publications across the political spectrum. At the end of a week in which Chirac has put his foot in his mouth about the Syrians in an interview with the *Washington Times* and Reagan has admitted selling arms to Iran, both in order to bargain the release of hostages in Lebanon, there's plenty of scope for sharp-tongued debate about the hypocrisy of leaders. Soon the joint is jumping with verbal fisticuffs, flailing arms waving for attention, sarcastic one-liners, all the fun of the fair from a culture that gave us *La Cause du Peuple*, Daumier's caricatures and *Le Canard Enchaîné*. It's a circus of irreverence, presided over by the Bacchic pipe-smoking Polac; more anarchistic than *Question Time*, more intelligent than *Spitting Image*, two hours of adrenalin argument.

The adrenalin sweeps us all into the night, and we wind up in Bofinger's brasserie at the Bastille talking our heads off with Polac and his team and the journalists until 3 am. Polac tells us that the privatisation of TFI is going to happen very fast now. But he seems unperturbed; *Droit de Réponse* has very good ratings, and has come to stand in people's minds as proof that France is still a land of liberty of expression. And it's just very good, involved television.

Back in London next night: after a brief nap, a working dinner at Le Caprice so that Peter Brook, who's arrived in London to see actors for the *Mahabharata* and to help the Royal Shakespeare Company raise money to bring it here, can meet Jeremy and explain how he plans to put the show on television. Peter does his exposition. I'm sure he sees it as a kind of performance – not a show-off, but a reiteration tested anew each time for its truth and freshness. Just like a performance of one of his own productions. As he sits there with his hands clasped, his upper body motionless, his pale blue eyes sweeping the table, there doesn't seem to be any division between the way he makes his theatre and the way he lives his life.

Jeremy listens with equal stillness, interjecting the occasional sharp question: 'You will only shoot with one camera when you're in India, won't you?' He seems impressed. There's talk about the Royal Opera House, whose future concerns Jeremy, a member of its board. Peter thinks that what's been called the 'schizoid' solution – part of the season with international stars flying in, the rest with a home team of good British singers in coherent, properly rehearsed productions – is the best. Then I encourage him to explain to Jeremy his other project, a feature film. This is a mistake, too much for one evening. Jeremy displays signs of restlessness – fingers drumming, gaze straying over other famous faces in the restaurant. Why must I always try to cram too much in?

Brook monopolises much of my Monday in the office. I show him tapes of programmes with some relevance to a television version of the *Mahabharata* – *The Mysteries*, *The Possessed*, *A TV Dante*, *Born in the RSA*. He goes off to lunch with the RSC and two Bombay millionaires, the last

potential sponsors for the London visit of the show. When he comes back
with Bill Wilkinson, the RSC's finance director, it's clear that this last hope
has failed. The millionaires, in their Carlton House Terrace apartment,
treated Brook like some upstart film producer looking for backing. They
gave him lessons in the *Mahabharata*, said that the thing they would be
interested in would be a kind of *Dallas*-version of the epic, a lifelong
serial with endless episodes, and a rich source of profit in home video
sales. Now London won't see the show until autumn 1988, after Zurich,
Los Angeles, New York, Perth, Adelaide, Calcutta, Benares and our
filming. Secretly, I think Peter might be a bit relieved: he'll be able to
put back the start of rehearsals by a month. But if it had gone the other
way, he would have accepted it with equanimity.

Next day, my birthday, I'm in at 8.15 to catch up on the mail, and then
to see Jeremy with Colin Leventhal about the Callas film. The situation
is complex. Tony Palmer's Shostakovich film is part of a four-film
package for which he is on the point of securing finance from a Swiss
bank. The other films include a film biography of Maria Callas for *The
South Bank Show*. The Swiss bank's finance enables us to contribute only
half the budget of the Shostakovich film, which will cost about a million
pounds. The bank expects to get its investment back from sales of
the other programmes on the basis of a revenue forecast. The only
likely-looking 'property' in the portfolio is the Callas film.

But Jeremy has commissioned a treatment of another Callas film for
us, from a young film-maker and a Callas groupie. I have said it could
endanger the financing, put Shostakovich into jeopardy, and throw Tony
Palmer into a fit of depression at the worst possible moment. Gillian
Widdicombe has argued equally forcefully against it. The best that Jeremy
will say is that if our Callas film puts the Shostakovich film in difficulties,
he would consider raising Channel Four's input.

There are birthday cards all over my desk when I get back to the office.
I have a breezy routine meeting with Stephen Phillips and his producer
about arts stories on *Channel Four News* between now and Christmas.
Michael Vyner, who runs the London Sinfonietta, comes in for a
friendly natter. We talk about future commissions for Opera Factory, the
Sinfonietta's forthcoming Russian tour, and Michael's need to take a break
from the treadmill and really think and look and listen afresh.

My lunchtime birthday treat, becoming an annual ritual, is to attend
the *Evening Standard* Drama Awards. In the men's loo I meet Luke
Rittner, secretary general of the Arts Council. I'd written to him asking
if there was anything we could do when the first news of a gravely

inadequate arts budget appeared, and now I ask him how bad things really are. 'I wish in some ways it could have been worse,' he says. 'The government's fudged things cleverly. It's bad, but no so bad as to force us to cut the budget of one of the big national companies. Equal misery all round, I suspect.' A gloomy conversation in, as it were, the stalls. The government and the arts world seem locked in a two-step of mutual mistrust and recrimination. Is the government philistine and dogmatic or are we simply getting it tactically wrong?

I find myself sitting next to Elaine Page, the star singer of *Cats* and now *Chess*, a chirpy person carefully nursing her food and drink because she's doing an eight-show week and already finding it hard to summon the energy to do a matinee and an evening on Saturdays after two shows on Thursdays. 'Couldn't you have contracted for your understudy to go on for the Thursday matinee?' I ask. 'I'm afraid it's me they want to see,' she says. 'When I insisted on taking one day off to finish recording an album, I was swamped with complaints and spent a fortune buying tickets for other performances for the disappointed punters.' Now that's called being a star, and knowing what it entails.

The absent arts minister Richard Luce gets a roasting in the speeches for being afraid to turn up and face his constituency. He told the *Standard* he had a previous commitment to open a building in Maastricht, Holland. My prize for best speech presenting an award goes to Patrick Barlow, who in the persona of Desmond Olivier Dingle, director of the National Theatre of Brent, conquers what must be an intimidating professional audience with a sharp script and impeccable timing. Desmond is particularly anxious to stress that the stories accusing him of making a personal fortune out of his work at the NT of B are completely unfounded: 'My trip to a remote resort in the Swiss Alps was purely in the interests of research for the next National Theatre of Brent production, a version of the Heidi myths . . .' I look forward to commissioning the scripts for his next series.

Back in my office I open the bottle of champagne that Colin gave me this morning, and share it with Jenny, Caroline and Lucinda. My cousin Danny comes in with two blokes (keyboards, bass) who are starting up a new band with him. Danny used to be lead guitar with the original Tom Robinson band when I was running the ICA in the late sixties. People used to compare his guitar-playing with Keith Richards's. Girls would come up to me and ask, 'Are you Danny Kustow's cousin??!!' Danny plays me two songs from their demo disc, moody, infectious stuff, and tells me about the mechanics of getting a record deal. It's a good way to wind up a birthday, drinking with the other member of the Kustow tribe who broke the mould of expectations and attempted a creative rather than a business or professional career. I feel for him; it's cost him a lot emotionally.

Mike Dibb's *Arena* film about Lorca, which I go to see next day at a Wardour Street preview, distils Lorca's poetry and life in a film that never loses touch with primary things: water (Andalucian fountains and streams whisper through the film), music, dancing, history, politics, sexuality, death. The film's guide, Ian Gibson, Lorca's biographer, is informed, passionate and utterly, surprisingly Irish. There are many distinctive Spanish voices, singing *cante jondo*, confiding or chanting Lorca's poetry.

Lorca quotes a friend hearing Manuel de Falla play and saying, 'All that has dark sounds has *duende*.' In the rest of Spain, this word simply means 'goblin'; in Andalucía, and for Lorca, it is the word for demonic, mysterious inspiration beyond reason or plan. 'These dark sounds,' Lorca goes on, 'are the mystery, from which we get what is real in art ... *Duende* likes the edge of things, the wound, it is drawn to where forms fuse themselves in a longing greater than their visible expressions.' Dibb makes television with *duende*.

That idea, those words, have had precise and elusive meaning for me ever since I read them as a student nearly thirty years ago. Brook, Bausch, Brodsky and Birtwistle have *duende*. Miles Davis and Caravaggio have it. Michael Dibb and Christopher Nupen and Gina Newson and the American video-maker Bill Viola are some of the television people who have it. The television they make is a television of exploration that invites you to join a journey, not a television of assertion that presses you to agree a position. Everyone recognises authentic 'dark sounds'; we all have an innate sensor for *duende*. That is why art is not for an elite.

Many of Tony Palmer's films have *duende*, though he needs to approach some personal cliff-edge to seize it. When I meet him for dinner to discuss Shostakovich and break the news that there will now be a rival Callas film, I find him already in depression. It's partly fatigue. Scarcely off the plane from Tokyo, where he's been shooting our Mitsuko Uchida film, he's flown to New York and back chasing Martin Sheen and doing a producer's job trying to hold down the money promised from WNET. Today he's just stepped off the train from Wigan, which will be the film's Russia. And tomorrow he's off to Germany, where they want him to stage an opera. Meanwhile, the deal with the Swiss bank, and the Swedish financiers they have introduced, is not in place, and he's paying for pre-production out of his own pocket.

With a mixture of jokes, outbursts and unfeigned affection, I try to lift the storm cloud. Then I have to tell Tony the news about the Callas film. He goes completely blank, doesn't immediately freak out, says he'll call from Germany tomorrow. I guess he'll be in delayed shock by the weekend, since the news may upset his financing plan for Shostakovich.

Next day includes a further instalment, at Programme Review, of the debate about whether to put out self-acknowledged gay programmes; viewing a series we have pre-purchased from Austrian television which takes as arresting a view of Schubert as *Amadeus* did of Mozart; discussing with an American producer a programme of unknown Kurt Weill sung by Teresa Stratas; going down the road to see former colleague Carol Haslam at Superchannel, where she's programme director, and being reminded of early Channel Four days, kit-of-parts offices seemingly just assembled, racks of circuitry still being installed, proof copies of the initial schedule, starting transmission in January. Carol talks, in the jargon of supra-national broadcasting, about the satellite's 'footprint'; I'm feeling more than a bit crunched today by television's seven-league boots. I am a camera, said Isherwood. For me, it's more a case of I am a satellite dish, bombarded by hordes of scrambled unregulated superimposed signals.

I topple into bed early, my brain wakes me at six, I'm in the office by 7.15, drafting a memo about the situation of LA SEPT. By nine am I'm looking at a VHS tape of the re-edited *Born in the RSA* and weeping buckets. It got me first time round when the black actor says, 'Fuck you fuck you fuck you for what you've done to the children. And fuck you fuck you fuck you for what you've done to me,' and then the singing, that full-throated harmony of struggle, starts up. And it gets me again this time round; more, because the images of the endings are tighter, better organised, less theatrical. *Duende*, perhaps. I'm paper-thin with tiredness and eventfulness at the end of this week.

I ring Tom and tell him I'm on my way. I've slotted in a portrait session this morning, even though it's Friday. It's quiet at Tom's. Drawings are strewn around of Jeremy King, who runs the Caprice, Tom's next sitter. Above my head, Tom has painted in the Greek comedy mask, standard Beaux-Arts model, which he bought in Paris, took with him to Baghdad, and has had marble-painted in Camberwell. It beams down, benign and abstract, a counterpoint to my melancholy. It lifts the picture. 'Everything in this picture is a fake,' says Tom as he starts working. 'Including the sitter?' I say. 'I mean the mask's a fake, my copy of Titian's picture behind you is a fake. Well not really. The mask is a real tool for teaching art, and a line back to antiquity. And my version of Titian is an interpretation; I've distorted the proportions a lot.' 'The work of art in the age of handmade reproduction?' I suggest.

Tom seems happy, as if a chess game were coming out well. 'I'm not doing a lot today,' he says, 'but I know what I'm looking for. You have to be on duty with a picture.' I ask him whether he's past the point of fucking the whole thing up. 'There's no chance of that now. The head's settled. It could still go wrong, and go right again, but it's found.'

At about which point the first accident in all our sittings happens. Tom smudges my portrait's forehead with some purple he hadn't realised he had on his hand. He rapidly wipes it off with a turps-stained tissue. A few minutes later, it happens again.

Two days later, I wake up with purple blotches on my forehead. Either Dorian Gray lives, or I really am getting agitated about my life and work.

WEEK 48 *November 24–30*

The week begins in the cutting room, looking at an assembly of Andrew Snell's Harrison Birtwistle film. Harry's face alters enormously: sometimes a red-haired baby, sometimes like ancient granite. When he goes back to his home outside Accrington – 'Arcady invaded by a power station' – he's at his most boyish, and you get some sense of the determined, nature-entranced shape-maker he was to become. Of his loneliness as a child, too.

At this stage, Andrew's film is struggling to find its pitch. It has wonderful observational documentary of Harry conducting the Grimethorpe Colliery Band; good talk from conductor Elgar Howarth and Harry himself, talking to Nigel Osborne; performance, of chamber pieces and of *The Mask of Orpheus*; landscape, rehearsal, analysis, analogies. My usefulness now to Andrew and his editor is to be both close and detached; to open up with them an image of an eventual film and see if it makes sense. The way the first half hour looks begins to suggest to me a film which reflects Harry's compositional processes in its own form. As always, it's important that it makes its own rules clear to the viewer in the opening moments, especially if it's trying to go beyond the known forms of the portrait or the description of how something is made.

The way people talk at this stage in the cutting room – the way I do, anyway – always sounds over the top. Metaphors sprout, trying to be evocative: this morning I talk about references to painting or landscape invading sequences 'like swarms of bees'. Actors used to frown in puzzlement when I used images like that in rehearsal. It seems to work better in the cutting room. 'I think you should be making a film that is musical, and happens to use documentary material among its elements,' I say to Andrew. It could be a film that embodies the important aesthetic principles in Harry's music, which have nothing to do with tonality or romantic expressiveness, but are as organic as geological forms, as impersonal as Aeschylus.

Walking back to the office, I stop off at Nigel Greenwood's gallery to look at Jeffrey Camp's new paintings. Couples arched in voluptuousness float above the Thames and City of London skyline, the Grand Canal and St Mark's. They levitate like Chagall figures, but they are sexy as wiry fashion models. And the paint, which whirls and whorls, is more Turner than Chagall. Then there are solitary male nudes approaching precipitous cliff-edges. The ecstasy and the anxiety in these pictures – did they grow from personal experience? There's something cool, watchful about their abandonment.

There's a copy of a letter from Tom Phillips to Jeremy when I get back, explaining that *A TV Dante* is alive and kicking, indeed has benefited from its delays and detours, and asking Jeremy to meet him and Peter Greenaway. I urged Tom to write this letter. Peter says that he has six months free from autumn 1987, after his next feature, and wants to crack on with their Dante. Having hurt Tom by his apparent lack of interest while making *Belly of an Architect*, he's now enthused him again. But it's very late in the day to claw back proper money into next year's draft budget, which our finance director tells me is 7 million pounds too big. Will Jeremy be swayed by Tom's seductively handwritten plea?

I get a message to drop in to see Jeremy at the end of the day to discuss Michael Tippett's new opera. We will be meeting Tippett's representatives later this week, with the director of Welsh National Opera, to try to wrest it from the BBC and Glyndebourne.

First I run a meeting between the producers, writer and script editor of *The Impressionists*, and a possible director of the series. Julian Bond has written scripts for an eight-episode series, fed by the research and comments of a batch of bright young art historians. Now we need a second draft to tighten the storytelling, make Cézanne and Monet more prominent, and open up the form so that it moves as far as possible from the Hollywood bio-pic. Julian needs to work on the rewrite with a director who has a vision of the style and convention of the ultimate film – but who also has the logistical ability to manage the long shoot which a series, as opposed to a feature, requires. We talk for an hour with one director whose last feature film has visual distinction and a sense of history, who has worked with contemporary artists, and who is interested in nineteenth-century France.

It all starts to come alive again as we talk. I don't know whether this director, of a number we are seeing, will be the right one. What I do know is that if *The Impressionists* is to go ahead – and it would be the most expensive single programme I've ever done – some alchemy between the vision of Monet or Cézanne and the style of shooting, editing and storytelling needs to happen.

When I go down to Jeremy, he's sitting with Justin Dukes, our managing director. Doubtless they're talking about tonight's board dinner and tomorrow's board meeting, which will discuss the report from Professor Alan Budd of the London Business School about whether Channel Four should break the ITV connection and sell its own advertising. Justin leaves when I arrive. Jeremy, with a half-smile, hands me back a copy of my memo about LA SEPT with his marginal comments: 'Good luck. 1) Don't get involved with projects your budget can't afford. 2) Don't offer projects to more than one European broadcaster at once. 3) Do spend some time in your office.'

I ask him whether there's anything else he wants to talk about. He says no. I talk about my new assistant, Annette Morreau, and how she will work with my opera and jazz consultants. He thumps the couch. 'It's all such a mess,' he says. 'You've wound up with three people working to you with overlapping expertise in music. That's what happens when people are chosen for a job description and not for themselves. We're starting to get a whole layer of people like that among the assistants.'

Then he immediately thinks of three examples of commissioning editors whose assistants are not ordinary or run-of-the-mill. But he's still angry. 'The Channel's getting too cosy,' he growls. 'I'm sitting through all these sodding interviews for a religious commissioning editor. Endless nice vicars. We need a shake-up. Anyway, I'm not going to be here after the end of 1988. And nor are you after 1989.'

I'm shaken by his vehemence. I argue my corner, but he doesn't take the cue. There's a glowering silence between us. We gaze at each other. I get up, we exchange mutters, I go.

I drive as fast as I can to Hampstead, and arrive half an hour late for a drink with Margaret Gardiner in Downshire Hill. I'm feeling numb. Suppressing feelings of panic at paternal disapproval, I suppose. I haven't felt these symptoms since the late sixties, when I was running the ICA and continually feeling I was defying daddy.

I lived in Downshire Hill then, in the garden flat of Fred Uhlmann, a German painter who had come to Britain as a refugee and married Lady Diana Croft, rebellious daughter of an aristocratic family with a castle named after them near Hereford. And it was then that I got to know my neighbour Margaret Gardiner, a striking, determined woman who wore bold jewellery and had works by Ben Nicholson, Barbara Hepworth and Naum Gabo in her front room. She contacted me to help her with names for a series of full-page advertisements opposing the Vietnam war. This must have been when I was working with Peter Brook on US, the theatre-piece about the British, the Americans and Vietnam. Margaret often reminded me of Peter Brook: a slight drawl in the voice, and a natural authority.

She opens the door, looking as I remember her, elegant, smiling, apple-cheeked, now over eighty. She's telephoned me several times wanting to meet. We swap chatter about the intervening fifteen years. Her front room is much as it was, the Nicholson still above the mantelpiece, with its astringent edges and smooth, flat greys. And Margaret still strikes me as an exemplar of the intellectual and political aristocracy of the thirties, a tradition I felt I was entering, continuing and altering when I ran the ICA and met Herbert Read and Roland Penrose.

Margaret wants my help. Ten years ago she gave her personal collection of abstract paintings and constructivist sculpture to the Orkneys, where she has a cottage. She wanted the people of the islands to be able to see works of art. She persuaded, enticed and ensured that there would be a fine building for the collection – the Pier Gallery at Stromness, with a back wall looking out over the sea – and enough money for its running costs, through limited grants from the council and the Scottish Arts Council, and a sponsorship from Occidental Petroleum. Now Occidental, who must be feeling that there's a limit to the conscience money they must pay for their oilrigs, are to end their funding, and the Pier Gallery may have to close. A film about it, says Margaret, would be interesting in itself and helpful to its future. I'll think about it, I say.

Lunch next day with Melvyn Bragg, our best and most open since I started this job. I've lost the chip on my own shoulder about him, the competitiveness. We talk to each other today as what we both are: outsiders – he a Northerner, me a Jew – together at the same Oxford college. We talk about the brass tacks of our jobs and lives with no bullshit, about holding on to a sense of self, about writing and doing, about family, about how things we once thought self-evident have been overtaken. Just like Justice Shallow and Silence . . .

We talk about Dennis Potter, another of our contemporaries at Oxford, whose series *The Singing Detective* is blazing out of the BBC each Sunday night. 'I had a very weird feeling watching it last week,' says Melvyn, 'that he was doing a final farewell to all the aspects of his life, a summary before the end. And that once the series was finished, he wouldn't last much longer himself.' The strange thing, I tell him, is that when we were watching it, Orna said she was afraid he'd die within a year. It has all these reverberations because everyone knows now that Dennis Potter suffers from the same excruciating skin disease as his hero. Another example of television blurring the borders of fiction and reality, the screen character and the real self.

There is one scene in a working men's club in which Potter's protagonist is attacked for betraying his father. It reminds Melvyn of a television programme featuring the young Dennis Potter when we were all undergraduates. Full of early-sixties fire and brimstone, author of a Jimmy Porter-ish book about sick Britain, *The Glittering Coffin*, and chairman of the university Labour Club, he had taken his father to pieces in front of the camera. 'Everyone from our sort of background at Oxford needed to struggle with his own father,' says Melvyn, 'but not all of us needed to do it in public. Maybe he's making amends for it still.' *The Singing Detective*: a stocktaking and a leavetaking.

Udi Eichler is waiting when I get back, slimmer, browner and calmer after a late holiday than in the summer when I last saw him. Then he was distressed about the uncertainty of future work, tetchy at me and at Channel Four for not bridging the gap between this series of *Voices* and the next, and worried about upheavals in his personal life. From Spain he had written me an epic letter of accusation, furious and warm at the same time. I had replied at inevitably lesser length, sending him Susan Sontag's story about what we do when we write letters to the distant beloved. Now we talk more easily, about the Catholic peasant roots he rediscovered in Spain, about the next *Voices*, which he wants to be a sustained investigation of a single person's concerns and obsessions, someone like Carlos Fuentes or the philosopher John Searle.

Udi is a very special person in television, a philosopher/producer. This year he became an even more special person, a philosopher/psychiatrist/producer; he passed his exams, and is now qualified to put up a brass plate and treat patients. We joke about it as we finish. 'You could really make a lot of money treating television people, Udi,' I say. 'You could be the only psychiatrist who advertises in *Broadcast*. I can just see the ad: "Udi Eichler, Shrink To The Industry! Special Rates For Independents! Treat All That Aggravation For One Per Cent Of Your Production Fee!"' As he leaves, handing out sweet fruit from his orange grove in Spain, he says that it's taken him four years to work through the consequences, professional and personal, of leaving Thames to become an independent, 'and I don't think it could be done any quicker'.

Lunch next day with Marina Warner and Gina Newson. They have delivered their script for *The Surreal Muse*, the film which will combine fiction and documentary to explore what men do to talented women they elect as mythical muses. Their script tells the story of a director preparing such a film, based on the life of Leonora Carrington and Max Ernst, and his relationship with three women: his disenchanted wife, his clued-up, moderately feminist screenwriter, and the young woman he elects as the object of his creative and real-life *amour fou*. Invading the fiction will be the real presence of Leonora Carrington, now a feisty seventy-year-old living in New York. Her impact on the young woman – who, like her, is a painter – changes the course of events. The past transforms the present.

Sitting in Heal's restaurant (which could well be a location for the film, so gracefully yuppie and Californian it is), I talk it through with Gina and Marina. It's still carrying too many birthstrings of research and reference, I say. And I don't quite believe in the producer of the film within the film. And the time scheme doesn't squeeze out everything it might from the characters. Perhaps I'm being too quickly critical; my time-sense is a bit jangled this week. I apologise for going too fast. 'All a writer wants to hear is praise,' says Marina. But Gina is listening, interpreting my imprecision. Gradually, we sort out what needs doing.

That evening, to see Derek Jacobi in Hugh Whitemore's play about Alan Turing, *Breaking the Code*. Turing, a mathematical genius who was an inspired cryptographer during the war, wrote a landmark paper in which he compared symbolic logic to the operation of a machine and paved the way for computers. He was a homosexual, harassed by the police; he committed suicide in 1954. Jacobi makes Turing boyish, restless, wrenched by a stammer as if his quicksilver intelligence were impatient with the flesh. He has two long and complex speeches about mathematics where you can almost touch the breath of thinking. His defencelessness in love or desire is almost intolerably naked.

Next day Brian Macmaster, director of Welsh National Opera, arrives for the Tippett opera meeting. Brian is small, wiry, soft-spoken, chain-smoking. A ferocious musical strategist, he has made Cardiff the junction point of burgeoning native musical talent and the Continental school of fiercely imagistic staging.

Gillian Widdicombe joins us, and we go down to Jeremy's office to meet Tippett's agent and musical adviser. We have to wait a few minutes: he and Justin are closeted with our chairman. Yesterday's board meeting discussing whether we should sell our own advertising was apparently inconclusive and extremely acrimonious. Rumour has it that the board lined up against the chairman, which would be its first serious internal split.

When Jeremy appears, however, he is avuncular and convivial. He got back from the Channel Four festival in Berlin earlier in the day, and is full of it. 'Am I Lenin or am I Trotsky?' he asks gleefully, referring to a *Financial Times* clipping which compared him to Trotsky, keeping the Channel in a state of permanent revolution. They take these metaphors seriously in West Berlin. 'I did an interview,' he continues, 'and they sat me on this white couch and there was a red motorcyclist's helmet in the studio, so I took it and placed it beside me all the way through. The interviewer was forced to ask me what it meant. I said the helmet was to stop me being mugged by independents, and the visor was to shield people from television's lethal rays. Catch the Intendant of a German television station talking like that!'

We then proceed to make our pitch to Tippett's agent and adviser. The Channel is prepared to put up almost half the commissioning fee, WNO a third, and Brian has been paging the opera houses of Europe and America for additional commitments. We put forward our ideas about the stage director, about London performances, and about how to bring the work to television. We underline our commitment to Tippett's work: *The Knot Garden* last year, *King Priam* this week, a full-scale film of *The Midsummer Marriage* next year. Tippett's agent chews his fingernails and listens impassively. He's heard a similar offer from the BBC.

Next morning I leave for Berlin, to present a day of our arts programmes to conclude the Channel Four festival at the Akademie der Künste. I haven't been to Berlin since 1973, when I was stuck at a theatre conference in East Berlin the day the Yom Kippur war broke out. Alexanderplatz was full of electronic billboards announcing the imminent arrival of the Egyptian army in Jerusalem, where they would doubtless slaughter my relatives. That had been my second trip to Berlin. The first was almost as traumatic. In 1961, a few months after the Wall went up, I came to

the city as a member of Planchon's theatre company, playing in West
Berlin. Like all theatre buffs at the time I spent as much time as I could
in East Berlin to drink deep at Brecht's Berliner Ensemble. On my last
night, I got lost in East Berlin at 2 am. All the Le Carré props were
there: faded flags and banners of Walter Ulbricht, bombsite rubble in
dark deserted streets, the rumble of the S-Bahn, the imagined tread of
steel-shod boots following me. I never imagined I'd be so glad to see the
garish neon of the Kurfürstendamm again.

We drive in to the Kempinski hotel, past the Goethe Pub and the Kant
Kasino, grand nineteenth-century buildings and broad boulevards, a
fairground near the Zoogarten, abstract paintings hanging behind gleaming Mercedes in the car salesrooms. Berlin may be sliced in half, but it
has the lineaments of Germany's only true metropolis.

I do my interview for a film which Kraft Wetzel, the festival organiser,
is making about Channel Four, then walk back to the hotel with him.
Moustached, garrulous, speaking American English, he is dead keen and
has no irony at all. But such young men can change things, and Kraft
has a mission to bring the Channel Four gospel to Germany.

We go into a bookshop by the Technical University, and I buy books
of old photographs of Berlin. One about the Berlin barrel-organ, the
street instrument that Kurt Weill immortalised in Mack the Knife's
cynical ballad. One photograph from 1928, the year of *The Threepenny
Opera*, shows an organ-grinder turning the handle of an ornamented
instrument strapped to a little cart. Two stilt-dancers in Bavarian folk
costume pose next to it. The man has leather braces, ankle socks and a
Hitler moustache.

Next morning I have breakfast with Renee Goddard. She's a native
Berliner who came to England as a fourteen-year-old refugee. Her
Bloomsbury polish is grafted on to a Berlin scepticism and a refugee
anxiety. This is the first time I've seen her on home ground. As we drive
through the Tiergarten to the Akademie der Künste for my first session,
she says, 'I remember coming back here after the war and seeing all the
elm trees gone. People had burned them to stay alive in 1945.'

The Akademie der Künste is a well-appointed arts centre in Berlin's
park. At noon on a Saturday, the kind of thoughtful bohemians you might
see at the ICA are roaming the lobbies. Introduced by Kraft Wetzel, I
tell them how I came to Channel Four, how the arts have been treated
on British television, and the guiding principles of my work, with a nod
in the direction of Walter Benjamin, whose *Berlin Childhood* memoir is
one of my source-texts about this city.

The projection of our programmes begins, and I'm free until the final evening. I walk through the Tiergarten to the Nationalgalerie, one of Mies van der Rohe's modernist landmarks. It reminds me of the American embassy in Grosvenor Square. The permanent collection is in the safest place, the basement. There's a big Joseph Beuys installation, a scatter of blackboards and a hanging walking stick, after-traces of Beuys's one-man anti-university. SHOW YOUR WOUND says the chalk text on one of the blackboards. Nearby are the Max Beckmanns, raw paint capturing nightclub truths from Weimar Germany: a woman giving birth backstage in a circus, a nightclub singer backed by a male chorus like trussed chickens, suspended by their feet. Strident unquiet, which the intervening years have not softened.

After a siesta, I go down to the bar to meet Thomas Brasch with Renee. He is a film-maker, playwright and novelist, author of a bestselling book called *Sons Die Before Their Fathers*. His father was one of the Germans in exile Renee knew when she was interned as an enemy alien during the war. Brasch senior, a communist, was elected leader of the Free German Youth in Exile. Brasch junior was born in Hampstead, two years before the end of the war. Immediately it finished his father took them all back to East Germany where he became Youth Minister, then Minister of Culture and a member of the Party Central Committee.

Thomas, who now sits opposite me getting through double Scotches at a fair rate, grew up as the son of a member of the political establishment of the Deutsche Demokratik Republik. In 1968 he was arrested and imprisoned for handing out leaflets protesting against the Russian invasion of Czechoslovakia. After his release he came to live in West Berlin with his girlfriend, formerly a leading actress of the Berliner Ensemble. It was an explosion of freedom for them, says Renee; they lived in a commune, plunged into West Berlin Bohemia, unfettered talk, art, drugs, drink, disaffection. He's been in the West ten years, is recognised as one of the truthtellers about the German experience.

He is my age, dark, unshaven, with something about him of a reluctant child dragged out to meet a boring uncle. He starts to talk sparingly in reply to my questions. It turns out he is the model for the hero of the Trevor Griffiths–Ken Loach film *Fatherland*, which tells the story of an East German coming to the West. He met Trevor at a film festival, told him his life story, and was amazed to receive the screenplay a few months later. 'I said to him, every writer has a right to use their own life, you must change this.' So Griffiths changed the protagonist from a writer to a pop singer. 'I did not like the ending of this film, where the singer has to choose between a profitable commercial engagement and singing at a rally for peace. He chooses the peace rally, of course; it is too –' and he raises a clenched fist in the air.

I ask him what he writes about. 'The impossibility of the private life. The political and the erotic. It is in bed you see that there is no more possibility of a personal life with meaning. When I came to West Berlin I looked at all these women, perfectly dressed and made up. If my relationship with my girlfriend Katerina finished, I thought, could I imagine making love to one of these women? I could not. There is no real self there, it is all a . . . you say, masquerade?' He smiles, drinks more whisky, says he's learned a lot about the West from whores, puts prostitutes' stories into his play. He talks with a burned-out restlessness, a man displaced by history, bombarded from both sides of the divide, determined to root out how it got this way.

He has a programme proposal to put to Channel Four. Next year is the 750th anniversary of the founding of Berlin. Already the city is being spruced up, an arts festival prepared, the machinery of official commemoration trundled into place. Not surprisingly, Thomas has a completely different kind of response in mind. 'I want to make six "Letters From Berlin", documentary portraits of people and places I know. The first would be about a seventy-year-old man who's been a policeman all his life. From the Spartakists in 1919 to the rioters in 1968, he's only had one watchword: law and order. I'd shoot him in the Museum of Egyptology, where he works now as a guardian two days a week. Then there's the man who used to run the canteen in the theatre of Gustav Gründgens – the man whose story was told in the novel and film *Mephisto*. Then a hotel doorman, great friend of Fellini, has a big collection of Fellini's drawings. Berlin's oldest department store, a description of a place where nothing but buying and selling has happened for 150 years. An East German waitress in a place where lots of West Berliners go across to eat. An old drug dealer from the twenties. And the British boy who, together with a Russian soldier, is guarding Rudolf Hess in Spandau, and doesn't begin to understand the whole thing.'

Next morning, after the final session at the Akademie which left me feeling that Germany was defenceless against the forthcoming satellite TV blitz, I wake up out of a nightmare, something to do with stealing a book, this book. They were putting handcuffs on me. Policemen were going through my drawers, seeing what books I set for my Harvard courses. 'Don't plant anything on me,' I said. A junior policeman whispered that I'd be able to make a huge insurance claim for wrongful arrest.

WEEK 49 *December 1–5*

When I get in, I'm told that Jeremy has gone through the roof because one of the programmes I've offered for scheduling in week 2, immediately after Christmas, won't be back from the labs in time; they're closing for a fortnight over Christmas. Is it just my imagination, or is he scrutinising the way I work more closely these past few weeks? I ring John McGrath – it's his programme of Gaelic songs and stories, *There is a Happy Land* – and find out there's no way he can meet the transmission date. Our scheduler has an alternative slot two weeks later, which will work. I write an explanatory note to Jeremy. I expect a sharp marginal scribble back.

Lunch with Naomi Sargant, our Senior Commissioning Editor, Education, is to some degree an exchange of lamentations. I tell her about the difficulties I've felt with Jeremy over the past few weeks; she tells me her saga of the College of the Air. This project, funded by the Manpower Services Commission and industry, will aim to use television and direct teaching to provide further education more linked with vocation and work than the Open University. Naomi was persuaded to apply for the top job, and was interviewed three weeks ago. As a former pro-vice-chancellor of the Open University, she has good educational credentials. As commissioning editor of a range of lively and accessible education programmes on the Channel she has a strong television track record.

The controller of BBC Education got the job. Naomi thinks she was set up. Telling me the story, tears come to her eyes. But tears come very easily to Naomi, something which wrongfooted me at first, until I came to see past the tears to the tough and unfashionable truths she often stresses. In debate she's one of the strongest characters in the Channel, and now that she doesn't think of me as an opponent I can even make her laugh. Occasionally at her own tendency to see all the cards stacked against her.

At the end of the day I sit down with Patrick Barlow, alias Desmond Olivier Dingle, the founder and leader of the National Theatre of Brent. Patrick has come in to discuss a number of possible programmes the NT of B might do for us next year. My favourite is his wheeze about an entire evening of programmes from NT of B Television, their plucky underfunded versions of all our innovations and alternatives, from *Diverse Reports* and *Brookside* to *Eleventh Hour* and video art. By next Christmas, when we'd hope to do it, it will be time we exposed our central beliefs – always at risk of becoming orthodoxies – to their amiable subversion.

Next day Richard Francis explains the Tate Gallery North, of which he's the new director. It opens next spring in an imposing Victorian warehouse in Liverpool's Albert Docks, a monumental brick edifice above a sheet of still water, tucked between the Maritime Museum and Granada's just-completed newsroom which is equipped with the latest satellite technology. Richard starts to reel off the exhibitions which he's planning, in the hope that we'll make programmes around them. I interrupt him. 'Richard, instead of making films about other art, why don't we take advantage of your environment and commission new works from artists specifically for TV? You've got the gallery itself, a calm staging-post for art and artists; you've got the enclosed dock, a wonderful space for performance and big images; and you've got Granada's hardware, technology and world-access on your doorstep. Let's do something together that is first-degree art for the television age, not just a report or a reflection.' Richard goes away enthused. The juices still seem to be working.

David Lodge and Colin MacCabe come in to discuss their programme on literature and linguistics. Colin, who has breathless enthusiasms, rang up last summer to sell me 'an unmissable idea'. Twenty years ago, he said, there had been a landmark conference on literature and linguistics which had firmly put semiotics and structuralism on to the map of literary studies. Now at the University of Strathclyde, where Colin was teaching until he came to the British Film Institute, he and colleagues had organised another international conference to re-examine the territory two decades later. Jacques Derrida, Raymond Williams, David Lodge, literary Marxists and flocks of academic honchos from American universities would be there. It would, said Colin, be definitive. Would Channel Four like to televise it? Oh by the way, said Colin, it would be happening in three weeks' time.

After I'd huffed and puffed and shouted at Colin about lack of notice for something which must have been at least a year in the pipeline, we pulled our socks up and got the entire weekend videotaped, asking David Lodge to be an occasionally quizzical observer and guide to the proceedings. I have seen a tape of highlights of speeches, interviews and encounters which is promising. Now Colin has brought David in to discuss adding a new layer to the programme. It's clear that David, who has written a draft script drawing both on his knowledge of linguistics and on his comic view of academic gatherings, is not won round by Colin's idea.

Colin feels that the conference – and the last-minute absence of some participants – excluded certain elements of the subject. He wants to surround the documentary account of the Strathclyde event with a pastiche *Right to Reply* programme. David feels that this is unnecessarily subverting his role as presenter and raisonneur. And the *Right to Reply* team are dubious about lending their studio and presenter.

I sympathise with Colin's wish to make the programme comprehensive, and contesting the programme's own basis seems in the spirit of the movement of ideas which has displaced literary pantheons and announced the death of the author. But there's something too prankish about the idea as it stands. And there are other ways of footnoting and offering alternative readings. I show them *A TV Dante*, with its footnotes and screentexts. It exerts its usual spell, and starts Colin thinking afresh about the form of the programme. David, who is quieter and more reflective than the pyrotechnic and ebullient MacCabe – Stan Laurel to Colin's Ollie – seems happier by the end.

Ronald Fraser follows in, to talk about 1968. He's just finished his book of oral history about that year and its meanings, focusing on the student generation in Western Europe, Britain and the USA. I tell him about our ideas for marking the twentieth anniversary, and ask him if he has an overview of what happened. 'To understand 1968 you have to begin in the fifties. What the students of '68 did was to open up a new political space. As it was gradually stifled, at different rates in different countries, they moved into the terrorism of the early seventies.' We talk about the parallel cultural trajectory, from the sensuous and gestural utopianism of the sixties to the seventies' retreat into theory, from a generosity that was often naive to a guarded purity on the left and a vengeful revisionism on the right. Will Humpty Dumpty's egg ever be put together again?

The day ends with an abrupt gear-shift from these philosophical and historical considerations to some urgent firefighting about finance. The Swiss bank which told Tony Palmer it would finance Shostakovich and three other films has got cold feet. This has left Tony, who forged ahead with the filming of one and pre-production of another, out of pocket to the tune, he says, of over £150,000. Will Channel Four advance this sum until the various deals and pre-sales of the films are in place, he is asking. It's too risky for us to do so, but we are looking for other ways to help him out. It's at times like this that Tony needs the full-time producer I haven't been able to find him. If the pressure continues on him like this, what state will he be in when he comes to the Shostakovich shooting?

Next day, my last before leaving for a week in New York, is stuffed to bursting. Two cutting room visits: first, to John McGrath's *There is a*

Happy Land, which is fresh and moving, now has some breathtaking scenery to complement its performances, and only needs fewer lingering shots of misty-eyed Highland audience members to make it as vivid as it should be. John also tells me he's nearly finished Annie Cohen-Solal's biography of Sartre and would like a commission next year to script a six-part series on his life and work.

I take a taxi from Soho to Islington, and from film to video, to look at *Dancelines* in a tiny edit suite near Sadler's Wells. Siobhan Davies is with Terry Braun and Peter Mumford, agonising over one of her pieces. But she and we know that she's always in agony at this stage. The piece needs no agonising, in my view. Slow tracking shots around dancers moving within a structure of walls. Some of the walls have apertures through which there are glimpses of birds sweeping over water, close-up faces, a bulletin-board of torn press photos, diagrams for the work being danced. The music is cellos and unaccompanied voices. I see something happening in it about couples and observers, and even more, about boundaries between the stationary and the moving, inanimate material and the body. My perceptions seem to help, though I feel like I'm busking.

Two crises at the end of the day. David Thomas and Nigel Wattis, who have been busy making the *Great Writers* series, come in and tell me that LWT has clamped down on their use of crews and resources, which they'd been pushing to the limit, getting fourteen minutes of drama in the can each day. Unless a further £100,000 can be found, the remaining programmes in the series will have to be made on a tighter rein. I don't have it, we discuss sponsorship or shortening the series. They will study the options while I'm in New York. Then the Lyric, Hammersmith phones to say that the local council want to prevent the performance of a play from South Africa because it contravenes the council's endorsement of the African National Congress cultural boycott. There's an emergency meeting tonight. I can't go, but send a message saying that the play, about two white anti-apartheid fighters in jail, one a militant and one a gradualist, is on the side of seeing clearly and should not be penalised.

I dictate, scribble, shift tapes and papers for an hour. I go home, watch television with Orna, pack. The telephone keeps ringing. Separation anxiety from programme-makers, at the end of the day. Extended lines of communication. Nothing personal.

WEEK 50 *December 6–13 New York*

This week, because of the revelations about arms sales to Iran and funds diverted to the Nicaraguan Contras, reality is billed to break through the

parade of movie simulacra and TV spectacle which the Reagan presidency
has been. Already the president's face is beginning to look like a collapsed
paper bag, his voice a sandpaper rasp. But there's every chance that one
unreality will, as in a Genet play, simply be supplanted by another.

The proceedings of the House Foreign Affairs Committee are broadcast live on PBS, introduced by an avuncular white-haired male, signifying
A Solemn Occasion. First to appear, as I sit making telephone calls in
my hotel room on a Monday morning, is Secretary of State George
Shultz. His humorous Bert Lahr face makes a pleasing counterpoint to
his donnish tutorial about the need to fight communism in Nicaragua.

At the end of his two-hour testimony, there is a rare moment when he
appears to be using television to tell his countrymen what the democratic
tug-of-war of pressure groups, lobbyists and competing interests is like
in Washington. 'It's never over. It's not like running a company or a
university. It's a seething debating society, in which people never give
up. Including me.' There's a politician giving the low-down. Predictably,
it's not included in the main news summaries of the hearings.

Next day's hearings star the ineffably emotional Colonel Oliver North,
all liquid eyes and tremolo, hailed by a Californian right-wing senator
with a rejigged version of Kipling's 'Gunga Din': 'It's Ollie this and Ollie
that/And go away you brute./But it's the saviour of his country/When
the guns begin to shoot.' Not to be outdone, a Democrat ripostes with
what he calls another Kipling quotation: 'To thine own self be true, thou
canst not then be false to any man.'

Would the level of literary quotation be any higher if we had the
American courage to broadcast British parliamentary committee proceedings live and in vision? Probably not, and I don't think we'll find out for
a long time yet. Meanwhile actors back in London are rehearsing a
ninety-minute programme of highlights of the trial in Australia about
Peter Wright's MI5 book. We'll put it out next week, as soon as the trial's
over – television's equivalent of instant street ballads about notorious
heroes and villains.

My main reason for being here is to meet the programme fund head
of the Corporation for Public Broadcasting, with Harvey Lichtenstein,
director of the Brooklyn Academy of Music, about a new strand of arts
programmes on American public television and Channel Four. The
series, which we would aim to start transmitting in 1989, would combine
work by British, American and European artists and programme-makers,
and investigate interactions between television and art, rather than use
TV to reproduce existing art. The first season would start with Peter

Brook's video version of the *Mahabharata*, which Harvey is presenting in
Brooklyn, followed by six single programmes by the likes of Twyla Tharp,
Pina Bausch, Peter Greenaway, Laurie Anderson. Production costs would
be carefully monitored, to reduce the enormous financial disparity between the USA and Britain or Europe. Corporate sponsorship would be
sought from American multinationals; for the first time ever, they would
be offered exposure on British screens as well as on American public
television, and the possibility of buying ads on Channel Four.

All these points I make to Ron Hull, the man from the CPB, in the
coolly elegant Madison Avenue conference room of Harvey Lichtenstein's lawyers, shirt-sleeved and winning and equipped with knowing
jokes. Sliver-like minimalist paintings line the walls. Listening to myself
doing the pitch, I think, this isn't half bad, you could grow addicted to
the hype business if you lived in New York. Dangerous addiction . . .

The other temptation of working with the Brooklyn Academy of
Music's Next Wave Festival – indeed with anything successful in American culture these days – is the danger of becoming the fashionable
avant-garde, of culture chic. To raise money and keep one's profile high
above the New York hubbub, you need media attention and social
charisma. I know Harvey well enough: he cares for the classic as much
as the contemporary, he can tell the difference between the genuinely
new and the stridently novel. But in the swirl of fundraising and publicity,
with Bianca Jagger and other glitterati on his committee of Friends,
distinctions can get blurred. And I have an ambivalent attitude to American celebrity and power, whether at BAM or the Getty Trust. Part of
me wants to preach to it (an old mother-country reflex); another part
wants to join the beautiful, powerful people, with their gleaming teeth
and sporty clothes.

I read in the Sunday edition of the *New York Times* a story about a
hostel for the homeless across the street from Brooklyn Academy of
Music. People living there, watching the limousines and furs of the art
crowd coming for the Next Wave Festival, have complained about BAM
never doing anything for them. 'I and my kids care about culture,' a Mrs
Ramirez is quoted as saying. It's a microcosm of so many inequities and
contrasts in this city, where the sleeping homeless in the subways are
starting to multiply as the temperature drops, and bag-ladies huddle by
the heating vents of smart galleries showing works with a lot of style and
little substance.

Erika Munk, theatre editor of the *Village Voice*, captures some of this
unease in a piece this week called 'A Few Notes on Experiment Under

Reagan', starting out with an anatomy of a currently fashionable phrase about new art: 'The cutting edge seems to be what we now have where we used to have the avant-garde . . . But there's something wrong or at least unsatisfying about this difference, no hope in it. Bohemians, radicals and their cheap, scruffy neighbourhoods have practically disappeared: new forms and forbidden subjects are almost instantly chomped up by the corporate maw and spat out as media or fashion.' The cutting edge, she concludes, 'involves neither the disjuncture of an avant-garde nor the disaffiliation of an alternative'.

Something like this, only with less money washing around to lubricate it, is what lies ahead for Britain if public funding is weakened and business sponsorship and corporate promotion take over. Sanitised new art, connoisseurship and the shrinking of any shared public space for art are the inevitable result. Cultural life as a giant shopping mall of the spirit. For the time being, BAM walks the tightrope and more often than not avoids the abyss.

Middle-aged ladies with careful hairdos and impeccable clothes – an older species of culture-vulture than you find at BAM – crowd into the smart Park Avenue auditorium of the Asia Society for an all-day Saturday event about 'The Goddess in Civilisation'. I've come to watch Diane Wolkstein perform her version of *Innana*, the Sumerian poem about the world's first goddess. I catch the end of a lecture about goddesses in Eastern antiquity. A pretty art historian from Princeton is explaining to a breathless house the myth of Isis and Osiris and how her raising of his 'phay-llus' (graphically illustrated by slides of Egyptian wall-paintings) is, of course, a fertility symbol.

In this atmosphere, reminiscent of Bloomsbury spirituality, flavoured with Jungian fervour and feminist scholarship, Diane's performance of the poem becomes even more priestess-like. The film about Innana, which Jane Weiner, an enterprising American independent producer, has asked Gina Newson to make, will have to reach past preciousness to the moving insights of the ancient text itself. Otherwise Innana and her secrets will remain inside specialist enclaves like the Asia Society.

More culture-vultures cluster round Van Gogh's last paintings at the Metropolitan Museum when I visit its latest megashow a few days later. A Chanel-suited matron peers at the paint surface through a giant magnifying glass, supping up every brushstroke of the great artist. Her hair is fixed in circular coils, which exactly echo the whorls of starlight Van Gogh painted in his night skies. Art ardour can go no further.

Like the prisoners exercising in Van Gogh's high-walled courtyard, the flock of art spectators, earplugged into its taped teleguides, trudges through the exhibition, which offers an almost day-by-day countdown to Van Gogh's suicide at Auvers. The acid greens and blues seem like an index of his distress. Because of the Metropolitan Museum's clout, virtually everything he painted or drew is here, in telling chronology. You realise how much he poured into how few elements – his cell-like room, the asylum garden and its lofty trees, one particular field enclosed by a wall, quarries, wheat, a rare rain-shower in the Midi. Then the final two canvases: black skeletal crows staining the radiance of a yellow wheat field, the only pure black in all the paintings; and grasping roots and tubers, claw-like, arthritic, torn up from the earth.

You exit into a museum shopping mall, crammed with customised Van Gogh ephemera. Van Gogh catalogues, Van Gogh notecards, Van Gogh posters, Van Gogh shopping bags in two handy sizes. Is this the democratisation of art, or its domestication? Imagine all those Park Avenue matrons penning cute thank-yous for dinner invitations on the back of Vincent's wheat field and black crows. These museum stores aren't so much the triumph of the work of art in the age of mechanical reproduction as the mechanisation of response, the multiplication of simulacra, the merchandising and undermining of real work.

Lincoln Kirstein paints a wonderfully irascible picture of museum and genius worship in this week's *New Yorker*. 'People make cathedrals out of museums,' he says. 'The museums have been taken over by the dealers, and the appreciation of art is really the appreciation of negotiable value, if you want to be realistic. No one looks at the paintings. They have just been in the precincts of status and they can rub some of this magic off on themselves. It's rather like the medieval systems of placating objects that represented saints, or lighting candles, or rubbing the toes of St Peter.'

I go to WNET to see Rhoda Grauer and her boss Jac Venza about a television history of classical dance, with Lincoln Kirstein as its mastermind. If we could find a form that is not just a repeat of Kenneth Clark's *Civilisation*, a form that dances itself as well as tells people about dance, it would be well worth doing.

The television monitor in Jac's office is showing another White House conspirator beetling his brows with concentration as he answers the questions of the congressional committee. Nearly twenty years ago Jules Feiffer wrote a political farce called *The White House Murder Mysteries*. At the time it was greeted as a cartoonist's amusing fantasy, conflating the criminal world with the business of government. Now it looks prophetic. As does *Pravda* in London. We are living in times when satire becomes documentary at dizzying speed.

Jac and Rhoda are a little subdued, I find. They've just come from an emergency meeting about one of their productions. 'The producer's gone down sick two weeks before we start shooting,' says Jac. 'The doctor is calling it mononucleosis, but . . .' His rueful shrug signals AIDS. If so, it won't be the first time he's gone through it; his head of music died of AIDS this summer.

The other reason they're depressed is that Exxon, the oil company which has sponsored *Great Performances*, has definitely decided to cut back its money by two-thirds for next year, and will taper off completely by 1988. Jac's transmission wall-plan is full of repeats, and he's considering doing a shorter season. Public funding cannot make up the shortfall. *Great Performances* has been the flagship arts programme for PBS for more than a decade. But it's not proof against a drop in world oil prices and changes at the head of a multi-national corporation.

One project we are developing with WNET is a series with the great American folklorist Alan Lomax. Lomax, whom I remember hearing on the Third Programme in the fifties playing recordings of Appalachian banjo music, has a unique collection of tapes and videos, ranging from Muddy Waters, Jelly Roll Morton and Howling Wolf to old Yaqui Indians doing ritual dances in which they pretend to be babies. He believes there is a universal grammar of melody and music, and has invented a science, cantametrics, to prove it. He is a hero of the old American left; through his recordings, an alternative history of America can be reconstituted, a grass-roots people's history.

He may be a kind of genius. Mike Dibb and Mark Kidel have been spending the week on a Channel Four development viewing and listening to Lomax's treasure trove of tapes and videos. Mark and Mike are excited by Lomax's material, but he expects their total dedication. 'I told him I couldn't just drop everything and spend the next year being the mouthpiece for his testament,' says Mike. 'And there's a whole side of him that's a crusading academic, suspicious of slick television types. But I think we've begun to win him round. And he's wonderful when he relaxes. He sings and dances and you can see how the stuff he's recorded has all got inside him.'

Another big man inhabited by his dancing music is Dave McKenna, jazz pianist in the tradition of Erroll Garner and Earl Hines, and one of my idols. I see from the paper that he's giving a solo concert on Sunday afternoon, and walk across Central Park to it in the gathering dusk.

Someone puts a quarter in a beggar's hat. 'Don't overwish,' he growls, 'keep it reasonable.' McKenna, a big burly man with the face of an amiable sea bass, hauls himself on to the altar of the Church of Heavenly Rest, Fifth Avenue at 90th, swivels his head round to watch us and, as if his hands were independent agents, starts to play.

He plays standards, Hoagy Carmichael, Cole Porter, Nat King Cole, Harry Warren. The invention is intricate, the stride never falters, the heart beats through. There's a Coney Island joy about it, infectious innocence, rollercoaster pleasure. In a final Christmas medley, his version of 'Santa Claus Is Coming To Town' grafts Thelonious Monk stubbornness on to oceanic Erroll Garner drive, a reconciliation of pianistic contraries. McKenna's solo piano, swinging up into the nave, untouched by the world of immunity virus or White House malefactors, a taste of American Eden for a congregation of middle-aged scruffy jazz lovers in the Church of Heavenly Rest.

There's so much life in the great American popular forms, so many ways in which they can be turned inside out for new contents, without losing their original appeal. Sondheim keeps testing how far the musical can be pushed, and the audience eventually catches up with him. In the New York bookshops this Christmas there is a funny, touching and appalling book called *Maus*, by Art Spiegelman. It tells the story of his father, a Polish Jew who was sent to Auschwitz and survived. Now he lives in Queens, a forgivable, infuriating, memory-haunted Jewish dad. Art Spiegelman's mother committed suicide in the sixties. *Maus* tells these stories through comic strips. All the characters are animals: the Jews mice, the Poles pigs, the Nazis sharp-fanged cats. It's the encounter between Walt Disney and Primo Levi.

Jules Feiffer, who has written an endorsement on *Maus*'s cover, enthuses about it when we have dinner. It's as if he's glad to have found someone from the younger generation of cartoonists who continues his own playfulness, poetry and graceful subversion. Jules has had a summer plagued by illness. I always forget he's at least ten years older than me. With his beaming face, ginger hair and egg-dome cranium, he looks like the two-year-old baby he and Jenny are bringing up. He's writing a screenplay for Showtime cable network about Huey and Bernard – the two male characters from his film *Carnal Knowledge* – two divorces, twenty years and a lot of pain later. Knowing him, I'm sure it will be as much about the Reagan years as about sex.

He's acerbic tonight: about the glibness and hype of much of the so-called avant-garde ('Laurie Anderson is Las Vegasing herself'); about the blurring of hierarchies in contemporary culture ('poor old Dwight Macdonald and Harold Rosenberg were the last critics to make these distinctions'). When we say goodbye on West End Avenue he hugs me, but there's a flash of realism, triggered by alcohol, in his affection: 'I miss talking to you, I wish you were here more. It's because we flatter each other, I suppose.'

Fifth Avenue is crammed with slow-moving phalanxes of shoppers. Santas ring bells incessantly. Little girls with Victorian dresses and big ribbons in their hair are herded into New York City Ballet matinees. 'It's the Nutcracker season,' says the headwaiter of an ultra-full restaurant near Lincoln Center. Nobody knows where anything is: a waitress, probably hired yesterday, can't remember the specials; a taxi-driver, Russian, hears West End when I say West Tenth.

I have breakfast with Susan Sontag. Her mother died last weekend. 'She wasn't much of a mother,' says Susan; but she has spent a lot of time weeping. 'I know many people have a struggle with their same-sex parent, but my mother simply wasn't there.' Does my affinity with Susan, the fraternal sense I often have with her, start in that shared wanting, her for a mother's, I for a father's acknowledgement? Her latest story, in a recent *New Yorker*, is about AIDS, a sort of whispering gallery of characters gathered around the bed of a terminal patient, sharing and comparing, huddling for comfort. 'I went to a weekend congress of doctors and immunologists about AIDS. They invited me because of my essay "Illness as Metaphor". They were universally apocalyptic. Who could have foreseen an epidemic like this? War, famine, environmental disaster, maybe; but this?'

She likes my calling her story a whispering gallery. 'I call it polyphonic voices. I think I'm doing something with fiction that no one's done before. I can't stop it coming. I wrote the AIDS story after getting a phone call that someone I knew had it. After the phone call, I just lay down. Then I got up and had a bath, and the story started coming, so I leaped out of the bath and started scribbling it down straight off. The whole thing only took two days. Then someone called up and asked me to write a play. Of course, I said, and without thinking began to tell them its plot.'

We talk about something she might write or make for me, for the new joint venture with BAM. She'd like to make a film about rehearsal mixing documentary and fiction, or a camera essay in Japan, or – what I'd like most – something about 'the lyric impulse' in people, the need not just to sing, but to live singingly. Some people think there's a lot of musicality in your essays, I say, but she doesn't want to write any more essays for the time being. 'There are lots of things I'd like to read me on, but the stories come first.' I help her choose an image for the covers of a new standard edition of her books. Already she's chosen drawings by Seurat and Jasper Johns, soft-focus black and white. For *Against Interpretation*, I pick a segment of an eighteenth-century architectural drawing she has on the wall, a spiral staircase with a window looking out into space. On her walls she has only black and white prints, nothing coloured. Plans and elevations, street layouts, Piranesi prisons. The black ink is stamped crisply into the thick paper. It makes an indelible mark, like Susan's own black mane of hair, strong face and lanky, customarily black-clad, body.

'There is a hierarchy in the arts, and literature is at the top. Because it exists purely in the mind, not in the sensoria,' says Joseph Brodsky next evening, looking much fitter and brighter than he did in London. 'It's being home,' he says. Home is a cluttered basement apartment in one of the few Greenwich Village streets which curves. On his table is the December issue of *Vogue*, in which he's written a memoir of Mikhail Baryshnikov, with whom he grew up in Leningrad. 'Baryshnikov thinks he is only a sensitive athlete compared with me. In Russia, they still know these things. When we used to pick up girls together in Leningrad, his girl would point me out to him and say, "Look, that's the poet."'

We talk about the programme I'd like to make with him and his fellow poet Derek Walcott, about the poet's psyche. It would start by videotaping a long conversation between the two of them and some of Walcott's students; we'd edit that and build words and images on to it. I know that it could touch elusive truths about poetry and experience. It's also at the outer limit of what can be done by television. And Joseph's English takes a little getting used to. But against doctor's orders, he's still trying to bum cigarettes, so we'd better make the programme while we can.

I ask him if he's writing, and he promises to make copies of a batch of new poems. He's also reviewing a biography of Anthony Blunt. Gnomically, puffing away at a stray fag some previous visitor dropped on the floor, he says, 'Of course there's a connection between scholarship and spying. Art historians deal with the contingencies of artists' lives.' I'm still trying to work that one out.

I buy Teresa Stratas's record of Kurt Weill songs. On the sleeve, she says, 'Who am I to congratulate myself on my "artistry" or my musical gift, or the instant celebrity that seems to go with it, when that Biafran or Indian or Ethiopian woman has no milk in her tit to feed her child? But look around us. There are so many people eating out of garbage

cans, right here on Broadway, right here in America. How can I close
my eyes to this and live only in "artistic loftiness"?'

47th Street Photo, where I go to buy computer discs before I leave, is
a melee of discount customers and a babble of Yiddish peppered with
words like 'Sony' and 'Hewlett-Packard' as the ultra-orthodox salesmen,
fringed, bearded and skullcapped, serve the milling crowd. Rabbis of the
electronic era, adepts of computer cabbala. It is snowing as my taxi crawls
across George Washington Bridge to the airport, big flakes beginning to
blanket Manhattan's multitudes. My taxi-driver is Bulgarian. The car
radio is talking about congressional hearings and rocket silos.

I get back to London, reconnect with Orna and home, drift in and out
of jet-lag over the weekend. On Saturday, Colin Leventhal invites me to
a sponsored tennis competition at the Albert Hall which we are televising.
As we sit in a box watching Yannick Noah, the black superstar of French
tennis, he brings me up to date with Charlotte Street events. There's
been a lot of speculation about the future. Will Jeremy go to the BBC?
Who's after his job internally? Who will be Channel Four's new chairman?
I say that it's beginning to sound like any other organisation. Colin talks
about another colleague: 'He's okay. But we didn't make Channel Four
just to be okay. I know it's only television, but no one in the world gives
television the time and attention we do.'

On Sunday I sit for Tom. The portrait is nearly finished now, starting
to be a picture with its own inner dynamic and rhythms as well as its
reference to my face, to the world. I tell Tom about the Van Gogh show
in New York, and particularly about his two wonderful paintings of irises.
'Yes, Van Gogh was good at flowers,' he says. 'But Cézanne couldn't
paint quickly enough. All the flowers in his paintings are paper.'

WEEKS 51–52 *December 15–25*

The countdown to Christmas has begun: a merry-go-round of familiar
faces at year-end parties in production offices, cutting rooms, hospitality
suites; sackloads of Christmas cards from facility houses reminding you
they're there, from production companies you commissioned during the
year and from the ones you didn't. 'Are you still enjoying being Maecenas
to this community?' asks Michael Ignatieff mildly at one of the seasonal
parties. Personal and domestic life starts to seep back, softening the drive
to activity. Orna has nearly finished dubbing and subtitling *Chateauvallon*;
there is light at the end of *le schlock*. She looks up from the video when
I tell her about my New York meetings. 'Did you give them a piece of
your mind then?' she says. That's our shorthand for when I get carried

away by my own earnestness ... But there's a great deal to do before
home takes over. I watch two films on the Steenbeck editing machine
before transmission. The final film of John McGrath's Highland trilogy,
bringing the songs and struggles of the Gaels up to the era of raids
against landlords and protests against NATO bases, is combative and
stirring without being sentimental. The other film I view is also Scottish
– Timothy Neat's *A Tree of Liberty*, about the songs of Robert Burns.
Serge Hovey, the American composer and musicologist who has devoted
his life to Burns's songs, is dying of muscular deterioration in California.
The footage I saw this summer of him, linked to a breathing machine,
unable to speak or write, was almost intolerable. Now Tim has edited
pictures of the wide-eyed wasting musician into a whole that is both
complex and sublime, with the power and humour of Burns's songs riding
through faces of miners, farmers, fresh-faced girls and children, and the
grandeur of lakes and clouds, earth and shifting light.

I take an early plane to Paris next morning for a meeting of the
programme committee of LA SEPT. The walls and streets around the
Assemblée Nationale have a morning-after feel, aerosol slogans attacking
the education minister and government racism already fading. But last
week's massive student demonstrations have reopened old social wounds
and undermined political certitudes. I ring Peter Brook and after an
update on the *Mahabharata*, ask him what sense he makes of it all. 'It
began as a genuine manifestation for civil rights,' he says, 'completely
unpolitical, and in that sense unlike 1968 – although it's now being
claimed by all the groups and factions on the left. When the police
cracked down with such violence, and the editor of *Figaro* magazine wrote
that young people were suffering from "AIDS of the mind", it mobilised
even the country's right-wingers against the government.'

The sense of treading a political knife-edge hovers over the meeting
at LA SEPT. It is businesslike and down-to-earth, working through a mass
of proposals for fiction films, documentary and performance programmes
with the beginnings of real debate about a future policy and transmission
schedule. The urgency in the discussions comes from the need for La
Sept to establish itself as a valid and valuable presence in what will
obviously continue to be a changeable political environment.

On TF1 when I get back to the hotel, an access programme has been
handed over to the students, who have made a lyrical anthem of their
last fortnight, all slow-motion banners, vibrant voices and heartbeat rock
and roll. Maybe that's what it was in reality, a hopeful demand for
recognition, for dialogue with authority, a festival before the onslaught

of the batons. In any event, there won't be many more programmes like this once TFI is privatised in 1987, especially if it gets into the hands of Robert Hersant, a pugnacious newspaper mogul who owns the vitriolic *Le Figaro* and a network of right-wing provincial newspapers.

Before leaving next day, I manage to take a peek at the newest museum in Paris, the Musée d'Orsay. Under the former railway station's steel nave, the culture of the nineteenth century has been marshalled. I have time only to roam inside the entrance, at what would have been the terminus of the platforms. Massive winged statuary rears operatically in the monumental space; through slit windows I see unrhetorical Pissarro landscapes. Architecture, graphic art and illustration, furniture, photography, the construction of the Opera, the invention of the cinema: all the cross-currents meet here. The team working on *The Impressionists* series must come here before they embark on second-draft scripts.

This has been a spectacular year for new museums in Paris: the Musée Picasso, the science park at La Villette, the remodelled modern galleries at Beaubourg, and now Orsay. And they're still working on the controversial pyramid extension to the Louvre. French presidents from Pompidou to Mitterrand, irrespective of political allegiance, have memorialised their eras in these cathedrals of history, identity and invention. Where are the comparable monuments of Heath, Callaghan, Thatcher? 1986 in Britain has been the year the Victoria and Albert Museum failed to open on Fridays. Well, our television is healthier than theirs. For the time being.

Straight back from London airport to the *Dancelines* cutting room. Terry and Peter have now edited documentary workshop material around the new pieces; we will show the kitchen as well as the meal. The piece which Siobhan Davies has made with Susan Sontag's story about letter-writing, shot in Chiswick House, has a grave lyricism and masked emotion; Ian Spink's post-nuclear piece, shot among Docklands debris, is a bleak warning, full of frightening images of survivors, and on the very edge of dance and performance-art documentary.

Back to Charlotte Street to talk to David Freeman about a triple bill of Maxwell Davies, György Ligeti and Kurt Weill from Opera Factory next summer. At home with Chomskyan linguistics, anthropology and gut theatre values, he talks about the Ligeti as though it were the very birth of sounds, notes, language and music; he's a director with a vision of opera and theatre, of opera as theatre, who has really hit his stride this year and will change both.

Frantic phone calls from the Lyric, Hammersmith: the local council has called an emergency meeting to censure the theatre for presenting a play from South Africa. I can't get to the meeting, send my proxy vote against this reaction. Banning the play would be acting like the South African government which has just stifled its last honest newspapers. It will demoralise artists and leave the regime untouched.

Stuart Hall, professor at the Open University, comes for lunch next day with me and Alan Fountain to talk about our plans for marking the twentieth anniversary of 1968. He is anxious about reports in the press that the Channel Four board is considering selling advertising directly, which he thinks would drive innovative, minority and experimental pro- grammes out of the schedule. 'The Open University and Channel Four are the only two good things to come out of the Wilson era which are still alive and kicking,' he says.

From there I go to the Coliseum to meet Peter Jonas and David Pountney and talk about our future relationship with English National Opera. The BBC has been talking to them, too; competition is hotting up. After a serious post-mortem on what went wrong with *Rusalka*, we talk about operas by Britten, Shostakovich and Sondheim which we'd like to do, with the help of sponsorship and cooperation from the unions, who still automatically envisage large sums of money whenever television is mentioned. Tomorrow, ENO will be told its Arts Council grant, and like all the national companies they are apprehensive.

Next day, the last working Friday before Christmas, things pick up a little more still. In rapid succession I have meetings about next year's Glyndebourne *Traviata* directed by Peter Hall, work out a strategy for the original dance-film which Pina Bausch is preparing in Germany, hear Jeremy Marre's account of where he's got to with his film on the biology of music ('if it works, it should make clear why the shift from major to minor in Mozart moves us so much'), and think how I can describe the arts programmes I'd like to do with Harvey Lichtenstein in America without either betraying them or frightening the funding sources, who need a grant application by early January.

After lunch, Mike Phillips and I stomp around the office like a pair of teenagers watching the cassette of Christopher Swann's programme about Loose Tubes, which has arrived hot from Granada for a New Year's Day transmission. 'They're a hooligan cooperative,' says the band's manager Tony Lazzerini in the film, 'a revolutionary society in microcosm.' Fighting talk, which hasn't been heard much since the sixties; but the exuberant individuality and collective inventiveness of

Loose Tubes bear it out, and the shape of the programme mirrors both their needle-sharp planning and carefree improvisation.

When Marina Warner and Gina Newson come in to talk about their surreal muse film, a wonderful coincidence happens. Marina, trying to explain to my cost-controller what the director of her film-within-a-film is doing, says, 'It's not as if he's doing a cinema adaptation of . . .' and then gropes for the name of a well-known novel. Simultaneous with her, I come out with *A Tale of Two Cities*, and we both burst out laughing. My two are obviously Paris and New York, emblems of intelligence and instinct. I wonder what Marina's are, and what kind of affinity the coincidence signals.

At day's end, an hour or so before the Channel Four Christmas party at the Video Café, I have a drink with Justin Dukes, who says he's much relieved at our board's decision neither to accept the option of selling our own advertising, nor to rule it out at some future date provided the Channel's purposes can be maintained. He and Jeremy have been working hard lobbying board members, who apparently outvoted our chairman Edmund Dell on the issue.

When we've finished, I come out and see Jeremy fulminating about a message that's just reached him. 'The prime minister's cassettes!' he exclaims. 'I always forget about sending her programmes to watch over Christmas, and we never have anything suitable. I can't send her Michael Clark and his punk dancers, can I?' He eventually sends her Placido Domingo in *Carmen*, and *The New Enlightenment* series about neo-conservative intellectuals, though she may feel she has enough of all that in real life . . .

We all pile into the Video Café and cram together, dwarfed by big-screen images of our younger selves, taken from some video promo made at the start of the Channel. I congratulate Liz Forgan on the dramatisation of the Peter Wright spy book trial in Australia, which went out hot on the heels of the closing speeches last night, reality satirising itself. Three glasses of red wine go straight to my tired head and I lope home early before I start acting like some daft executive at an office knees-up.

Hung over next morning, I make my way down to Tom's for what will probably be the last sitting. I stop at Chapel Street market to buy vegetables. I love the bustle of busy street markets, barrows and bellowed costermonger patter, big Hogarthian women and their wiry husbands, fairy lights and blaring pop records, all the fun of the fair.

I spot a little Italian delicatessen on the corner and go in to buy *amaretti* and *panettone* for presents. The owners and his wife are handing out little glasses of liqueur with cherries in them and wishing people *Buon Natale*. Apart from upwardly-mobile Islingtonians, the customers are mostly whiskery old London Italians and their buxom wives. They drink their liqueur and chatter in Lombardy accents. Little local shops like my father's, immigrant London: still my home patch.

The final touch to my portrait Tom wants to add today is the copy of James Joyce's *Ulysses* in the bottom left foreground. It's there because it's the right colour green, because it balances the mask of comedy in the top right corner and completes the web of classical allusion, because Tom and I got to know each other at Oxford when I was playing in a stage adaptation of *Ulysses*. Carefully, he sketches in its outline, fills in the colour, fiddles with the perspective. I come round to look at the result with him. 'It plugs you back into the picture,' he says, and it's true, I no longer float forward in some undefined foreground. The diagonals of the book are echoed in the lines of the imitation Titian behind me; pinned into the picture space, my sad face is lifted by the comic mask above my head.

I have given Tom the first third of this book to read, because I hope he'll do a jacket for it and because I want his reactions. He's pretty severe to begin with, talking about its self-importance, and I sit there thinking, oh God, I'll never get beyond self-dramatisation. Then I begin to listen more carefully, put what he's saying into perspective with what he hasn't read yet, what I learned later on in the writing.

'There's not enough of the quotidian, of everyday life. Everything you do is a big deal; doesn't anything ever turn out disappointing?'

He's got me in one: a street-market barker, always talking up my own life.

'Some things I've shared with you, Mike, and you're simplifying your reactions. And all these phenomena you experience, they're isolated, they have no threads back into your life. Why don't you give yourself time to spin out the interconnectedness of things, their umbilical cords back into your past?'

'Because I seize novelties, Tom, and fear continuities. Because I was trying to catch myself on the wing. Because there was never time to make a definitive –'

'You won't ever have time to be definitive. But you could make it a deeper immediate document.'

I spend most of Sunday starting to pick apart the beginning of this book and put it together again. The last episode of Dennis Potter's *The*

Singing Detective goes out, an object-lesson in following the consequences of one's imagination through to the lyrical, purgative or bitter end. Its hospital ward, says a doctor friend who works at Bart's, is the most authentic ever shown in television drama. Nearly seven million people have followed it each week.

The Singing Detective, Potter's *Samson Agonistes*, is a tribute to the BBC's continuous commitment to an awkward customer like Potter, rows about censorship and writer's irascibility notwithstanding. The result is an extended work of fiction in a mass medium which goes as deep into the individual and collective spirit as any trumpeted novel or play of the past ten years. Channel Four should hope to produce something as good after such a sustained relationship with a writer. Somewhere in one of his interviews, Dennis Potter said that by the time he died he hoped to have squeezed every bit of juice out of himself. As long as such artists consider television a proper instrument for their work, television's still in good shape. And the shrill ideologues and political economists busying themselves rearranging 'the audio-visual landscape' should have their earthmovers restrained so that things like *The Singing Detective* can take root.

In half an hour on the year's last working Monday, three bits of next year which I thought I could rely on fall down: Tippett chooses the BBC and Glyndebourne to commission his new opera over us and Welsh National Opera, dates shift for the recording of Britten's *Rape of Lucretia* next August and the studio is no longer free, and a good potential producer for our late-night live debate show turns it down. Enough adversity to get the adrenalin up after the break.

On the positive side, Tony Palmer phones to say that Ben Kingsley wants to play Shostakovich. One of his reasons, apart from his admiration for Tony's other films, is his excitement about David Rudkin's script. He told Tony that he was a fan of Rudkin's plays when he was at the Royal Shakespeare Company in the sixties. He thinks Rudkin has had a hard time, like many of his generation of writers, and hopes that the film will restore his status. It's good to find a star actor whose horizons aren't bounded by Hollywood. Tony believes that with the help of Channel Four's letter of intent and other pre-sale commitments, the rest of the money will be guaranteed and he will be able to start shooting in February. Wigan and Liverpool will be his Moscow and Leningrad.

The other good news is that at the end of a meeting with Peter Greenaway and Tom, Jeremy agrees a three-year commitment to *A TV Dante*. Peter has promised to split his time each year between a feature film and Dante; we will transmit the thirty-four episodes, one for each canto, in three annual blocks; by the third year, if they sustain the level of invention with which they have begun, we should have a work of television art which anticipates the high-definition technology of the next decade.

An 1100-line picture on a wall-size flat screen with impeccable sound is going to change people's television expectations and demands, perhaps more so in the long run than the proliferation of delivery systems and apparent choices which lies immediately ahead. *A TV Dante* could be the type of a new generation of programme for people who want from television what they can get from music, poetry or painting, and especially for the young with an appetite for work that is contemporary and has substance. There is a sizeable worldwide audience of such people already, even if it's easier to measure by attendances at exhibitions and perform-ances, or sales of new music records, than from the ratings figures and appreciation indexes of existing broadcast television.

Having taken the decision, which will provide half of the likely total budget and leaves Tom and Peter's producer to raise the balance, Jeremy relaxes, talking about the underfunding of the arts, saying how little money it would take to improve the situation, wondering whether it would be worthwhile organising a deputation to Downing Street. 'As long as there are philistines at Cabinet level, nothing's going to change,' he says.

I'm delighted that he's decided to support Peter and Tom's work; it's the kind of decision I'd always hoped and expected him to take but, because of what I've felt to be our estrangement, could no longer be sure of. Already in the routine meeting I had with him yesterday, he was visibly more affable. Neither of us referred to the tensions of the past weeks, though he mentioned the burden of the arguments over selling our own airtime, and said he was relieved that the memorial evening for Tamara at Wigmore Hall had gone off well. At the end of what must have been a difficult year, and with his repeated statement that he won't stay at Channel Four beyond the end of his contract in 1988, what does he envisage doing in future?

There are continued murmurings about his becoming Director-General of the BBC, although he keeps saying he hasn't been asked and there are a lot of good internal candidates. Would he really want to take on the huge task of turning around that mammoth vessel and making it shipshape? Is it the natural culmination of everything he's done in broadcasting, or are there things he cares about more than television – like opera and the arts, British cinema, cricket, his own programme-making? Does the Scottish Jew he keeps calling himself really want to rise to a summit of the establishment and exercise nonconformist power, the way Hugh Greene did when he was BBC Director-General? The hub and heart of public-service broadcasting is certainly going to need someone as good and experienced and self-questioning as he is over the next decade. And Channel Four will need a chief executive with his range and originality. Already people are beginning to worry that much of what makes the Channel good depends on Jeremy's being there.

As a Christmas treat, I give him the funniest programme proposal I've elicited in 1986. It's from Desmond Olivier Dingle, chief executive and artistic director of the National Theatre of Brent, alias Patrick Barlow. It's a modest proposal that NTOB Television take over an entire week's programming on the Channel next Christmas.

'We at the NTOB have long marvelled,' writes Dingle, 'at the way Channel Four present all these programmes single-handed night after night and all from one not overly large studio in Queen Charlotte Street. It is in fact nothing short of a miracle in my opinion. However, I do feel that round about the Christmas season – when all the other companies and the BBC and that are pulling out their biggest stops and guns and so forth – then Channel Four must feel very deeply alone and profoundly overburdened indeed! It is for this reason, therefore, that we should like to offer our assistance at this time with a wide variety of popular programmes totally done and presented by the National Theatre of Brent.'

The NTOB goodies include *Dingle*, 'an entertaining, penetrating and powerfully controversial chat show with Desmond Dingle interviewing the celebrities of the moment (5 minutes)'; *Your Garden and You*, 'a gripping insight into the world of gardening. Hosted by Bernard (2 minutes)'; *Madam Butterfly*, 'the fabulous opera starring Dame Kiri Te Kanawa (if available) leading the NTOB ensemble (condensed version 5 mins)'; *Eleventh Hour*, in which 'Bernard will interview a major minority group (1 minute)'; *Whoever Heard of a Fourth Channel?*, 'the dramatic and moving story of the first days of Channel Four Television vividly brought to life by the NTOB. Starring Desmond Olivier Dingle as Jeremy Isaacs'.

The chief executive's mouth puckers, he suppresses a chuckle. It pleases the antic in me to wind up the year proposing both Dante's *Inferno* and a week of National Theatre of Brent micro-programmes, a combination I could only hope for in Channel Four.

Drinking with David Rose at the end of the day, he asked me how this book is going and I say it has turned out a good year to be writing about, not only because of all the big shifts and changes in television, but because it's the year in which I have really begun to see what making television can be, yet without losing my sense of being only a visitor to television.

'We've all noticed that, dear boy,' says David, who usually pulls my leg when I start getting solemn.

'But who can really feel at home in television, David?' I say. 'It's too –'

And we both rotate our hands and wiggle our fingers, as if to say 'prolific', 'provisional', 'ephemeral', 'engulfing', 'restless', 'ungraspable', 'omnivorous' or 'elusive' and he nods, takes a thoughtful slug of red wine, and does not continue to send me up.

WEEK 2 *Monday January 5 1987*

On the first working Monday of the new year, I get up before daybreak, and by mid-morning I am in Paris on a cold damp morning. The Russian film director Andrei Tarkovsky died last week. We co-produced his last film *The Sacrifice*, and I had a message from Jeremy's office asking me to attend the funeral as the Channel's representative.

It was partly coincidence that I should be asked: Jeremy was out of London, and so was David Rose, who actually commissioned *The Sacrifice* as a *Film on Four*. There was also, I thought, a personal subtext. One of the last public activities of Tamara Isaacs was to take a leading part in the campaign to get the Soviet authorities to allow Tarkovsky's son to leave Russia and join his father. I remember Jeremy telling me how Tamara had insisted on standing outside the National Film Theatre leafleting the audience on a cold night last November, only months before she died.

The funeral is to be in the Orthodox Russian cathedral on the rue Daru, not far from the Arc de Triomphe and the Salle Pleyel, where the great virtuosi give recitals. Before I left I rang Michael Ignatieff, who was brought up in the Orthodox Church, to ask him what I should expect. 'After the service you should go to the Russian restaurant across the road from the church and have a vodka and a piroshke to wish him on his way,' said Michael. 'It's called A La Ville de Petrograd.'

I have visions of an elegant terraced restaurant, filled with distinguished White Russian émigrés in beautifully tailored old-fashioned clothes. A La Ville de Petrograd, opposite the gold-leafed onion domes of the church of Alexander Nevsky, is a little bistro with formica tabletops. Folk-painting murals of Cossack girls roguishly slapping their thighs cover the walls. There is a samovar, babushka dolls, loaves of black bread, a panoply of different vodka bottles behind the bar and on it a copy of the official registry of the Russian nobility, in case any upstart comes in and makes false claims.

Since it's cold and there are nearly two hours to go before the ceremony, I go in. Seated next to a French businessman and his secretary scoffing blinis, I order food and drink and try to remember Tarkovsky. I met him once only, in David Rose's office, just after he'd arrived in London, a wiry, weatherbeaten man in his fifties. He'd made one film, *Nostalgia*, since he'd arrived in the West, but it hadn't been a commercial success, and Channel Four and the Swedish Film Institute were at that time the only sources of funds for *The Sacrifice*. It was hard talking to him through a translator.

Later in the year, David Rose came back from seeing the shoot of *The Sacrifice* in Sweden, shaken by Tarkovsky's maniacal perfectionism. 'He's completely ruthless,' said David. 'He measures things down to the last inch. Won't tell the actors what their parts mean, just wants them to be on the exact spot for his long takes.' Tarkovsky's sustained choreographed takes and tracking shots, sometimes almost ten minutes long, are the secret of his power. They give his spiritual fables the force of documentary testimony. The first time they ran the final scene of *The Sacrifice*, in which the protagonist burns down his house, the camera jammed, and they had to rebuild the house to burn it down again. There was no standby camera: Tarkovsky's films are wagers without a safety-net.

It's time to go across to the church. I climb up the steep flight of steps to the entrance, where I am told to remove my hat. David Gothard, who used to run Riverside, and started the campaign about Tarkovsky's son, greets me. 'It's small in there, and crowded already,' he says. 'You'd better go in.'

Inside it's very dark, except when flashes and flares of news cameras explode. The church is high, it's like being inside an upended stained-wood boat, or a rocket on a launch pad. Hieratic figures have been smoked into the curves of the domes. I push my way through and stand on one side of the altar. I realise I am standing with Tarkovsky's relatives: stocky fiftyish men with the slightly rodent-like features he had, scarved women, two boys who must be his sons. People are holding candles, with cardboard discs to shield their fingers from the wax.

We wait for a quarter of an hour. The lenses buzz and click as people who might be personalities arrive. But it doesn't feel like a fashionable event, more a congregation of transients. Behind me is a fleshy-faced woman in a big black fur coat. 'From the Soviet Embassy,' someone whispers. Priests scurry past, I can hear them muttering as they put on their robes behind the icon-hung wall. Smothered in flowers, the coffin stands between four candelabra.

The service begins, in Russian with French interpolations. Resonant singing sweeps round the space, it feels puzzlingly close and distant at the same time, then I see the choir across the nave and realise how immediate the acoustic is. For fifty minutes the chanted Mass rolls through us in waves of steady harmony. Time, which Tarkovsky sculpted in his films, stands still. Cameras, the instruments through which he saw and spoke, capture his last rites, except when the head priest, a tall man with saturnine features, asks the cameramen to refrain while the Gospel is read.

A nun in a grey wimple lights a taper from one of the central candelabra and passes the flame to people holding candles, who pass it to others. The interior glows with candleflame. I am finding it hard to swallow.

After his family one by one come forward, kneel and kiss the coffin – to a renewed locust-rasp of lenses – the flowers are removed from the coffin and we follow it out into the courtyard. Three hundred and fifty people stand outside listening to speeches which the wind makes inaudible. David Gothard and I inspect the wreaths: a huge one from the embassy, another from the union of Soviet film-makers, and one from the cinema censorship commission, which made it impossible for Tarkovsky to make more than five of the twenty-five screenplays he submitted.

'There's Rostropovich,' says David. The balding white-haired man at the top of the steep flight of steps has produced a cello, and begins to play the slow movement of a Bach sonata. For six minutes he plays, in the bitter hard air, his head cocked to the neck of the instrument, his long fingers making the melody vibrate, his bow scooping up handfuls of harmony like earth.

Spotlights focus on Rostropovich of course, tape and film whirs, lens-tongues clatter. But they don't seem to impinge at all. The mind's ear blanks them out. The burnished sound outrides everything.

POST / PREDICATION 1837

Art, especially literature, is a great hall of reflection where we can all meet and where everything under the sun can be examined and considered. For this reason it is feared and attacked by dictators, and by authoritarian moralists.

Iris Murdoch, The Fire And The Sun

You should accept the political and economic climate in which we now live and make the best of it.

Richard Luce, Arts Minister

The rectangular floor tiles guide our sight toward the semi-robed Christ. He leans against a column on which rests the stone statue of a Greek hero with a raised hand. Two henchmen simultaneously lift their whips. Their strokes will be regular and indifferent like the ticking of a clock. The silence is complete, without the victim's moans or the executioner's odious breath . . . We view Piero della Francesca's *The Flagellation of Christ* as through a thin pane of ice chained, fascinated and helpless as in a dream.

Zbigniew Herbert, Barbarian In The Garden

We have moved, with other editors, press and marketing people, into new offices in a block across the road from the main building, spacious and eerily calm. From my window I catch glimpses of Jeremy and other unsuspecting colleagues in off-guard moments alone in their offices. Jeremy seems to spend more time reading the morning papers than I imagine he used to. Like James Stewart in *Rear Window*, I quite often find myself gazing down, feeling a bit of an exile, cut off from the hubbub of my former fourth-floor habitat. But that too has been turned upside down, people being shunted from office to office and floor to floor. This is a springtime of upheaval whose logic is not yet fully apparent.

In February Jeremy suddenly decided to apply for the position of Director-General of the BBC. He did not get the job, but he will leave next year to run the Royal Opera House. Next month our chairman Edmund Dell retires, to be replaced by Richard Attenborough, currently our vice-chairman, who should maintain the editorial emphasis of the Channel. Our Programme Controller Paul Bonner joined ITV in April, Liz Forgan was promoted to Deputy Programme Director, and commissioning editors have been organised into five groups, to provide a framework and continuity for whoever succeeds Jeremy in 1988. I will no longer have the same direct, if sporadic, relationship with Jeremy. Channel Four's era of benevolent autocracy is ended, although in truth it's been over for at least a year, as the number of commissioning editors has grown and contact with Jeremy has decreased: the new structures simply acknowledge this.

We are all now facing the certainty that we will lose our leader in 1988, and that the Channel must reshape itself to receive whoever will play that most difficult role, successor to an illustrious pioneer. The changes in Channel Four will coincide with big shifts in British broadcasting in the 1990s. Some will be prompted by technological innovation, some by market forces, some by ideological zeal. A decade from now, Channel Four will exist in very different context: greater individual 'mixing and matching' by viewers with access to satellite dishes and cable services, more multi-national ownership and production of communications, less monolithic and bureaucratic structures in both BBC and ITV.

Three developments will affect Channel Four particularly. High-definition television will offer better pictures and sound; will it also create a demand for less disposable programmes? Enlarged opportunities for independent programme-makers in BBC and ITV will mean greater security for the many talented people who took the plunge and went independent with the advent of Channel Four, for those brave mavericks who had already done so, and for those newcomers who decided for the first time that television could be something worth doing. Will those alternative outlets also threaten the distinctiveness of Channel Four, or simply make it more competitive in its turn?

And, as the basis of financing television is re-examined by the government in the light of its anti-monopolistic and pro-market convictions, Channel Four may be encouraged – or obliged – to 'float free' from the ITV companies and sell its own advertising. Would the pressures of the advertising agencies, with their ritual complaints each quarter that forthcoming schedules don't do enough to deliver audiences to their clients, mean that Channel Four would stifle its courage in order to survive?

These and other questions are already pulsing across the magnetic field of television in the first half of this year, awaiting echoes and answers. Meanwhile the journeyman business of television – putting out the best programmes you can make and trying to capture the best audience you can get – continues. As transmission hours expand on all channels, first with breakfast and then with daytime television, Channel Four stays on air until 3 am three nights a week, starting with a season of Russian films on Thursdays, a gangly charismatic young talk-show host and open-ended discussion on Fridays, and risqué comedy on Saturdays.

Arts programmes which have been cooking through the past year, sometimes longer, are served up over the first six months of this year. *State of the Art* gets enthusiastic previews, along the lines of 'the first time television has dealt seriously with contemporary art' and – with the exception of the *Guardian*, *Screen* magazine and Biff Comics – hostile reviews. When it's not attacked with the kind of knee-jerk philistinism that makes merry with bricks at the Tate and tampons at the ICA, it's pilloried, especially by people on the left I respect, like Anthony Barnett and Peter Fuller, for going along with postmodernism.

I'm as bruised and bewildered by the vehemence of the attacks (including an onslaught from my colleagues at Programme Review) as the programme-makers are. I agree with critics of the series that, in seeking to circumvent an authoritative host-figure and substituting a collage of quotations spoken by off-screen voices, *State of the Art* is less approachable or 'user-friendly' than earlier series fronted by Kenneth Clark or Robert Hughes or even John Berger. I don't think that all the actors sound as if they understand the quotations they're speaking. And many of those quotations, written for the printed page, could have been re-edited for the ear. With these improvements, the series could have been less initially intimidating. But it would still have grated sensibilities, as did John Berger's *Ways of Seeing*, coming as a rebuttal of the gentlemanly connoisseurship of Kenneth Clark's *Civilisation*.

State of the Art takes on the historical relativism, stylistic knowingness, and commercial fashion-machine of much art of the eighties; its form echoes the scepticism and allusiveness of many of the artists it presents; it also explores, without heroics, what its writer Sandy Nairne calls 'strategies of resistance' to the postmodern position and the manipulations of the art world. Unlike most television, it accepts the demise of what Jean-François Lyotard has called 'the great narratives' of explanation – Marxism, Freudianism, even Modernism. Therefore it does not appeal to some trustworthy common sense that the viewer can rely on; it doesn't even offer the viewer identification with a perplexed Everyman journeying through its labyrinth. What it does give is a detailed and disabused account of this labyrinth, the web of ideas and images and practices in the art of the eighties. And this is what makes *State of the Art* both clear-eyed and comfortless. Meanwhile it elicits the most virulent viewers' postbag since the National Theatre of Brent's *Messiah*, when someone wrote in from Glasgow warning that God would smite me dead for blasphemy.

Our four-week season of the music of Harrison Birtwistle is received more warmly, perhaps because Birtwistle has over the past year stood forth as the leading British composer of his generation and, after the triumph of *The Mask of Orpheus* in particular, there is a genuine curiosity to know more about his elusive personality and impassively original music. Andrew Snell's documentary which opens the season uses visual analogues – the sculptural intricacy of an Assyrian bas-relief or a Henry Moore, the morphology of rocks and stones, the formality of Piero della Francesca – to elucidate Birtwistle's music, and peers behind his masks to glimpse the thoughtful child among the Northern rockfaces and the relaxed force of the adult artist. The film will be the Channel's entry for this year's Prix Italia music prize.

Also warmly greeted is the first programme in the new series of *Voices*, in which George Steiner – febrile, polysyllabic, pipe-clutching – insists that Freud's effect has been to devalue inner personal life. The psychoanalyst Bruno Bettelheim, facing him with a Buddha-like stillness which drives Steiner to even greater verbal and intellectual display, unnervingly contrives to suggest that he's missing the entire point. Perhaps the widespread attention this programme receives in the press reveals that a high percentage of TV critics are familiar with the shrink's couch. In any event, none of them can agree who won the debate.

This spring's *Dance on Four* season, which has become an awaited annual event, opens with *Dancelines*, welcomed by dance critics as an overdue opportunity for choreographers to create work specifically for television. None of the new pieces is longer than ten minutes; my hope for next year's *Dancelines* is that the choreographers will make more extended dance television works.

Now that Peter Greenaway and Tom Phillips are definitely going ahead to complete their television version of Dante's *Inferno* over the next three years, we air the pilot programme of *A TV Dante*, Canto Five. The graphic intricacy and contemporary allusiveness of this fifteen-minute video of the Circle of the Lustful and the tale of Paolo and Francesca enthuse viewers and reviewers alike. 'Roll on the other thirty-three cantos,' writes the *Daily Telegraph*.

The programme also brings me my first brush with the IBA as regulator of taste and decency. Tom and Peter have used a nude actor and actress to portray Paolo and Francesca, and I am asked to send a tape of the programme to my 'minder' at the IBA. His scrutiny takes place in the shadow of a Tory backbencher's bill which would bring broadcasting under the provisions of the 1959 Obscene Publications Act. Although the bill is talked out in the last parliamentary session before the election, everyone's saying that it will be back, along with new legislation governing broadcasting, if Mrs Thatcher is re-elected. I send the tape of *A TV Dante* over to the IBA, with a wodge of Peter and Tom's arcane storyboards and scripts for the entire poem. After a week, the lapidary answer comes back: 'We are content.'

But all those programmes are over and done with. This spring Tony Palmer has started shooting his Shostakovich film in Wigan, even though the New Zealand bank which is guaranteeing his budget hasn't signed its contract. At all hours, he rings. 'Just thought you'd be amused to know that the bank's bloody lawyer's secretary spent three hours trying to find the key for the desk where they keep the floppy disc for the contract that has to be air-couriered to Auckland tonight.' 'Tony here. Thought you'd like to know I've just had a car crash and I'm stranded in deep snow up a high mountain in Switzerland, all alone.' 'Hello, this is Tony. Thought I ought to tell you since you're the only one with the slightest interest in this film that I've stopped filming and I'm half way down the M1 on my way home. Nobody gives a damn. I've paid £120,000 out of my own pocket so far, I've co-written the thing, designed it, and I'm trying to direct it, when I'm not popping into phone booths trying to raise the rest of the money. Well, that's it, I've come to the end of my tether.' Six weeks later: 'Only two days more filming to go. The rushes look all right. But good rushes don't make a good film. I'm never going to go through all this again. One thing *Shostakovich* has taught me: as a film maker, I've really got nothing to say. I'm going to give up making films after this.'

I try to offer the soothing counsel or the soft shoulder or simply the attentive ear that is required. I field other people's appeals for reassurance, calls for support and demands for attention. I'm nursing a late-night talk show which is meant to start at Easter; guest-editing the inaugural twelve-hour broadcast of LA SEPT in France, which is like riding a bucking bronco; and trying to train my new assistant Annette Morreau, who has arrived from fifteen years in the Arts Council and, like every newcomer to Channel Four – a vehicle now travelling at considerable speed – finds it hard to get her bearings.

Orna's father dies. We go to Israel for the funeral, three hundred people from all over the country in the hot sun in a graveyard by the sea on the slopes of Haifa's Mount Carmel. For days afterwards people crowd into her parents' apartment to offer condolences, to reminisce about Yakov.

By the time I knew him he was a sedentary, deep-voiced, elephant-eared old man with a wicked sense of humour. I once got him out of his armchair and away from his heaped ashtray for a walk round what remains of the old city of Haifa. He showed me the *hammam*, the Arab bath-house, and the places where his father used to ply his profession as an apothecary and folk-doctor. In restaurants he talked Arabic to the waiters, who replied with a mixture of humour and respect. At the rabbinical court a few days before my wedding, a panel of hairy elders asked him the formal question: how could they be sure I was who I said I was? 'Because I say so!' he boomed out, with the authority of the son of a local dynasty. I think he was proud of me as a son-in-law, and although I saw him infrequently I got along with him fine, when he wasn't pulling my leg.

We stay for five days of his wake. I shelter from the day-long stream of Hebrew behind a book in the corner of the apartment. I can't get into

War and Peace, so I borrow my sister-in-law's copy of the biography of Frank Sinatra, and lose myself in its five hundred unauthorised pages.

Back home, I notice that my appetite for this job is less keen than usual. I put it down to overwork, and to post-natal sadness at the completion of this chronicle of 1986. You're adapting to not having your weekly write-up to do, I tell myself. But some of my disaffection has institutional roots: have I been passed over in the choice of leaders for the five groups into which commissioning editors have been reorganised? Organisational paranoia, such as I haven't experienced before at Channel Four; soon, like the protagonist of Joseph Heller's *Something Happened*, I'll start worrying about closed office doors and the relative sizes of desk diaries.

Another, perhaps determining, factor in my mood is Jeremy and his forthcoming departure. We all felt the shock of imminent deprivation when Jeremy went for Director-General of the BBC. I felt a personal sense of abandonment as well. Jeremy has been the latest, perhaps the last, of the succession of father-figures I have elected through my life so far. Most have become friends, colleagues and equals; all began awesome, and I needed to shine in their esteem.

Jewishness played an important if mostly unspoken part in getting close to Jeremy, as did a shared passion for the arts – alongside his passions for good journalism, political debate, underdogs, cricket and mischief. At the end of our regular meetings there would usually be an off-duty exchange, about family or books read or the state of his feelings about the job. Once or twice he vouchsafed scathing criticisms of colleagues to me. *Vouchsafed* is the right kind of word for the archaic undercurrents of our relationship.

I started this chronicle of a year uncertain of my own future but clear about Channel Four's. I end it with a new contract which will take me to the end of this decade, certain only that the Channel will change, perhaps in ways none of us can envisage now that Jeremy has opted to leave broadcasting and run the Royal Opera House instead. He made the decision the day after the BBC turned him down.

We had known of his interest in the Opera House for some time, but two days before the BBC interview I asked him why he was applying. 'I love opera, as you know,' he said, 'but I can go on enjoying it whatever I'm doing. The BBC touches national life in so many more ways. Anyway, I've been encouraged to go for the BBC.'

I saw him three days after the interview, and he was still shaken. 'The longer the interview went on, the greater the gulf between those governors and me. Halfway through one of them said, "Mr Isaacs, don't take what I'm about to say as a criticism, just a statement of fact – but you don't seem to me the sort of man that takes well to discipline."' That single phrase seems to sum up the climate of jittery toughmindedness surrounding the BBC last year, in the wake of Alasdair Milne's sudden departure as Director-General. In such an atmosphere it was almost unthinkable that a man with a reputation as an awkward customer, like Jeremy, would get the job.

I had come from the arts into television; he was quitting television to run an arts institution. Would he miss the big swirl and scope of television, find himself cramped? Or would he enjoy concentrating on the problems and rewards of one house, one line of production? And where would he place his democratic fervour in an institution which has been so identified with money, class and privilege? These past few weeks he's been muttering about the appalling underfunding of the arts compared with television. 'No matter how much each of you complains about his budget, in real terms you've had more each year. Out there, in the publicly funded arts, the money has either stood still or been cut back.' If he can raise standards at Covent Garden, clean out restrictive practices backstage, get the true cost of making opera acknowledged and met, and make the place less socially intimidating, the move will be justified. Meanwhile broadcasters shake their heads at his departure, friends wonder whether he's not having second thoughts, and we who work with him begin to prepare for life without him.

On the last Saturday of May, after several weeks in which we've seen little of him in Charlotte Street (is he already getting sucked into the Opera House? already making space for new structures and procedures to be put into operation?), I meet him in the bar of the pavilion of the Oval cricket ground. It's a special occasion: Tom Phillips has hired the ground for the day and invited three hundred friends to celebrate his fiftieth birthday watching a match between Tom Phillips's XI and The Rest Of The Art World XI. Dressed in a white coat and staring sternly down the wicket, Jeremy has been umpiring all morning. Now he's discussing the finer points of the game with a real Surrey County umpire, and clearly relishing the late-imperial splendour of the surroundings: the polished wood, the oil paintings of famous Victorian players ('that one was donated to the club by the player's mother, Michael – he must have been Jewish'), the framed photographs of illustrious batsmen of the twenties and thirties.

'When Roger de Grey and I walked out onto that turf this morning at the start of play, my heart beat faster. It was like walking out on to a great green stage. The human race, Michael, is divided into those who appreciate cricket and those who don't.'

'I'm here more as a spectator than a player, Jeremy.'

'You're here, that's enough. You qualify.'

I lead him through the long-room, crowded with white-clad guests, high on the game and on the pink champagne we've been plied with since our arrival. Tom has financed this spectacular event with a raffle, for which each of us pays a tenner and gets a signed print, Tom's self-portrait. I hope he breaks even; I overhear the catering manager saying, 'We were told to cater for two hundred and fifty, we're going to run out of strawberries.' We squeeze past an elated player. 'Do you know that the ball actually speeds up when it reaches the outfield here!' he exclaims. And the captain of The Rest Of The Art World XI toasts Tom 'for making a lot of grown-up schoolboys' dreams come true'.

In the dining room Jeremy and I join a table with Iris Murdoch, a museum curator and three of Tom's fellow members of the Royal Academy. Some of them have seen Tom's portrait of me at the RA Summer Show. One thinks it's 'very inward', another says it's overcooked, a third wags his hand in a too-hot-to-handle gesture. Does that mean it's intense? awful? some terrible give-away about me?

Jeremy is deep in conversation with Iris, asking her to give him arguments he can use to justify opera. Iris, who revealed this morning that she was a good all-rounder in her school first XI, pauses for thought, and then pronounces: 'First, any attack on opera would be a first step in an attack on all the arts. And then, the real reason opera matters' – Jeremy leans in to make sure he catches this – 'is that it keeps the myths alive in the world.'

After lunch Jeremy leaves for Glyndebourne, missing a dramatic afternoon's play, the presentation of the raffle prize by David Attenborough and Adrian Mitchell's calypso, written throughout the day's play and mock-heroically celebrating Tom's pulled tendon and innings of one run. Jeremy certainly seems to be bringing everything to bear on the Opera-House challenge – toughness, determination, care and forceful argument about fundamentals. Maybe he will be able to shake up Covent Garden and further the reinvigoration of opera in Britain, as he has spurred on the renewal of television.

In the last Programme Review meeting of May the debates have a new pressure and urgency. The commissioning editors are starting to take responsibility for life at Channel Four after Jeremy – or at least to try and set up a working structure so that Jeremy's successor finds a company that can't be pushed around too easily. Liz Forgan, who now chairs these meetings, has not only turned them into a proper forum for the Channel's underlying concerns – we've discussed sex, violence and censorship, our relations with ITV and with independent producers – she also proposes a new way of making the annual decisions about budget allocations and schedule priorities, which are the very heart of the Channel's identity.

Instead of each editor having an individual budget meeting with the chief executive (which often became an uneasy tug-of-war between Jeremy's editorial diktat and the pressure of financial targets), the process will be extended to allow commissioning editors to express views on the entire output and priorities of the Channel, not just their own patch. Then decisions will be taken by the main executives and the heads of the five groups of commissioning editors. It means that one thing Jeremy fought to avoid – a middle layer of management between the chief executive and the people responsible for programmes – has been created. But for months now, most editors have only been able to have at best sporadic face-to-face contact with Jeremy anyway.

At Programme Review, Alan Fountain seizes on Liz's plan and pushes it further, calling for maximum open debate compatible with efficient decision-making, warning about the erosion of commissioning editors' autonomy. Other editors, especially those with experience of the BBC, are worried in case organising commissioning editors into groups leads to territorial rivalry.

It seems that we are engaged in the classic manoeuvres of any political movement which has been led by an autocrat. The succession of power after the reign of a dominant pioneering leader is always a risky moment for the goals and ideals of the movement – and this applies equally to the Bolshevik revolution after Lenin, China after Mao, Israel after Ben-Gurion, or the politics of television. I put my faith in what I liken to a parliamentary process of open and uninhibited debate, with commissioning editors the equivalent of MPs representing the constituencies of programme-makers and viewers.

Fellow editors with more bitter and direct political experience, like Alan and Farrukh, are less sanguine. Farrukh objects to my analogy: 'We're not like a parliament, nobody elected us and we're not responsible the way MPs are. Channel Four is more like Cabinet or collegiate government.' Alan says that, although he's pessimistic about getting backing for radical programmes after Jeremy goes, because no one else will overrule an entire roomful of advisers the way he has, the opening-out of debate must be pursued: 'Every other alternative is worse.'

At the end of the meeting Gillian Braithwaite-Exley, who has the demanding and meticulous task of constructing our programme schedules, intervenes to urge the commissioning editors to seize this last chance to take responsibility for the Channel's future. 'I've been in ITV a long time, and I know how quickly a company can be turned inside out and become quite different.'

Liz Forgan has begun inviting commissioning editors to present a paper each month to the Programme Review meeting on any topic of their choice. I deliver mine to a July meeting, conscious, as all editors now are, that this summer is the last chance for any contribution to decisions about the Channel's future, which will begin to be made in earnest with the choice of Jeremy's successor this autumn.

I start by saying that I would like to imagine that my arguments will be read by my successor. Whoever takes over from me must be at perfect liberty to contest all my assumptions; yet I would like them first to be understood. This summer's statements from commissioning editors could become a collective stocktaking at an important crossroads for the Channel, a sort of out-of-breath, temporary testament.

'The goal has been art television,' I say, staking out once more what the most distinctive Channel Four arts programmes have attempted, 'not simply the arts on television but television that is shaped and altered by the insights and practice of art and artists. As *Dancelines* was shaped by the interaction of choreographers and a TV director/editor; as *A TV Dante* arises from the encounter of a painter and a film/video director. As future works may come from artists learning the techniques and possibilities of television, the way painters learned the technology of engraving and printmaking, the art of multiples.

'My hunch, unsupported by any surveys or research, is that people watch the Channel more actively and selectively and with greater curiosity than other television. We have an image in people's minds of "something different and special", of unpredictability. As well as being perceived as a channel of entertainment and information, the Channel is appreciated as a television of culture and communities. Culture in the widest sense: the culture of ethnicities as much as the culture of connoisseurs; the culture of the dispossessed, the under-provided and the excluded; the culture of survival. And communities, not just in the most broad-brush sense, but communities of interests and hobbies, of continuing self-education, of buried memories and allegiances. Communities which we try to address not as herds, but as individuals.

'One of the strongest things you can do in arts television is to convey the intensity of music, opera, theatre or dance performed in unbroken time and ripened in front of a succession of audiences. But how to convey that intensity? Relays from the stage shot in real time (*Rigoletto* or *Gloriana* from ENO)? Studio reinterpretations on video of the stage production (*King Priam*, *Yan Tan Tethera*)? Film recreations yoking the power of the original to the language of the camera and the editing table (Peter Brook's *Carmen*)?

'When the alchemy of stage and screen works, it combines camera precision and the grammar of the screen with what Kenneth Tynan, referring to Olivier, called "high-definition performance". It helps if you can afford, as we did with the *Oresteia* and *The Mysteries*, to record several real-time performances and piece the thing together in post-production. When you are dealing with the orchestra and chorus of a major opera house, this can be prohibitively expensive. But now that most of the big national companies have had to curtail or stop touring, television's role as a disseminator matters even more.

'We haven't had much concert performance of orchestral and instrumental music on Channel Four, because pointing cameras at people blowing, scraping or hitting instruments makes, by and large, pretty stolid television. Nor is it the equivalent of the way we perceive instruments in the concert hall, where physical distance and the presence of the actual sound make us see in a more diffused way, of which the camera close-up is the enemy.'

I go on to talk about the visual arts, and our attempts to transcend the stereotypes of the art film or series, especially about art of the past; I worry about the tendency of all prestigious and costly documentary series to become doggedly encyclopaedic; and I raise a flag for poetry on television. 'The devil's advocate inside me,' I conclude, 'says that poetry is verbal, and better suited to radio or print. I answer that since its origins poetry has been fleshed out between people, the Homeric storyteller conjuring up Odysseus to listeners and viewers round the campfire, the bard in the crowded banquet hall recounting *Beowulf*. Television is the best medium to restore this human circle to poetry, because it can give the voice and speech of poets and their audience in space and time, not just a disembodied text.'

After his initial encounter with television production in the making of *A TV Dante*, Tom Phillips wrote a slightly shell-shocked account of the difference between making a painting and making television.

'Painting,' he wrote, 'is a solitary activity and – despite the wild myths of *la vie de bohème* – regular: it responds only to its own pressures. It is not expensive to perform and you don't have to have a meeting every time you want to buy a brush or work late in the studio. Competitiveness exists but it is implicit: often one is competing with colleagues who have been dead for hundreds of years.

'As long as he is willing to be poor for the first years of his career, the artist is not in any way accountable to others; he needs neither to propose to others what he is going to do, nor explain why it is taking him so long, nor cut it down to smaller size once he has finished. His is the ideal dreamworld and nightmare of the primary creator.

'Television is a monster that daily devours the hours that take weeks to produce. Its dietary preference, however, is for the long and thin; creativity is the garnish rather than the substance of its meals.'

Tom's response to television is as true and untrue as all blanket descriptions of this amorphous, omnivorous medium. It would apply equally to the differences between any solo, cheap, low-tech art – such as painting, writing poems or composing sonatas – and the collective, costly, technological arts such as television and the cinema. Yet it is a salutary reminder of the ephemerality of our medium – which is why we festoon it with so many festivals and prizes, trophies against the floodtide of oblivion.

Channel Four *is* different from other TV. If Tom's implied strictures are to be answered, and if Channel Four in all its programme areas is to continue to stand out in world television and British culture, it will do so by echoing this country's many voices, by contesting orthodoxies of thought and expression; and above all by preserving a television fit for primary creators.

'Television,' concludes Tom, 'is a tribe that awaits its anthropologist.' I am certainly not that anthropologist, though I have been both tribe-member and fieldworker. Sometimes I feel no less of an outsider looking in than when I first arrived at Channel Four, though by learning to think and make television I have also become an insider looking out. Committed to television, my allegiance to the arts and to something more than information, entertainment or industry gives me a rudder to negotiate television's tides and currents.

Looking back over this book of a year in Channel Four, I am all too conscious of its lacks and absences. My workdesk is piled with books and articles from whose insights I had hoped to argue a thoughtful analysis of the phenomenon of television. Walter Benjamin's essay 'The Work of Art in the Age of Mechanical Reproduction' rubs shoulders with Fredric Jameson's 'Video Art and Postmodernism'; the gnomic jokes of video artist Nam June Paik – Zen sage of TV and video – sit next to monographs on the history of photography, for I suspect that many of photography's early debates – is it simply a technological/industrial process, a copy of reality, or can it become art in its own right? – are being replayed about television. But, tied to the tempo of television and the timescale of a diary, I haven't been able to pursue such intuitions, and they must await calmer times.

There are some themes, however, which my diary keeps touching. The proliferation of channels, whether terrestrially broadcast or transmitted to our homes by satellite through dish or cable, has already begun. It will reach bewildering proportions over the next decade, a glut of programmes hose-piped into our heads. National boundaries, and cultural and linguistic communities will be bypassed by the new technology, differences and distinctions will be smoothed over. But little work has been done on the perceptual and cultural effects of this image glut. Children with itchy fingers on the remote control have grown up accustomed to channel-hopping – called *le zapping* in France, as if programmes were being shot down in flames like Vietcong. In 1986 young people's programmes like *The Tube* or *Network 7* began to be increasingly interrupted and overlaid by teletext listings and electronic menus of items coming up next, as if the programme-makers were nervous of viewers switching their abbreviated attention-span to another channel. All part of the information cult of the eighties, addiction to overload, knowingness irrespective of experience, the brand-label outlook, as enshrined in the listings and capsule reviews of *Time Out* and its clones in every world metropolis.

There's little point in denouncing this avalanche. Like most of the phenomena of late-capitalist modernity, it has a double aspect. On the one hand, the usury of images, their resonance leached out as they are hijacked into pop videos and commercials. On the other, a wide landscape of reference, the possibility of witty and elliptical expression, a lingua franca of television conventions, from which new work with more gravity can be built.

This 'postmodern image maelstrom' flows through some of the strongest contemporary works of art: Peter Greenaway's films, Eduardo Paolozzi's prints and sculptures, Pina Bausch's dance-theatre pieces,

Robert Wilson's theatre works, Philip Glass's music, Laurie Anderson's performances, for example. Works that embody allusiveness or quotation, that acknowledge they come *after* – after nineteenth-century art, after heroic modernism, itself now a classic. And their way of making art has permeated some television – Robert Ashley and John Sanbourn's seven-part video opera *Perfect Lives*; Geoff Dunlop's Talking Heads film *Once in a Lifetime*, and his *State of the Art* series; and, still in progress, the Peter Greenaway–Tom Phillips *TV Dante*. These are works in which a great deal happens per square second, per square inch of screen, works not just for viewing but for recording and re-viewing, tight-packed television for an age of overload in which most TV is too weightless, too thin.

In the year covered by this book, it often seemed as if everyone was using the idea of pan-European television as a rallying-cry or an alibi. Enrico Berlusconi, who created a chain of crass and glossy commercial stations in Italy which rivalled the state-run networks, proclaimed his European ambitions in 1986 and acquired a channel in France, studios in Spain, partners in Germany. Channel Four sat down with German, Austrian, Swiss and French television to create a European co-production association. LA SEPT gained access to TDF1, the French communications satellite, and prepared to launch a European cultural channel in 1988. And the EEC kept holding conferences about the challenge of European TV.

There are strong economic arguments for creating a 'European space' for the production and distribution of television. American programmes dominate the world TV market because America is big enough for expensive programmes like *Dallas* or *Dynasty* to recoup their cost at home. All foreign sales then become pure profit, and such series can be sold to European and other foreign televisions at a fraction of what a comparable native drama series would cost. So American stories, images and idioms circle the world.

But – it is argued – if Europe could offer a consolidated market instead of a patchwork of linguistically differentiated national territories, if European televisions could agree to collaborate on stories and pro-grammes which would appeal across national frontiers, then American cultural imperialism would no longer colonise large tracts of world television.

The problems are what European stories and programmes? what shared European values? In arts television, it's easy enough to collaborate on anniversary homages to the mighty dead or to monumental events –

Mozart, the French Revolution – but much harder to find partners for the unfashionable living or the unruly immediate past – Czeslaw Milosz or 1968, for example.

European broadcasters need to find ways of coming together around shared but differentiated European themes and topics, matrix ideas that don't grind down cultural distinctiveness into bland 'Euro-pudding', as my colleague Renee Goddard calls it.

1986 was not a good year for public-service television, or for public television *tout court*. The BBC was harassed and intimidated by Norman Tebbit and the bullies of the Conservative Party Central Office. The Peacock Committee held scholastic debates about pay-per-view and consumer sovereignty, and attacked self-perpetuating professional elites – as did Mrs Whitehouse and her knight-errant Gerald Howarth MP, with his bill against 'grossly offensive' programmes, supposedly foisted on viewers by a depraved mafia of broadcasters. A French socialist government which had never had the courage to release television from state control and instal real competition with the private sector suddenly lunged into commercial television, creating two private channels virtually overnight. Meanwhile the technology of video recorders and 'time-shift' sapped whatever shared experience – millions watching the same pro- gramme at the same time – television could still lay claim to, privatising the act of viewing.

The moguls moved in to privatise European television, a phalanx of media barons sweeping governments along with them, irrespective of their political colouring: Berlusconi, Bertelsmann, Kirch, Murdoch, Maxwell, Hersant, Bouygues. Their war cry is, 'We must create a modern European television, capable of competing with America'; their weapon a cheque- book, as they scurry around buying up the star performers, newspeople and producers nurtured by public television, outbidding each other for big new movies, Hollywood backlists, imported soaps and series (whose prices they drive up, to the glee of American producers), stealing exclusiv- ity on major sport from public television – doing everything, in fact, that a bustling, thoroughly modern, fully entrepreneurial television should, except inventing anything new for the medium, any fresh or bold inno- vation which people will be able to recall as a landmark.

In this battle between private and public televisions, Channel Four has been coopted by both sides. Public television upholds the Channel as shining proof that 'cultural television' (which is how the Europeans, and especially the French, see Channel Four) need not be boring, worthy or pedagogic. Free marketeers and deregulators praise Channel Four for being unbureaucratic and cost-conscious, for creating an independent production sector, for undermining the vested interests, restrictive practices and featherbedding of a duopolistic industry. The Channel's example has triggered the British government's insistence that BBC and ITV employ independent programme-makers for 25 per cent of their output. How many of these will be true independents or simply previously employed staff, and to what extent this penetration of 'fortress television' will lead to calls to dismantle the public sector altogether remains to be seen.

The risk of a partially or fully privatised television system is that needs people didn't know they had (which public television frequently awakens) will be met less and less. The logic of ratings, marketing and statistics will take over. The concept of an important minority programme will vanish. No need will be met that cannot be described, quantified and promoted in advance of its satisfaction. The reliable formats, familiar talents and safe repertory that characterise the print or screen publishing of the great communications conglomerates of the 1980s will begin to fill every channel, every mind.

'People engage in an almost bizarre variety of different activities in front of the set: we eat dinner, knit jumpers, argue with each other, listen to music, read books, do our homework, kiss, write letters and vacuum-clean the carpet,' writes Jane Root in the book of the Channel Four series about television, *Open the Box*, referring to the Oxford psychologist who put a video camera inside the TV sets of twenty families and taped them watching, or not watching, television. There have been many contradictory jeremiads about the reductive effects of TV-watching – it shortens the attention-span or drugs people into a trance; makes them hypercritical and sceptical, or subservient and imitative; it collapses politics into show business, helping an actor become a nation's president, or it deepens democracy by giving voice to people excluded from the official consensus.

My concerns about the reductive powers of television can be pinpointed in the words we use to describe consumers of broadcasting. We speak of viewers of television (or of listeners to radio); but people who go to a play, opera or concert we call an audience. It is the difference between domestic and communal experience, between something private or solitary and something shared.

Why should this matter? Television brings the wonders of the world and the pinnacles of our culture within reach of a fingertip on a remote control. But it does so at a price, and that price is considerable in the area of television in which I work, arts television. There, television domesticates high things, it scales them down, and substitutes spurious intimacy for absorption and involvement.

In part this is a result of the technical limitations of current broadcast television: the picture is too coarse, the sound too cramped. But there is more to it. An audience is more than an agglomeration of the individuals who compose it; some sea-change occurs in their responses and sympathies, some enlargement and alchemy of their perceptions. They become more open to what Lilian Baylis, the founder of the Old Vic, called 'awe and wonder'.

Television isn't an ideal medium for awe and wonder. That's why it's at its best presenting the democratic and the demotic, vernacular drama, familiar music, art already well known through widespread reproduction in other media. Not because its means of reproduction are inadequate, but because television addresses itself to the home, to individuals or often inattentive groups. As viewers we are domesticated, we are attuned to privatised experiences, unused to ascending the ladder of perception, the way we can as members of a live audience, sharing a time and a space.

Sometimes I think that trying to make television speak like a painting or a poem or a song or a dance is a misguided and quixotic enterprise. Then I tell myself that television reaches so many people we've just got to push it to its limits. Viewing habits and expectations can change. I remember a telephone call to Channel Four one evening in the middle of *1980* by Pina Bausch, an expressionist dance-theatre piece lasting nearly three hours. 'I just wanted to tell you all that I came home to watch the football match but it was rained off,' said the caller, 'so I switched over to your channel and I've been watching this thing for the last two hours and I can't make head or tail of it but I can't stop watching, so could someone please explain why I've stayed with it for the last two hours?'

New television technology will change viewers' expectations. One of the most influential figures on my generation in the 1960s, and the person who first made me think about technology, was the American designer-architect, Buckminster Fuller. Bucky believed that most of the world's political, social and cultural problems could be solved by better design and information-sharing. His utopianism was inspirational in a time of affluence and turbulence. Since the 1960s, we have become more wary of grafting utopian hopes on to hardware; still, the next generation of television and video will at least sharpen perceptions. Over the past two years 'high-definition television' has been developed in Japan, the

USA and Europe. As with every new device, a bitter battle has broken out between the proponents of rival systems, but essentially what the customer gets will be the same: high image resolution, with nearly 1200 lines scanning pictures. Today television in Europe has 625 lines, and in America only 525 lines. The picture will be steadier and brighter, the sound clearer and richer. High-definition television will also be able to be shown in cinemas, either by transfer to 35mm film without grainy horizontal lines, or directly by electronic projection with the same quality.

High-definition television may become the technical medium for work that requires layering of imagery and sound, density of information, poetry of expression. And such work could combine real-time relay with highly crafted segments, as only television can do. Finally, the possibility of exhibiting high-definition work in cinemas, to audiences rather than domesticated viewers, could open the way to shared 'awe and wonder' through television. It will come; but in the foreseeable future only to yet another privileged minority, able to afford the hardware.

This chronicle of a year began with my high-pitched argument with Jeremy about the relative originality of television and theatre. It ends in this last week of May 1987 with a visit to a theatre for the making of a television programme, Inger Aby's film about Gluck, the 200th anniversary of whose death falls in 1987.

It is being shot in Drottningholm, an eighteenth-century theatre built in the park of Gustavus Adolphus's royal palace, an hour's boat ride from Stockholm. I come out for a weekend to see the shoot and work on the script, which has been translated from the original Swedish and needs improvement.

I'm completely bowled over by this little theatre, a box of baroque marvels whose understage, like the creaking wooden hull of a man-of-war, is crammed with winches, windlasses, rollers, ropes, pulleys and hoists for instant scenic transformations, the miraculous spectacles of the pre-camera age. And I'm touched by its simplicity – bare-boarded dressing rooms heated by tiled stoves, through their check-curtained windows a view of trees, grass, a lake. Everything is wood – the low, shallow beds in each dressing room, the gappy catwalks above the scenery flies, the coffin-like box with rocks inside which is seesawed to make the sound of thunder.

I rediscover my pleasure in the power of artifice, watching Inger shoot a tempest and transformation scene in Gluck's *Iphigénie*. In a sudden, noisy rush, the flats painted with stormclouds are whipped out and tranquil pastoral flats slotted in: the eighteenth-century equivalent of a quick cut, naive and self-evident. You can imagine the technology but it doesn't stop you delighting in the illusion.

Next door to the Drottningholm theatre is a little museum with paintings of *commedia dell'arte mimes*, fairground buskers and street theatre clowns. Their rude cavorting figures speak to the showman in me; heads peeking from curtained booths in marketplaces recall fantasies of unleashing marvels on an audience, the impulse to hide and show, which propelled me into the theatre, into the arts. And the fluctuating, illusory imagery of the painted walls and cloths of Drottningholm, made to be seen by flickering candles, vulnerable to daylight and to the stark, steady illumination of electricity, reminds me of the limits of photographic precision and the power of the half-tint, the emblem.

For the tenth time Inger shoots a danced combat of masked figures in a sea of swirling smoke. From the theatre's heavens an eighteenth-century opera impresario descends, couched on clouds, a *deus ex machina*. In the theatre, there can be a god in the machine; from the machinery of television, can we ever engender more than ghosts?

INDEX